Edith Wharton

Edith Wharton

A STUDY OF HER FICTION

BY BLAKE NEVIUS

Berkeley and Los Angeles

UNIVERSITY OF CALIFORNIA PRESS

1953

UNIVERSITY OF CALIFORNIA PRESS
Berkeley and Los Angeles, California

CAMBRIDGE UNIVERSITY PRESS
London, England

Permission to quote from the writings of Edith Wharton has been granted
by Charles Scribner's Sons and Appleton-Century-Crofts, Inc. A list of the
separate titles follows in the Acknowledgments.

Designed by Ward Ritchie

To
My Mother
and the memory of
My Father

Acknowledgments

I would like to express my gratitude to the following individuals for their various kinds of assistance in the preparation of this study: Mr. Donald C. Gallup, Curator of the Collection of American Literature in the Yale Library; Mr. T. J. B. Walsh and Mr. David Randall of Charles Scribner's Sons; Mr. Dana H. Ferrin of Appleton-Century-Crofts, Inc.; Mrs. Gerald D. Meyer and Mrs. Elsie Leach, both of Los Angeles.

I am grateful also to my colleagues in the English Department of the University of California at Los Angeles, John J. Espey, Leon Howard, James. E. Phillips, Jr., Hugh G. Dick, and Bradford A. Booth, who read the manuscript and gave me the benefit of their suggestions.

To Glenn Gosling, of the University of California Press, I am particularly indebted for his wise and patient editorial guidance; and I am under a similar obligation to his colleague, James Kubeck, who saw the manuscript through the final stages.

The Research Committee of the University of California at Los Angeles came to my aid with a grant to cover certain necessary expenses in the preparation of the study.

Permission to quote from unpublished material was kindly granted by Mrs. Wharton's legal representative, Mrs. Royall Tyler, and by the Yale Library Committee.

My thanks also to Mr. Herbert R. Brown, Mr. Robert Carver North, and the editorial boards of *The Pacific Spectator* and *The New England Quarterly* for permission to reproduce portions of this study which, in slightly different form, appeared in their journals.

Permission to quote from copyrighted works of Edith Wharton is acknowledged as follows:

To Charles Scribner's Sons for *The Greater Inclination* (copyright, 1899); *Crucial Instances* (copyright, 1901); *The Valley of Decision* (copyright, 1902); *The Descent of Man and Other Stories* (copyright, 1904); *Italian Backgrounds* (copyright, 1905); *The House of Mirth* (copyright, 1905); *Madame de Treymes* (copyright, 1907); *The Fruit of the Tree* (copyright, 1907); *A Motor-Flight Through France* (copyright, 1908); *Tales of Men and Ghosts* (copyright, 1910); *Ethan Frome* (copyright, 1911); *The Custom of the Country* (copyright, 1913); *Xingu and Other Stories* (copyright, 1916); *A Son at the Front* (copyright, 1923); *The Writing of Fiction* (copyright, 1925).

To Appleton-Century-Crofts, Inc. for *The Reef* (copyright, 1912); *Summer* (copyright, 1917); *The Marne* (copyright, 1918); *French Ways and Their Meaning* (copyright, 1919); *The Age of Innocence* (copyright, 1920); *The Glimpses of the Moon* (copyright, 1922); *Old New York: False Dawn, The Old Maid, The Spark, New Year's Day* (copyright, 1924); *The Mother's Recompense* (1925); *Twilight Sleep* (copyright, 1927); *The Children* (copyright, 1928); *Hudson River Bracketed* (copyright, 1929); *Certain People* (copyright, 1930); *The Gods Arrive* (copyright, 1932); *A Backward Glance* (copyright, 1934); *The Buccaneers* (copyright, 1938).

Permission has also been granted by Appleton-Century-Crofts, Inc., to quote from Percy Lubbock's *Portrait of Edith Wharton* (copyright, 1947).

Los Angeles, California   B. N.

Contents

Chapter I

EDITH WHARTON TODAY

It is difficult to think of a twentieth-century American novelist, except possibly Cabell, whose reputation has suffered more from the change of interests and narrowing of emphasis in the literature of the 'thirties than has Edith Wharton's. To a generation of writers nurtured on social realism, young men for whom, as Leslie Fiedler recalls, "abandoning oneself to the proletariat and finding oneself as an artist seemed a single act," she had nothing to teach except by way of negative example. She had always been put down as something of a snob, but the experience of the depression years had the effect, among critics and writers at least, of exaggerating the limitations of her social ideal. The faint air of exasperation and the conscious hauteur which occasionally informed the pages written in her lonely old age did nothing to temper this impression. "At present," she complained in *A Backward Glance* (1934), "the demand is that only the man with the dinner pail shall be deemed worthy of attention, and fiction is classed according to its degree of conformity to this rule." No one was more aware than Mrs. Wharton of the prevailing shift of sympathy and its unfortunate effect on a reputation already undermined by the succession of second-rate novels she wrote in the 'twenties. As the triumph of proletarian literature became more obvious, the phrase "the man with the dinner pail," appearing in several of her essays, acquired the bitterly symbolic overtones of Yeats's "Huxley, Tyndall, Carolus Duran, and Bastien-Lepage." As with Yeats, it served the purpose of focusing her resentment on a scapegoat.

To readers who knew her only through her later novels, with their slightly rasping tone and their old-fashioned technical competence, she must have seemed merely a survival of the first generation of realists, whose fruitless attempt to react upon the drift of a changing tradition had soured her hopelessly, as similar attempts had soured so many gifted writers of her generation. Even those who judged her, if not by the wrong novels, at least by those which gave a limited view of her achievement (mainly *Ethan Frome* and *The Age of Innocence*), were too badly informed to be able to make any lasting evaluation of her work. Somehow, in spite of the reminders of such critics as Edmund Wilson, Diana Trilling, and Q. D. Leavis, the Edith Wharton who wrote *The House of Mirth, The Custom of the Country*, and *The Reef* has been neglected. Yet by any standard these three novels must be reckoned among her best. Technically, they are far superior to anything—the fiction of Henry James excepted—produced in that gray transition period between the death of Frank Norris and the First World War, and although as sociological documents they are less comprehensive than the novels of Robert Herrick, David Graham Phillips, and Upton Sinclair, they make their unique contribution to a survey of American society, conducted in the early years of the century, which is unsurpassed in our literature.

It is a sign, though not an infallible one, of her waning reputation that she has been slighted by recent anthologists. Twenty-five years ago, no account of the American experience abroad would have overlooked the evidence of her many novels, short stories, travel books, and miscellaneous essays, to say nothing of her efforts in behalf of the French cause and the French and Belgian refugees in the early years of the First World War; yet Philip Rahv's *Discovery of Europe* (1947) manages to do just that. Although the best of her early short stories have enabled her to maintain a precarious foothold in many college anthologies of American literature, the long-time best seller in this group, Norman Foerster's *American Poetry and Prose*, is unable to find room for her alongside such dubious immortals as O. Henry and Hamlin Garland, and the same is true of the text sponsored by her own publishers, Scribner's. The implication, I suppose, is that she can no longer hold her place by virtue of her craftsmanship alone and that her subject for the most part has been better handled by Henry James. Nevertheless, she is still read, if only by those who do not watch the barometers of literary taste, and the indications are that her audience is by no means small. She has had a kind of revenge on "the man with the dinner pail," for he symbolizes an era which already seems as remote as that chronicled in *The Age of Innocence*, and his sponsors have been the victims of a critical reaction no less overwhelming than that which she encountered in the 'thirties.

The objections to the view of life expressed in her fiction have not come entirely from the left. Even the conservative critics agree that she was too well bred, too narrow in her social outlook, too chillingly rational in her

3

treatment of experience to be able to convince us always of the genuineness of her sympathies or to maintain a real hold on the affections of the reading public. These are partially valid objections, and they have barred Edith Wharton from the first rank of novelists writing in English; but they do not apply equally to all her fiction and they are by no means, as some critics have implied, the whole truth about her art and personality. Those who think of her as merely well-bred and unexceptionably narrow should consider Arthur Mizener's anecdote of F. Scott Fitzgerald's visit to the Pavillon Colombe, where he had been invited by Mrs. Wharton for tea. Although the story has lost its freshness through successive retellings, its point, as I understand it, is still worth stressing. Fitzgerald, mildly drunk and on the defensive, set about to shock the genteel assembly. Having first told his hostess that she knew nothing about life and having been disappointed at the good humor of her reply, he invented the story that when he and Zelda first came to Paris they had lived for two weeks in a bordello. "Instead . . . of the horrified response that he had expected," Mr. Mizener relates, "Mrs. Wharton and her guests were all looking at him with unfeigned and perfectly sincere interest." When Fitzgerald, by now embarrassed, faltered in his account, his hostess urged him on: "But, Mr. Fitzgerald . . . you haven't told us what they did in the bordello." At which the guest excused himself and fled back to Paris to pour out his humiliation ("They beat me! They beat me!") to Zelda. "Nearly all of the Fitzgerald of the period," Mr. Mizener concludes, "and a good deal of the history of two literary generations, is in that anecdote." [1] I am not sure what is meant by this last remark, but it

---

[1] For notes to chap. i, see p. 253.

4

is clear that Fitzgerald and his contemporaries, like so many who have followed them, forgot all too quickly that Edith Wharton in her day had dealt candidly with her material—so candidly that, as she recalls in her memoirs, one indignant reader asked her if she had ever known a respectable woman. To give her credit where credit is due, she was less likely to be offended by plain speaking than by the kind of personal dishonesty that Fitzgerald displayed on this occasion.

That she sometimes found it difficult to preserve her detachment, is unfortunately true: many of her novels, particularly those she wrote after 1920, are weakened by the force of her prejudices. She resisted almost every tendency of postwar American culture, in manners, morals, and art. She does one thing unforgivable in a novelist: the characters whom she dislikes, whether by instinct or training, frequently alter under the pressure of her antipathy until they have lost their original outlines. Undine Spragg, in *The Custom of the Country,* is a notable example; so is Vance Weston, in *Hudson River Bracketed* and *The Gods Arrive.* Moreover, it is in the novels just cited that Mrs. Wharton's treatment of Middle Western culture slides into a burlesque which is at odds with her usual and most successful tone. Her protest is no more trenchant than that of Sinclair Lewis, whom she so curiously anticipates, but Lewis's arises from a close and even sympathetic knowledge of his subject, whereas Mrs. Wharton's appears to stem from uninformed prejudice.

On these and similar grounds she has been accused of being a snob. This is a touchy subject and one which in this country is likely to block discussion of a writer's possible merits. If it is snobbish to resist the common practice of basing social distinctions on any single criterion, such as money or talent or antecedents, then paradoxically she is a snob. But a great deal of cant distinguishes our use of the term. At the worst, she merely substitutes her own brand of snobbishness for the prevalent American article; instead of establishing the bank statement as the criterion, she discriminates on the broader basis of manners (not in the narrow sense, but as a cultural index), sensibility, and character.

Recent criticism has perhaps avoided her for still another reason: the paucity of biographical information. This would not be a deterrent except for the suspicion that her fiction is intensely personal in the manner, if not to the degree, of Thomas Wolfe's or the recent Hemingway's. We know little more about her life than she was willing to tell us in *A Backward Glance,* a book as interesting for what it leaves out as for what it includes, or than we can gather from Percy Lubbock's brilliantly supplementary *Portrait of Edith Wharton* (1947). Both of these memoirs are as indispensable as they are charming, but both leave the reader with the feeling that, for reasons he perhaps can appreciate, he has been drawn only slightly into the confidence of the authors. They are full of tantalizing "faint clews and indirections," and they are remarkable finally, not as biography, but as valedictories to a period, a way of life, a particular circle of friends. They raise almost as many questions as they answer, and they are questions which may or may not be satisfied when Mrs. Wharton's papers, now in the Yale Library, are made available in 1969. Until then, the critic will have to rely heavily on the two books I have mentioned, expanding their suggestions as far as he dares without falling into unwarranted speculation. Although

6

there are other, fleeting glimpses of Mrs. Wharton's career to be obtained from the memoirs and letters of her friends, such as Bernard Berenson, Mrs. Winthrop Chanler, Logan Pearsall Smith, and Henry James, they merely substantiate, without adding to, the impression we have from Mr. Lubbock's book.

This conspiracy of silence would be discouraging were it not that Edith Wharton seems to have been indebted to real-life persons and situations only in the limited and refined sense that all genuinely imaginative artists are. The modern American novel, especially since the heyday of naturalism, has been so overwhelmingly devoted to the *roman à clef* that it is difficult to credit the exception, but Mrs. Wharton appears to be one. I have been assured by Mr. Lubbock that her life, apart from its general significance and that of the background against which it unrolled, is not essential to an understanding of her fiction.[2] Although I am inclined to accept this statement only tentatively, it is nonetheless true that Edith Wharton's extraordinarily fertile imagination not only presented her with more suggestions than she could use, but, like that of Henry James, it was able without the aid of actual characters and their histories to develop the germ of an idea into a fully realized situation.

It would be unreasonable, however, to assume that Mrs. Wharton's themes and the particular treatment they received under her hand were not determined or at least modified by her experience. We have, particularly in her autobiography, in Mr. Lubbock's portrait, and in Henry James's letters, the suggestion (it is seldom more than that) of certain difficult episodes in her life which seem to be shadowed forth in her fiction—episodes arising from the incompatibility of tastes between herself and her husband, the latter's failing health, their separation and divorce, and her friendship with Walter Berry. It is impossible to note the reappearance in her novels of certain problems, situations, and character types without speculating on their common significance. Generally, and in a way I will shortly try to define, her novels deal with the trapped sensibility. The theme is so persistent that, with all due respect for the motives of Mrs. Wharton and her friends in their attempt to divert attention from her private life, it cannot be overlooked. For the most part, however, I have tried in the chapters that follow to meet Edith Wharton on the ground she would have chosen—that provided by her writings.

There are at least three reasons why Edith Wharton should have a permanent claim on our attention. They will be developed in chapters iv-vi (which contain the heart of the matter) and somewhat less explicitly in the following chapters, but I would like to sketch them in here.

It is largely of accidental significance that Mrs. Wharton is the only American novelist who has dealt successfully and at length with that feudal remainder in New York society which hardly survived the beginning of the present century. More important is the fact that in chronicling the twilight of her race, she made the most of her opportunity—limited though it was by her point of view—to enforce a contrast between the old culture and the new, to illuminate, as no other novelist of her generation was able to do, a major aspect of our social history through the dramatic conflict between the ideals of the old mercantile and the new industrial societies.

In the second place, she is, next to Henry James, our

8

most successful novelist of manners—not an extravagant claim in view of the limited competition in what to Americans seems to be an alien and difficult genre. It must be apparent to Mrs. Wharton's readers that the view of reality in her novels emerges characteristically through a sharp and very self-conscious differentiation of appearances, that it is embodied in names, in the inflexions of speech, in details of costume and decor, in the countless means by which, as Lionel Trilling has pointed out, any fairly homogeneous group within a culture expresses its separateness. For this reason, she sought like Henry James to locate her subject in the rich ground offered by a traditional society—that of old New York or of the Faubourg St. Germain, with their consciously developed systems of manners—rather than in the more representative hinterlands of American society. *The Age of Innocence* is her triumph in this genre, but *The House of Mirth*, *The Custom of the Country*, and *The Reef* are not far behind.

Finally, she overcomes what has seemed to many critics to be the narrowing influence of her subject matter by her exploitation of two great and interlocking themes. Both appear in her earliest work, but neither is prominent until after the publication, in 1905, of her first great success, *The House of Mirth*. From this point on, all of her novels and the best of her long tales—*Ethan Frome*, "Bunner Sisters," and *The Old Maid*—derive their chief interest from her attempt to come to grips with two complex and basically unresolvable themes. The first is provided by the spectacle of a large and generous nature—that of an Ethan Frome, an Ann Eliza Bunner, an Anna Leath, or a Ralph Marvell—trapped by circumstances ironically of its own devising into consanguinity with a meaner nature—that of a Zeena Frome, an Evelina Bunner, a George Darrow, or an Undine Spragg. There is no accounting for such disastrous unions except as a result of the generous but misguided impulses of the larger nature; there is no justifying their waste of human resources. Moreover, there is no evading the responsibilities they entail, and this acknowledgment, inevitable to one of Edith Wharton's training, opens the way for her second theme. Given the general situation I have described, the novelist next tries to define the nature and limits of individual responsibility, to determine what allowance of freedom or rebellion can be made for her trapped protagonist without at the same time threatening the structure of society. Both themes are as familiar as they are inexhaustible. The opportunities they provide are mainly for the novelists in what F. R. Leavis calls "the great tradition," for whom the drama of life unfolds itself preëminently in moral terms. The first theme, particularly, is inescapable in the novels of two members of this company with whom Edith Wharton is closely allied in craftsmanship and sensibility but who surpassed her in intellectual force: George Eliot and Henry James.

Because of this kinship, it is possible that the large public revival of interest in Henry James has prepared the ground for a reappraisal of Mrs. Wharton. She is generally thought of as a disciple of the master; and although she is much more than that, the half-truth may serve a purpose in redirecting attention, by way of what is valuable in James, to what is valuable in Edith Wharton. Almost by themselves among American novelists in the early years of the century, they helped preserve the artistic dignity of the novel, and there is a significant parallel in their careers. But Edith Wharton made it clear in her novels, and more explicitly in *A Backward Glance,* that she was unable to follow James in his later development, so that his technical influence is confined for the most part to her early short stories and that most Jamesian of her novels, *The Reef.* If Q. D. Leavis is stretching a point in claiming that "the American novel grew up with Henry James and achieved a tradition with Edith Wharton," it is just as absurd to think of Mrs. Wharton simply as a poor man's Henry James.

Her achievement can stand by itself. If we can be persuaded to read her with a portion of the tolerance and sympathy we reserve for such writers as Mark Twain and Theodore Dreiser, who embrace a more native tradition, her value may become apparent. The first notion we will have to scrap is that she spoke for a small, privileged group in society which was intent upon reinforcing the moribund claims of the past. There is nothing she scorned more than the pretensions of wealth or birth when they were unsupported by qualities of character, intellect, and sensibility. Much as she admired the society of the *ancien régime* in France, her sarcasm, according to Percy Lubbock, was never vented more freely "than on the claims and assumptions of that same old honourable tradition, when it is not the past that rules it with a living spirit, but convention with a dead hand." It was her misfortune, perhaps, to have maintained her transatlantic orientation at a time when American writers were most strenuously asserting their independence, but she spoke for Western culture as a whole. At a time when that culture is everywhere threatened, its values are nowhere better reaffirmed than in her fiction, essays, and, by no means least important, her books of travel.

Chapter II

RECONNOITERINGS

In her memoirs, Edith Wharton has a great deal to say about the obstacles she had to overcome in getting her professional career under way. As she describes them, however, they were mainly external and may even have been exaggerated to conceal an initial lack of impulse. She was well equipped for the task of literature. In spite of her informal schooling, she had read deeply since early childhood in the best English and continental literature, had been on terms of daily intimacy with the purest spoken English (a matter with her, as with cultured New Yorkers in general, of special pride), and was endowed with an extraordinary visual memory and a sensibility which responded to the finer gradations in the moral and aesthetic spectra. Before she was eight she had begun to make up stories in her head, and somewhat later she was putting them down on paper. By the time she was thirteen she could write a very respectable sonnet. But the promising talent announced by her slim, paper-bound volume of juvenile poems, privately printed at Newport in 1878,[1] was discouraged, we are led to believe, by her coming out "a year before the accepted age" and, later, by her marriage at twenty-three to Edward Wharton.

---

[1] For notes to chap. ii, see p. 253.

What followed was an apprenticeship quite unlike that of the average young writer. The indifference of her husband and their friends to the challenge of literature and her own stake in the game was, after all, merely another form of the indifference which every beginner has to contend with. But there was the added fact of her isolation. She was denied free communication with other members of her craft by the combined timidity and disdain which marked the attitude of her class toward the creators of all but the politest forms of literature. The American cousins of Matthew Arnold's Barbarians had developed a culture no less exterior than its counterpart in England, characterized by the same passion for field sports and the same regard for manners, good looks, and a distinguished bearing, but above all by the same insufficiency of "light." Their fear of innovation led to their distrust of literature, which all too often advocated new and disquieting ideas.

Nevertheless, Edith Wharton began to appear in print not too long after her marriage, and one asks the question why, after having defied the canons of respectability to this extent, she managed to publish only a handful of poems and short stories during the decade following 1889. Part of the answer would seem to be that for a while at least she found relief from boredom in the activities that were always to claim so much of her time: gardening, entertaining, interior decoration, and the annual trips abroad for Edward Wharton's health. "I am not sure," wrote one of her friends of this period, "that literature and the desire to write played so large a part in her life in these early days as one might suppose in reading *A Backward Glance*." [2] The advantages of too much money and too much leisure might in the end have defeated the writer in her altogether, except that the compelling need for self-expression was not satisfied by her other miscellaneous activities. At that, it was not until several years after the publication of her first book, while writing *The House of Mirth* under pressure from a deadline, that she learned how to work.

But there were other obstacles perhaps more serious. She lacked self-confidence, and her health was uncertain. There is sufficient testimony, in her letters to her editors at Scribner's, in *A Backward Glance*, and elsewhere, to the reality of the first inhibition. None of her friends failed to note her shyness, even after she had learned to obscure it behind a formidable manner. But the reminiscenses of her friends and her own autobiography give the impression that Edward Wharton was the only valetudinarian in the family and that the trips abroad were undertaken mainly for his benefit. Although by and large this may be so, Edith Wharton's letters to her publishers, from 1893 to the outbreak of the First World War, tell a somewhat different story. It is in this connection that the history of her first volume of fiction is interesting, because it challenges the view encouraged by her memoirs that her literary debut was postponed by circumstances imposed by her environment and, most clearly, by the demands of her social position.

As early as November, 1893, she was discussing with Edward Burlingame, editor of *Scribner's Magazine*, the collection of short stories that was to be published eventually as *The Greater Inclination*.[3] Apparently, many of the stories were already written and the problem even at this stage was one of selection. In March, 1894, after Burlingame evidently had balked at accepting two of the stories, Mrs. Wharton admitted that she was losing confidence in herself (this becomes a familiar cry), and in July she asked for another six months' leeway. Then a year and a half of silence intervened before Burlingame learned that his correspondent had been seriously ill since her last letter and was not yet allowed to do any real work, although she hoped to have ready for next year "the volume that Scribner's was once kind enough to ask for." Late in 1896, she forwarded the dialogue called "The Twilight of the God," which ultimately took its place as the weakest and most pretentious story in the collection; but once again the volume was delayed by her collaboration with Ogden Codman, Jr., on *The Decoration of Houses* (1897) and by the many details connected with the printing of this pioneer manual of interior decoration. In February, 1898, she wrote her patient editor: "I have been really ill and my matière grise is so soft and sloppy that I can't do much work." Later in the year, encouraged perhaps by his approval of "The Pelican," she was confident that the volume would be ready for autumn publication, and in August she announced that she had seven stories in final form and an eighth ("The Coward") that would be finished in a month. When he received "The Coward" and "A Journey" in September, Burlingame was able to send the complete manuscript to press, and *The Greater Inclination* finally appeared in March, 1899, nearly six years after it had been proposed. In April, it might be added, Mrs. Wharton was again unwell.

Although the nature of these early ailments is not specified, there are references in Mrs. Wharton's subsequent letters to flu, grippe, hay fever, earaches, and—most serious—eye trouble, which at one time took the form of conjunctivitis. These are respectable if undistinguished complaints, which do not necessarily betray unusual stresses in one's private life. There is no mention of the nervous condition which Edmund Wilson is inclined to blame on her marriage and which he suggests was responsible for her taking up authorship seriously,[4] although it might be inferred from the length of her illness in 1894–1895. To what extent her ailments reflect a failure of adjustment in her marriage is of course unknown. But, anticipating on the basis of the slight evidence available, I would not be surprised to learn someday that her health improved suddenly beginning about 1914, the year which followed her divorce and witnessed the beginning of her strenuous and devoted efforts in behalf of the Allied refugees.

The Greater Inclination was a careful selection, made with the help of her literary mentor Walter Berry, from her best apprentice work of the preceding decade, omitting the stories which had appeared in magazines and which their author regarded as "the excesses of youth . . . written at the top of my voice."[5] In spite of the general distinction of the collection, at the time all the more surprising because the author was unknown, its versatility is a bit too calculated, its cleverness too transparent. All of the stories except the unexpectedly realistic "A Journey" reflect a self-conscious attitude toward the arts and are full of the small change of literary conversation. For example, it is a sign of his "quality" that Mr. Carstyle, the obscure provincial lawyer in "The Coward," reads Montaigne instead of his law books and that during a walk in the country he holds forth on Diderot to his young friend Vibart. But, however lightly carried, Edith Wharton's culture is genuine, and in these stories as in her later ones, notably "Xingu," the manifestations of sham culture are treated with the blandest irony. Mrs. Amyot, the widow in "The Pelican," undertakes to pay for her son's education by lecturing to women's groups. Having exhausted the subject of Greek art, she questions the narrator about other possibilities:

. . . What did I think of a "course" on Raphael or Michelangelo—or on the heroines of Shakespeare? There were some fine steel-engravings of Raphael's Madonnas and of the Sistine ceiling in her mother's library, and she had seen Miss Cushman in several Shakespearean *rôles,* so that on these subjects also she felt qualified to speak with authority.

Nevertheless, it is largely because of its calculated range and cleverness that the collection produces no firm impression of Edith Wharton's talent. In this preliminary sampling of what Percy Lubbock calls her "odd cases, queer motives, and awkward episodes" only one story has an important thematic relation to her later and more characteristic fiction. "Souls Belated," once intended as the opening story in the volume, recounts the practical education of Lydia Tillotson, who has left her wealthy, uninteresting husband to join her lover Gannett, a peripatetic writer. While the fugitives are in Italy Lydia receives notice of her husband's divorce action. Gannett wants to make her an honest woman, but Lydia, who has been condemned for years to the treadmill of respectability, refuses to take advantage of her position or to defer to the conventions of a society they have both learned to despise: "We neither of us believe in the abstract 'sacredness' of marriage; we both know that no ceremony is needed to consecrate our love for each other." Gannett counters with the argument (one that Odo Valsecca, in *The Valley of Decision,* is shortly to employ with Fulvia Vivaldi) that Lydia surveys life too theoretically and that it "is made up of compromises." As for conventions, he adds: "One may believe in them or not; but as long as they do rule the world it is only by taking advantage of their protection that one can find a *modus vivendi.*" Altogether, this is a perfect formulation of the pragmatic creed which governed Edith Wharton's own life and the destinies of her fictional characters in a world where conventions are valued as expedients and compromise is the only path to such freedom as is possible.

The soundness of Gannett's objections is borne out by what follows. After months of hole-in-the-corner existence during which the lovers move from one obscure hotel to another to evade the curious attention of their compatriots, Lydia learns that they cannot remain forever in hiding. For one thing, Gannett needs the stimulus of society in order to continue his writing. As Mr. and Mrs. Gannett, they register at a fashionable resort and are immediately accepted into the exclusive, mainly English society ruled by Lady Susan Condit. Somewhat later, a Mr. and Mrs. Linton appear among the guests— the latter a flamboyant, loud-voiced type and her husband "a blond stripling, trailing after her, head downward, like a reluctant child dragged by his nurse." Lydia, taking her cue from Lady Susan, manages to avoid the newcomers until one day Mrs. Linton corners her, confides that her husband is really Lord Trevenna, that she is the notorious Mrs. Cope, and that after a publicized courtship they have fled to Italy to await her divorce. It has been clear to her from the beginning, she adds, that she and Lydia are "in the same box." Confronted by her own situation in the vulgar guise of Mrs.

Cope's, Lydia reacts at first as might be expected: she climbs hastily onto her moral high horse. But in recounting the scene to Gannett she admits her inconsistency and the folly of her earlier viewpoint: "Respectability! It was the one thing in life that I was sure I didn't care about, and it's grown so precious to me that I've stolen it because I couldn't get it in any other way." Gannett, seizing the opportunity, again urges marriage, and Lydia, after an abortive flight, capitulates.

No other early story marks out so precisely the ground on which the moral question in Edith Wharton's novels will be debated. Lydia Tillotson's decision sets the precedent for her fictional successors, for all those rebellious women, including Undine Spragg, who sooner or later heed the voice of respectability, bow to the conventions, accept the compromise. Julia Westfall, the heroine of "The Reckoning," in Edith Wharton's third collection of stories, *The Descent of Man* (1904), leaves her husband because, having tired of him, she decides that the marriage tie should bind neither partner permanently. Then, having remarried with the mutual understanding that each partner will be free to break the contract when he chooses, she discovers after a few years that her second husband is in love with another woman and insists on holding her to their agreement. In a moment of contrition, Julia visits her deeply wronged first husband to assure him that she now understands. Eighteen years later, Edith Wharton still finds enough interest in this tritely ironic situation to repeat it in *The Glimpses of the Moon*. The young lovers in that feeblest of her novels marry with the same tentative agreement, part on the basis of a foolish misunderstanding, and are reunited following a similarly disillusioning experience with their freedom.

Kate Clephane, in *The Mother's Recompense* (1925), having deserted her stuffy husband for a lover with a yacht and then having spent years of penitential exile abroad, knows that "the prison of her marriage had been liberty compared with what she had exchanged for it." There is only one kind of freedom possible for Edith Wharton's characters: that which they create within themselves with the aid of culture and which they may share with kindred souls in a republic of the spirit.

Many of these early stories testify to the apprentice's fascination with the world of artists and writers now at long last opening to her. Although only two of the stories in *The Greater Inclination* are concerned with what Robert Morss Lovett calls "problems of aesthetic morality," they foreshadow the importance of this interest in the volumes that follow. Five of the seven tales in *Crucial Instances* (1901) have as their central characters painters, authors, or collectors, and in general examine the artistic conscience and the relation of the artist to his public. The two remaining stories, "The Duchess at Prayer" and "The Confessional," are evidently, like "A Venetian Night's Entertainment" in *The Descent of Man,* by-products of the writing of *The Valley of Decision,* for both are romantic tales with an Italian historical setting.

Unlike Henry James, Mrs. Wharton was not at her best in exploring the human situation behind the work of art. Even in *Hudson River Bracketed* and its sequel *The Gods Arrive,* her most ambitious attempt to illuminate the writer's special problems and frustrations, her view of the artistic life remained an enchanted one, essentially the romanticized version of an outsider. None of her artists bears the stamp of authenticity. With the exception of Vance Weston, they are self-consciously devoted to an ideal of Art which exists mainly in the pages of sentimental fiction, and like Edith Wharton herself they are seldom caught unawares in their working clothes actually laboring at their craft. A Stephen Dedalus wrestling with the meaning, shape, and color of words would be an alien figure in their midst. The difficulties of their lives resolve themselves into social and moral crises which have only an incidental relation to their vocation.

It is significant that Mrs. Wharton is most convincing when she examines, as she so frequently does, cases of creative impotence, not merely because they are within reach of her irony but because, surrounded as she was most of her life by dilettantes, she can understand such cases better than that of the artist who is so absorbed in his task that he is all knees and elbows in the drawing room, and, secondly, because her own career was in one sense a triumph over the very obstacles that defeat her characters—social position, too much money, lack of sympathy, and an everyday environment that is indifferent, if not hostile to art. In the characterization of Vance Weston she fastened appropriately on the consuming egoism of the artist, but, having done so, she then went on to prove that, far from appreciating the positive value to the artist of this occupational trait, she was aware principally of its antisocial implications. *Her* art had to take its place always among the gardening, entertaining, and traveling that crowded her schedule. On occasion, her friend Bernard Berenson tells us, she could interrupt her more frivolous plans because "a fit of work" had come over her; but ordinarily "she never fussed about her work, never made you feel that it obsessed her." [6] The majority of the friends who have written about her com-

ment on the businesslike way she had of compartmental-
izing her interests, so that anyone who did not know
where she spent her morning hours would have difficulty
guessing, as did Sir Walter Scott's visitors, that she was
a writer. Although her closest friends expressed their
wonder that she got any writing done, the long bibliography of her works and the evidence in her manuscripts of
constant, painstaking revision prove that she had nothing
of the dilettante in her make-up. At the same time, it is
impossible to think of her in the same category with
James or Flaubert as being endlessly preoccupied by the
problems of the novel or as sharing their special devotion
to art as a profession and a way of life. How, if this were
not so, could she have made the extraordinary and un-
thinking demands on James's time and energies that
Percy Lubbock recalls—descending on him with her motor at Rye, confounding his working schedule, and bringing with her the distractions of the great world outside?
There was still something about Edith Wharton of the
divine amateur, and consequently her stories of artists
and writers retained something of the amateur's day-
dream which belonged to her youth.

Even so, the chef-d'œuvre of *Crucial Instances* (on the
whole, the least distinguished volume of stories Mrs.
Wharton published before the 'twenties) is "The Recovery," a parable about the artist in America. Keniston, a
well-known American painter, worshiped in his native
Hillbridge where he "took precedence of the colonial
State House, the Gilbert Stuart Washington, and the
Ethnological Museum," permits one of his wealthier dev-
otees to exhibit his paintings in Paris. He has never
been abroad, never studied the Old Masters, has taught
himself to paint and has produced slowly, not for want

of skill, but because in reality he has nothing to say. Europe is a revelation. He haunts the National Gallery in London and subsequently the Louvre. He refuses to attend his own exhibition. Meanwhile, his wife has been wondering anxiously how the knowledge that his work is inferior by European standards will affect him. Keniston meets the test: at forty he determines to start all over again and to learn his craft from the ground up.

Keniston represents the danger to the American artist of provincialism, a purely local standard of evaluation, and the protective adulation of a narrow, unsophisticated public. Even if the theme were not implicit in so much of Edith Wharton's subsequent work, it clamors for recognition in "The Recovery." At the outset of her career, she looked for guidance to those among her limited acquaintance in the literary world who represented the broadest and most traditional culture—men like Henry James, Paul Bourget, Charles Eliot Norton, and Edward Burlingame. To the end she remained skeptical of the artist whose background and inspiration were wholly native. She was fond of quoting Kipling's line, "How can they know England, that only England know?" She wrote in her essay on Paul Bourget: "En effet, c'est seulement en ayant vu d'autres pays, etudié leurs moeurs, lu leurs livres, frequenté leurs habitants, que l'on peut situer son propre pays dans l'histoire de la civilisation." [7] And she would have agreed with James that the American writer "*must* deal, more or less, even if only by implication, with Europe." [8]

It is difficult to quarrel with her premise, but it led her by degrees to conclusions that were extreme and unjustifiable and that betrayed more irritability than good sense. American life, she complained in her essay "The

Great American Novel" (1927), offers "so meagre a material to the imagination." [9] What she meant in the particular context was that it offers so limited an opportunity to the novelist of manners (an objection I will have occasion to consider later), but even on this ground her case has been undermined by novelists of a later generation. That she could even make the statement suggests how little real acquaintance she had with the imaginative literature of her own country, a fact that is underlined in her critical and miscellaneous prose, and especially in *The Writing of Fiction* (1925), by the paucity and at best the shallowness of her references to Melville, Hawthorne, and Twain, the most indigenous of our novelists. The importance of Melville particularly she never understood, but as late as 1924 classed him with Stevenson, Marryat, and the elder Dumas as a writer of adventure tales. With the important younger novelists of the turn of the century she had no community whatsoever, nor did she owe anything to Howells and his generation. It was only late in life and after years of almost uninterrupted residence abroad that she became genuinely interested in American fiction through the achievement of some of her younger contemporaries, such as Dreiser, Lewis, and Fitzgerald; but what she appreciated in them most was their traditional approach to the problem of technique in the novel—the fact that they gave aid and comfort in her crusade against Joyce and his disciples.

If the whole of nineteenth-century American literature had never existed, it is difficult to see how Edith Wharton's contribution would have been seriously modified. Her most indigenous work, *Ethan Frome*, was an attempt to alter the New England local color tradition as she thought she found it in the pages of Sarah Orne Jewett and Mary E. Wilkins Freeman, writers whom she accused too broadly of viewing their region through "rose-coloured spectacles." Otherwise, her literary origins are transatlantic. In both substance and manner, her fiction is closest to that of Balzac, Stendhal, George Eliot, and Henry James. From whatever angle she is approached, she is perhaps the least "American" of our important novelists, and it is well to recognize the fact from the outset.

Except for "The Recovery," none of the stories in *Crucial Instances* is worthy of the talent announced in her first collection. Setting aside the two romantic Italian episodes, the stories all conclude on a sentimental, optimistic note which we think of as foreign to Mrs. Wharton's characteristic tone. Keniston is not the only character to survive the "crucial instance" and, in fact, acquire new strength from his ordeal. For the heroine of "The Angel at the Grave," who has devoted her spinster existence to the memory of an illustrious New England ancestor, life takes on a new meaning when Orestes Anson's tarnished reputation is renewed through the discovery of a lost pamphlet. When the impoverished old dowager in "The Rembrandt" proposes to sell an Old Master that everyone but herself knows to be a fake, the other characters manage to save both her pride and her bank balance—and in the process try, like the principals in Chaucer's Franklin's Tale, to outdo each other in magnanimity. In their wholesale deference to the popular tone of magazine fiction, the stories in *Crucial Instances,* together with the long tale *Sanctuary* (1903), published about the same time, stand alone among Edith Wharton's earlier works. There is a marked reversion in these stories of contemporary life to the false sentiment and the conventionally "inspirational" endings of the stories she published in *Scribner's Magazine* in the early 'nineties.

One way to explain this sentimental interlude is to assume that the majority of the tales, excepting "The Confessional" and "The Duchess at Prayer," were written in the 'nineties or earlier and then rescued from the drawer for revision. Although the chronology of Mrs. Wharton's early short stories is bound to prove a vexing problem, thanks to the lack of manuscripts and her habit of constant revision, there is at least one bit of evidence to suggest that she refurbished early pieces in order to keep the market supplied. A version of "Bunner Sisters" (1916) was in existence as early as 1891 or, at the latest, 1892,[10] and yet there is nothing in the style of the published version, except possibly the curious mishandling of the dialogue, to remind us of the apprentice. Moreover, the particular segment of New York life that Edith Wharton chose to represent in "Bunner Sisters" relates it most clearly to "Mrs. Manstey's View," her first published story, whereas if we place it in the neighborhood of 1916 it seems, in both subject and treatment, a peculiarly isolated work. Although at this stage in her career Mrs. Wharton was neither a rapid nor a diligent worker ("uncertain" is her own term), the two years intervening between *The Greater Inclination* and *Crucial Instances* would ordinarily have been sufficient for the composition of the seven stories in the second volume. However, not taking into account the usual distractions that kept her from her desk, she had written her first long tale, *The Touchstone*, during the latter part of 1899[11] and by the first months of 1900 was hard at work on *The Valley of*

Decision, a task that involved long hours of reading and research as well as writing. During most of this year the projected volume of short stories was pushed aside. What better expedient than to rework her tyro efforts?

It is not difficult to determine from these early collections what Edith Wharton thought a short story should be, but if there is any doubt, one need only turn to her chapter on "Telling a Short Story" in *The Writing of Fiction,* where the theory fortunately agrees with her practice of twenty-five years earlier. The reader will find nothing original or provocative in the chapter and, as a matter of fact, nothing that will really help him to differentiate between Mrs. Wharton's stories and those of certain of her contemporaries with whom, in point of fact, she had little in common. The novel, she tells us, is primarily concerned with character, the short story with situation; but they are related in that "the art of rendering life in fiction can never, in the last analysis, be anything, or need to be anything, but the disengaging of crucial moments from the welter of existence." In the novel there may be a number of these "crucial moments," graduated in effect toward the most important; in the short story there must be only one. The significance of the episode is to be determined by its "relation to a familiar social or moral standard" and by its recognition of "the eternal struggle between man's contending impulses." The distinctive qualities of the treatment will be immediacy and compactness, which are to be realized mainly through a strict observance of the unities of time and point of view. Mrs. Wharton follows her friends Henry James and Paul Bourget in attaching a special importance to the intensity residing in "a personal, a direct impression of life" (the phrase is James's); consequently, in about a third of her stories she employs a narrator and in the others, where the story is told in the third person, our vision of events is limited to the view of one participant. In both cases she adheres to James's suggestion that—in her own words—"the mind chosen by the author to mirror his given case should be so situated, and so constituted, as to take the widest possible view of it."

Except for the restriction on the point of view, this definition of the short story is abstract to the point where it admits of no distinction between a short story by Edith Wharton and one, say, by James Joyce, although that is perhaps as it should be in a book professing to outline only a general theory of technique. In spite of Mrs. Wharton's analogy of the short story at its best to "a shaft driven straight into the heart of experience," the majority of her stories have less moral significance and less intensity than the slightest of episodes in *Dubliners;* her crucial moments seem faked in comparison to Joyce's muted epiphanies. Edith Wharton had a fatal weakness for the anecdote, for the situation capable of taking a surprising turn or of lending itself to an ironic or merely amusing treatment. Her recollections in *A Backward Glance* are punctuated with anecdotes related to her by Edward Robinson, Cecil Spring-Rice, Jean Cocteau, and others, all of them bizarre or ironic, and in which the situation, of course, is everything. Situations so defined are necessarily limited in their power of implication. Most of Edith Wharton's stories are so slight in subject and execution that the exceptions stand out. She wrote perhaps a dozen short stories good enough for any anthology, but she also wrote more than her share of ephemera.

E. K. Brown has remarked that, although the style of Mrs. Wharton's early stories (1890–1904) resembles that of James, she has not conceived of the short story in the same manner. Whereas James patiently develops every worth-while suggestion latent in his subject, Mrs. Wharton "l'embrasse [the subject] d'un seul coup et n'en present que l'élément essentiel et vital." [12] It is true that the assurance with which in too many of her stories Edith Wharton isolates her case, examines it cursorily, and makes her diagnosis has disturbed even her friendliest critics. Henry James, in a letter to Walter Berry, likened himself to an earth-bound worm and Mrs. Wharton to an eagle, suggesting that the latter, because he flies too swiftly and at too high an altitude, has no sharp impression of the terrain—specifically, the psychological terrain of the novel.[13] And Percy Lubbock remarked about her early short stories: "There is one gift we could occasionally wish for her, and that is the gift of forgetting that there are more picturesque chances and incidents in the world than one—the one for the moment under our eyes." [14] But Edith Wharton's reluctance to come to close grips with her subject is only part of the story; there is also the inherent failure of many of her subjects to sustain such an encounter.

It should be noted finally that these stories adhere to the formal tradition of the nineteenth rather than the twentieth century. Chekhov's prescription (which has had its effect in our time) that "when one has finished writing a short story, one should delete the beginning and the end" could not be applied to Edith Wharton's stories without fatal results. In contrast to the situations in Chekhov's and Joyce's stories, which seem to have been detached from life with a minimum of violence to their integrity, hers are rounded, enclosed, artificial. In a manner of speaking, her stories have no middle; their development is mainly exposition and climax. They are as remote as possible from the *tranche de vie* that she condemned so earnestly in *The Writing of Fiction*. And this is equally true of the stories of her last two decades. From a technical standpoint, she was no more an innovator in the short story than she was in the novel.

Inevitably, the name of Henry James has crept several times into the discussion, as it did into the reviews of Mrs. Wharton's first volume of stories. Since in what follows it will appear more, rather than less frequently, it may be well at this point to at least open the question of his influence on Edith Wharton. Early and late, from the publication of *The Greater Inclination* to the obituaries of its author nearly forty years afterward, it was customary to remark that she was a disciple of his and to let it go at that. Until all of the evidence is in (I am thinking particularly of the James letters to Mrs. Wharton which are part of the collection at Yale), it would be fairer to both writers to modify the usual view of their relationship by reminding ourselves that, roughly speaking, they started from the same position, proceeded by the same path, and that somewhere around 1900 they separated—with James taking a high road where the atmosphere, for Edith Wharton, proved too rare. It was in 1904 that she wrote to W. C. Brownell: ". . . The continued cry that I am an echo of Mr. James (whose books of the last ten years I can't read, much as I delight in the man) . . . makes me feel rather hopeless." [15]

Certainly the usual view is complicated by the fact that the two novelists' origins, background, and class outlook, as well as their literary ancestry, were almost identical. The most we can say for sure is that James led the way and that up to a certain point Edith Wharton found it easy to follow, and that rarely has there been so striking an affinity between two writers.

With certain departures, *The Writing of Fiction* is a highly simplified restatement of James's basic theory of fiction, but precisely for that reason—because of its orthodoxy and its determinedly impersonal quality—it is, for the student of Edith Wharton's own novels, an exasperating document. Mrs. Wharton had a mind of her own, but it expressed itself less in the form than in the tone and content of her fiction. If her literary intelligence was less patient and subtle than James's, it was usually more direct. Moreover, her strongest work is not her most Jamesian, so that any attempt to perpetuate a simple cause-and-effect view of their relationship is bound to be as misleading as the attempt to minimize Edith Wharton's debt to James in order to enhance her independent stature.

Although the general agreement in outlook and method between the two novelists cannot be deduced solely from Mrs. Wharton's early short stories, a certain area of it is already apparent. For James, his friend recalled, "every great novel must first of all be based on a profound sense of moral values ('importance of subject'), and then constructed with a classical unity and economy of means." [16] Leaving aside for the moment the question of form, we may protest, however mildly, that this is an oversimplification of James's doctrine as formulated first in "The Art of Fiction" and later in his preface to *The*

Portrait of a Lady. James was always more cautious than Edith Wharton in isolating and defining the various functions of a work of art. No statement so flatly confident, so open to a multitude of questions, as her paraphrase of his supposed doctrine would have been possible from him. His real position was more explicit and more tenable:

There is one point at which the moral sense and the artistic sense lie very near together; that is, in the light of the very obvious truth that the deepest quality of a work of art will always be the quality of the mind of the producer. In proportion as that intelligence is fine will the novel, the picture, the statue partake of the substance of beauty and truth.[17]

And seventeen years later:

There is, I think, no more nutritive or suggestive truth . . . than that of the perfect dependence of the "moral" sense of a work of art on the amount of felt life concerned in producing it. The question comes back thus, obviously, to the kind and degree of the artist's prime sensibility, which is the soil out of which his subject springs.[18]

This notion that the moral sense of a work of art is dependent, not on the subject (the artist must be granted his *donnée*), but rather on the quality of the mind that seeks to express it, is rather obscured in *The Writing of Fiction,* where we are told that "a good subject . . . must contain *in itself* something that sheds a light on our moral experience" (italics mine) and that it must first of all answer the normal reader's question, "What am I being told this story for? What judgment of life does it contain for me?" Nevertheless, in her early stories Edith Wharton tacitly recognized James's dictum by carefully assigning the point of view to the "finest" consciousness available, and in an unpublished critical fragment she acknowledged the dependence of the moral sense of a work of art on "the amount of felt life concerned in producing it" in her statement that "the immoral (or at least the harmful) novelist is he who handles a sombre or a complex subject without sufficient power to vivify its raw material." [19] Allowing for Mrs. Wharton's occasional oversimplifications, she and James are in perfect agreement. "The ultimate value of every work of art," she insisted, "lies, not in its subject, but in the way in which that subject is seen, felt, and interpreted." [20] Consequently, in her essay on Marcel Proust she took that writer gently to task for his failures of moral sensibility.[21] Her position is worth emphasizing because it will be remarked, first in *The Reef* (1912), but particularly in the novels she wrote following *The Age of Innocence* (1920), that her own moral sensibility is progressively inadequate to the demands made upon it by her subjects, with the result that her comments on Proust must strike the reader of *A Son at the Front* and *The Mother's Recompense* with an unexpected effect of irony.

What Edith Wharton said of George Eliot, that she "vibrated to *nuances* of conduct as an artist vibrates to subtleties of line and colour," [22] could be said of both her and James at this point in their respective developments. Unlike Miss Talcott, the heroine of her short story "A Cup of Cold Water," who is unable to "distinguish the intermediate tints of the moral spectrum," Edith Wharton sometimes allowed the intermediate tints to usurp the function of primary colors with the result that the dramatic texture of some of her early stories is perilously thin. Nevertheless, her problem was the same as James's:

how to express the nuances. And it is in this connection
that her most reliable and Jamesian cluster of metaphors
comes into play. Her characters, in the early short stories
and in *The Reef* particularly, are intensely aware of one
another; they respond to the slightest changes in the atmosphere of thought and sensation conveyed by another
presence; and they are equally alive to impressions gen-
erated by their physical environment. The general image
by which this empathy is expressed occurs in the reference to George Eliot just quoted: the individual becomes
an instrument capable of transmitting and receiving the
most delicate vibrations. When Edith Wharton is most
conscious of James's example, she falls most easily into
his manner. *The Reef* alone supplies countless variations of this central metaphor: ". . . Darrow, on meeting her again, had immediately felt how much finer and
surer an instrument of expression she had become" (p.
3); ". . . To the actual, the immediate, she spread vi-
brating strings" (p. 61); "He recalled with a faint smile
of retrospective pleasure the girl's enjoyment of her
evening, and the innumerable fine feelers of sensation
she had thrown out to its impressions" (p. 54); ". . . As
she walked by Darrow's side her imagination flew back
and forth, spinning luminous webs of feeling between
herself and the scene about her" (p. 116). The last example recalls the statement in *A Backward Glance* that,
to Henry James's intimates, his hesitancies of speech,
"far from being an obstacle, were like a cobweb bridge
flung from his mind to theirs, an invisible passage over
which one knew that silver-footed ironies, veiled jokes,
tiptoe malices, were stealing to explode a huge laugh at
one's feet." And in the same book we have a description
of Minnie Bourget, one of Edith Wharton's most cher-

ished friends, as a being "full of delicate and secret vibrations." It is impossible, of course, to pursue this subject of metaphoric parallels to its conclusion. Anyone familiar with the styles of both James and Mrs. Wharton will be constantly alive to the echoes. For example, the latter's heroines are often described as "spreading," "quietly beating," or "folding" the invisible wings of the spirit, or they may be simply aware, like Kate Orme in *Sanctuary,* that "whereas, before, the air had been full of flitting wings, now they seemed to pause over her and she could trust herself to their shelter." Another metaphor, by no means uncommon in fiction, but which is especially active in both James and Mrs. Wharton, is that of the moral or emotional abyss which is constantly opening at the characters' feet, dividing them from each other or from their own better natures. One recalls particularly those situations in James, frequently duplicated in Mrs. Wharton, where his heroes, confronted by a sudden demand on their feelings (usually made by a woman who has some claims on them), make a bridge of evasive words to carry them safely across this frightening abyss. It is apparent, in short, that the sensibility embodied in the point of view employed by both novelists is almost identical and therefore expresses itself in much the same terms.

In the early stories and novels the dialogue, too, is frequently Jamesian in its hesitations, seeming *non sequiturs,* and unfinished statements. In "The Twilight of the God," for example, we have what amounts to a parody of the master.

Oberville. ". . . You see I can only excuse myself by saying something inexcusable."

Isabel (deliberately). "Not inexcusable."
Oberville. "Not—?"
Isabel. "I had remembered."
Oberville. "Isabel!"
Isabel. "But now—"
Oberville. "Ah, give me a moment before you unsay it!"

But James's conversations are carried on in a denser and more highly charged atmosphere. Questions hang in the air unanswered, and the silences are oppressive. The air surrounding Edith Wharton's characters is of a thinner texture; remarks have a greater tendency to evaporate in it. Her dialogue is ordinarily brisker than James's and more emphatic.

Such parallels as I have suggested are confined to the realm of technique. The larger attitudes which these two novelists shared, their similar view of society and morals and their joint interest in the novel of manners, will be considered in their place. It would be easy, of course, to point up the resemblances in situation between *The Age of Innocence* and *The Europeans*, between *The Buccaneers* and *The Portrait of a Lady*, between *Madame de Treymes* and both *Madame de Mauves* and *The American;* but it could be argued that they are the natural result of two writers, related in background and temperament, working on the same general subject. It should be clear by now, however, that the reader who knows his James is at least half prepared to understand Edith Wharton on first acquaintance.

Chapter III

THE VALLEY OF DECISION

The beginning, middle, and end of Edith Wharton's career as a novelist coincide with the publication of her three historical novels. *The Age of Innocence* (1920) concluded the major period that had begun in earnest with *The Valley of Decision* (1902), and the posthumous appearance of her unfinished novel *The Buccaneers* (1938) belied the impression of nearly twenty years' standing that her integrity had been permanently sacrificed to the requirements of the popular market. Among these novels, only *The Valley of Decision,* with its setting in eighteenth-century Italy, ventured into a past antedating Mrs. Wharton's own recollections. Nevertheless, her attachment to the civilizations of vanished eras was sufficiently plain in her brilliantly written and permanently interesting travel accounts—*Italian Backgrounds, A Motor-Flight through France,* and *In Morocco*—and in her careful study of Italian villas and their gardens, books in which her professional devotion to landscape and architecture could be indulged with the utmost leisure and her interest in background isolated from the demands of story and characterization. In most of her novels, the Past—or at least that vital residue of the Past for which she pleaded—is summoned indirectly to comment on the shrunken and degraded present. It is in *The Valley of Decision* alone that the Past assumes an independent value and by the intrusion of its more material aspect manages to overwhelm the human aspect without which the art of the novel cannot justify itself. To a greater degree than in any of her other novels, Edith Wharton's attention is (to borrow a phrase that Henry James applied to Balzac) transferred from inside to outside, from the center of her subject to its circumference.

I have found no evidence to seriously shake Mrs. Wharton's statement that the writing of *The Valley of Decision* was not preceded by a laborious study of eighteenth-century Italy. "The truth is," she insisted in *A Backward Glance*, "that I have always found it hard to explain that gradual absorption into my pores of a myriad details of landscape, architecture, old furniture and eighteenth century portraits, the gossip of contemporary diarists and travellers. . . ." She seems in fact to have had some of Carlyle's genius for organizing and revivifying the scattered impressions drawn from literature, art, and random observation. At the same time, the dense and varied background of *The Valley of Decision* cannot be explained simply as the product of a kind of intellectual osmosis. The fragmentary notes that have survived the general ruin of her workshop indicate that she consulted a wide variety of sources and that to carry out the ambitious plan of the novel she had to pursue special investigations into such subjects as the history and intrigues of the Jesuits and the Illuminati, the domestic arrangements of the Italian nobility, the war of traditions in the theatre, and the influence in Italy of the French encyclopedists. On small sheets of expensive notepaper she jotted down the topics in fashionable drawing rooms, the eighteenth-century preference in house pets, notes on costumes, musical instruments, and theatrical masks and conventions. There is a long list of the scents and toilet waters to be found on the dressing tables of aristocratic ladies. From Evelyn she learned that "Bologna monks breed lap-dogs in great demand— their noses broken when puppies"; from Mrs. Piozzi, that countesses addressed their maids informally as "mia Sorella." Another hint from Dr. Johnson's quondam confidante helped her to imagine the vivid scene in Donna Laura's antechambers, with the servants idly playing cards and quarreling while the visitors go unattended.[1]

Much at home as Edith Wharton was in *sette-cento* Italy, her imagination could not have brought to life the rich, panoramic setting of *The Valley of Decision* without the stimulus and occasional details supplied by other observers. Working at the Mount in Lenox, far removed in space as well as time from her subject, she was able to bolster the vision of Alfieri's Italy formed by her travels and earlier reading by renewing old acquaintances and making new ones as she worked. Of such value were the accounts of Mrs. Piozzi, Arthur Young, Lady Mary Wortley Montagu, and Henry Swinburne, among the innumerable eighteenth-century English visitors to Italy, and of Goethe, Stendhal, de Brosses, and Kotzebue among their contemporaries on the continent; the memoirs of Gozzi, Goldoni, and Casanova; and the histories of the separate duchies, particularly those of Parma and Mantua, which together provided the model for Pianura. When the slender resources of

---

[1] For notes to chap. iii, see p. 254.

the Lenox public library failed her, Charles Eliot Norton and his library at Shady Hill came to her rescue with volumes unobtainable elsewhere.

This scholarly absorption in the milieu of a neglected period of Italian history was reflected in an unfortunate way in the novel. Seldom has a background so deeply felt and so authentic had as its fictional *raison d'être* a story and characters so lifeless and abstract. I doubt that Edith Wharton was ever deceived as to the vitality of her story. In the final essay of *Italian Backgrounds* (1905), she belatedly furnished the clue to the unity of that volume by defining her approach to Italy. "In the Italian devotional pictures of the early Renaissance," she wrote, "there are usually two quite unrelated parts: the foreground and the background."

The foreground is conventional. Its personages—saints, angels, and Holy Family—are the direct descendants of a long line of similar figures. Every detail of dress and attitude has been settled beforehand by laws which the artist accepts as passively as the fact that his models have two eyes apiece, and noses in the middle of their faces. . . . *It is only in the background that the artist finds himself free to express his personality. . . . One must look past and beyond the central figures, in their typical attitudes and symbolical dress, to catch a glimpse of the life amid which the painting originated.* Relegated to the middle distance, and reduced to insignificant size, is the real picture, the picture which had its birth in the artist's brain and reflects his impression of the life about him. [Italics mine.]

The passage applies to the novel. The foreground of *The Valley of Decision*, like that of the devotional paintings, is wholly conventional. The story of Odo Valsecca and Fulvia Vivaldi, in spite of its superficially tragic conclusion and the intellectual pretensions of its martyred lovers, fails in any significant way to break with the stock romantic pattern of the costume novel that had ruled popular taste in fiction for a decade. At tense moments the hero and heroine freeze into the noble attitudes of an heroic tableau: the renunciatory gesture, the gesture of despair or triumph, are as carefully rehearsed as the theatrically conceived speeches they accompany. Fulvia Vivaldi, like Romola whom she resembles, belongs to the second half of the nineteenth century; she is a victim of the genteel dogma in fiction, enunciated by the authors of *The Gilded Age* among others, that woman is either angel or devil, "the vestal of a holy temple" or "the fallen priestess of a desecrated shrine." For this reason, and also because she is acting under Mrs. Wharton's direction as the spokesman of a barely disguised feminism, her substance is almost refined away. She is remote, ethereal, wholly idealized, "the symbol of [Odo's] best aims and deepest failure." Her cavalier is several jumps behind the reader in acknowledging the abstract quality of her personality: "Perhaps her recent suffering had spiritualized a countenance already pure and lofty; for as he looked at her it seemed to him that she was transformed into a being beyond earthly contact, and his heart sank with the sense of her remoteness."

In the character of Odo, Mrs. Wharton sought to dramatize the intellectual and spiritual conflicts of the age.[2] Unfortunately, in order to funnel the various and often contradictory currents through a single representative consciousness she had to endow her hero with a mind and temperament pliable to the most diverse in-

41

fluences. It was necessary on the one hand that he be of an easygoing, skeptical, pleasure-loving disposition; on the other, that he exhibit a latent idealism and an intermittent passion for reform. These elements are never plausibly reconciled; the character of Odo remains largely blurred and amorphous. Perhaps to a certain extent *The Valley of Decision* may beg the questions of form and characterization by taking refuge, along with *Marius the Epicurean,* in the anomalous category of the philosophical romance; but the reader has the right to object that the only excuse for employing the novel form at all in such an enterprise is for the purpose, as George Eliot argued, of making ideas incarnate.[3] In *The Valley of Decision,* as in *Daniel Deronda,* that purpose is never achieved. The many-sided conflict of ideas which Odo embodies is not successfully dramatized. It is intellectualized, explained, but never made incarnate.

Percy Lubbock in *The Craft of Fiction,* following his friend and master Henry James, has emphasized the useful distinction between "picture" and "drama," between the pictorial and the scenic methods of development in the novel: "It is a question of the reader's relation to the writer; in one case the reader faces toward the storyteller and listens to him, in the other he turns toward the story and watches it." In *The Valley of Decision* Mrs. Wharton has relied mainly on the former. The pictorial method of development, to which the dramatic has been largely sacrificed, is employed to obtain a broad and representative rather than an intense and personal impression of life. "It is the method of picture-making," says Mr. Lubbock, "that enables the artist to cover his great spaces of life and quantities of experience," and herein lies the peculiar advantage of the novel over the play, the scenic method over the dramatic. The danger of exploiting this advantage at the expense of direct, that is, dramatic representation is obvious in *The Valley of Decision,* as it is in Thackeray and frequently in Balzac, whereas the "judicious blend" of the two methods for which Lubbock seeks may be found at its most successful in writers like James, Tolstoy, and Flaubert.

At the same time, it is her reliance on the panoramic method which enabled Edith Wharton to bring her milieu so impressively to life. The physical and intellectual backgrounds of her story provide a better testimonial to her future powers as a novelist than does her pallid foreground. To paraphrase her remark about Italian religious paintings: one must look past and beyond the central characters in their typical romantic attitudes and dress to catch a glimpse of the eighteenth-century actuality in contrast to which the drama reveals itself as so patently contrived. It is more than a glimpse, however. The novelist has taken no less than the whole of northern Italy—its spiritual as well as physical terrain—for her province. Odo Valsecca's odyssey, which includes lengthy stays in Turin, Milan, Naples, Monte Cassino, Rome, Florence, and Venice, provides a kind of Baedeker tour, with careful attention not merely to local monuments but to the details of local color. "Whatever other qualities the historical novelist has," Mrs. Wharton once wrote, "the essential one is the visualizing power. . . .

Our conception of the men and women who lived three or four hundred years ago is made up not from personal experience, but from literature and art—from the books they wrote, the pictures they painted, and the houses they lived in. From the books we obtain, with more or less effort of mental adjustment, a notion of what they thought and how they expressed their ideas; but much more vivid is the notion formed of them from their appearance and environment. And it is for this reason that the visualizing gift is of the first importance to the novelist. George Eliot did not possess it. Her letters from Italy show her curious insensibility to qualities of atmosphere, to values of form and colour. And for this reason her Florence, for all its carefully studied detail, remains a pasteboard performance. . . .[4]

Without questioning the justice of the last remark, we must grant that Edith Wharton was blessed preëminently with the visualizing power. Not only did she have an extraordinary sensitiveness to the local features of landscape and architecture, but, like James in *The American Scene,* she observed with a painter's as well as a traveler's eye, generalizing and composing the details of her subject and frequently calling the attention explicitly to her method (". . . the scene was such as Salvator might have painted . . . the roadside started into detail like the foreground of some minute Dutch painter . . . this prodigal response to fancy's claims suggested the boundless invention of some great scenic artist, some Olympian Veronese, with sea and sky for a palette"). Moreover, *The Valley of Decision* contains a succession of genre paintings remarkable, in the generally romantic context, for their realism. With the aid of contemporary diarists and travelers, the ordinary life of the road so beloved of the picaresque writers is frequently and sharply brought into focus.

Here were pilgrims of every condition, from the noble lady of Turin or Asti (for it was the favorite pilgrimage of the Sardinian court), attended by her physician and her cicisbeo,

44

to the half-naked goat-herd of Val Sesia or Salluzzo; the cheerful farmers of the Milanese, with their wives, in silver necklaces and hairpins, riding pillion on plump white asses; sick persons travelling in closed litters or carried on hand-stretchers; crippled beggars obtruding their deformities; confraternities of hooded penitents, Franciscans, Capuchins and Poor Clares in dusty companies; jugglers, pedlars, Egyptians and sellers of drugs and amulets.

Long after the story has blurred in the memory, we remain on familiar terms not only with the everyday background, but with the brilliant episodes of court life in Turin, the pageant of Venetian gaiety and intrigue, the glimpses of the theatrical life of the time taken at every level. It is not surprising that the subordinate characters, such as the Abate Cantapresto, Carlo Gamba, and the actress Mirandolina of Chioggia, have more actuality than do Fulvia and Odo; they belong more intimately to the physical background and in a large measure draw their vitality from it.

In reviewing another novel about eighteenth-century Italy, Maurice Hewlett's *The Fool Errant* (1905), Edith Wharton had occasion to remark that in the past century fiction "has been enlarged by making the background a part of the action, and it is only when the stage-setting fails to merge with the drama that its details become importunate."[5] As a daughter of the nineteenth century, she knew her Taine and Sainte-Beuve, her Balzac and Flaubert, and could hardly deny the importance of background in the general composition. Not only was it no longer possible to write a novel, and particularly a historical novel, with the thinly generalized, almost wholly factitious background of, say, a *Gil Blas*, but the means had to be found to relate that element in a vital way to the action and, as she argued in *The Writing of Fiction,* to make it subservient to the point of view.

The impression produced by a landscape, a street or a house should always, to the novelist, be an event in the history of the soul, and the use of the "descriptive passage," and its style, should be determined by the fact that it must depict only what the intelligence concerned would have noticed, and always in terms within the register of that intelligence.

This is admirably Jamesian (and Edith Wharton was always readier to agree with James than to follow him), but it cannot be vindicated in the pages of *The Valley of Decision,* where no such absolute interaction between foreground and background exists—rather where on occasion it is clearly denied. Thus, one lengthy description of a typical Venetian scene is brought casually into relation to the foreground with the remark that it "unrolled before [Odo] with as little effect of reality as the episodes woven into some gaily-tinted tapestry," and there are great clusters of representative detail which can be assimilated only in the most general fashion into "the history of the soul."

Here we have the dilemma confronting the chronicler of a fictional past—the dilemma stated a century earlier by Walter Scott in his preface to *Waverley.* The element of setting in a historical novel, especially a novel about so unfamiliar a period as the Italian *sette-cento,* must be disproportionately elaborated to help achieve the illusion of reality. The average reader cannot find his way about by himself, and his orientation places a heavy responsibility on the novelist. But in fulfilling this obligation, the novelist finds it difficult or impossible to subordinate every detail to the dramatic effect and the point of view.

For someone with Edith Wharton's tastes and interests, the dilemma was unresolvable. The setting was what absorbed her; the characters and story had to get along as best they could. It is mainly in such stories as *Ethan Frome*, which had a stark, contemporary background, that she was able to give us an example of the novel *démeublé*. As soon as she moved into the richly furnished past or the more elaborate drawing rooms of the present, the details threatened to become importunate. Even in *The Age of Innocence* and *The Buccaneers*, written long after the novelist of manners had found herself and was able to estimate more accurately the dramatic significance of appearances, her precise notation of costume and decor was every now and then merely ludicrous:

. . . A warm pink mounted to the girl's cheeks, mantled her brow to the roots of her fair braids, and suffused the young shape of her breast to the line where it met a modest tulle tucker fastened with a single gardenia. (*The Age of Innocence*, p. 3.)

Mrs. St. George shivered under her dotted muslin ruffled with Valenciennes, and drew a tippet edged with swansdown over her shoulders. (*The Buccaneers*, p. 9.)

It remains to ask whether there are any personal and contemporary meanings to be drawn from *The Valley of Decision*—whether Edith Wharton was attracted to her subject by any other motives than her love of Italy and her desire to do justice to a period largely overlooked in English historical fiction. Like her hero Odo, she possessed "a deep moral curiosity that ennobled [her] sensuous enjoyment of the outward show of life." At times,

47

the Worth tea gown barely concealed the hair shirt. Her great subject, the way in which her own "innocent" and irresponsible class coöperated—however involuntarily—with the new moneyed class that had emerged since the Civil War, to sacrifice the finer spirits coming within their orbits, had been only faintly adumbrated in her short stories, although it was shortly to be enlarged in *The House of Mirth*. To one for whom the past was so much a living part of the present, the resemblances between the social order in Italy before the Risorgimento and that of her own late nineteenth-century New York would have been inescapable. In eighteenth-century Italy, she once wrote, "people lived *au jour le jour*, taking pain and pleasure lightly, and without much sense of the moral issue." [6] The generalization is underlined throughout *The Valley of Decision*. The dominant social tone is that struck by the extravagant, hedonistic, and narrow-minded aristocracies of Venice and Turin rather than that of Sir William Hamilton's *salon* at Naples, where the chosen spirits of the age gathered in a liberal atmosphere to discuss the new ideas flooding into Italy from the north. To the reader of *The House of Mirth*, *The Custom of the Country*, and Mrs. Wharton's autobiography, what is it that is so familiar about the latent social commentary of *The Valley of Decision?* Why, for instance, does her description of Genoa set up such determined echoes?

. . . The splendid houses with their marble peristyles, and the painted villas in their orange-groves along the shore, housed a dull and narrow-minded society, content to amass wealth and play biribi under the eyes of their ancestral Vandykes, without any concern as to the questions agitating the world. A kind of fat commercial dulness, a lack of that personal distinction which justifies magnificence, seemed to Odo the prevailing note of the place.

Clearly, in such passages we are aware of the author and mood of *The House of Mirth*. The ornately hideous sixty-room mansions on Fifth Avenue built by the founders of the post-Civil War dynasties and the social ideal which they embodied are obliquely criticized in *The Valley of Decision*. The showy, irresponsible upper-class society of *sette-cento* Italy comes off badly in comparison with the subversive group of humanitarians and free-thinkers gathered about Professor Vivaldi, but no more so than the pleasure-seeking society to which Lily Bart is condemned in comparison with Lawrence Selden's "republic of the spirit." The following passage refers to Odo Valsecca and the court life at Turin, but without any inconsistency it could be introduced into *The House of Mirth* to describe Selden (or, with a change of pronoun, into the novel which followed it, *The Fruit of the Tree*, to describe Justine Brent), because in reality it gives us Edith Wharton's reaction to the commercial civilization of New York:

None was more open than he to the seducements of luxurious living, the polish of manners, the tacit exclusion of all that is ugly or distressing; but it seemed to him that fine living should be but the flower of fine feeling, and that such external graces, when they adorned a dull and vapid society, were as incongruous as the royal purple on a clown.

The reader who finds a double significance in the background and events of what otherwise might pass as an innocent, if unusually solemn historical novel may be teased by another question. Was it simply by accident

that during the heyday of progressivism in this country
Mrs. Wharton chose to write a novel so contrary in spirit
to that vast movement of philanthropy and reform sponsored by scientists, social workers, and even politicians,
and somewhat later by journalists and novelists—a novel
so devoid of optimism and so skeptical of panaceas? In
the light of her background and convictions, I think not.
I am aware that she has elsewhere warned her readers
that "the general conclusions which disengage themselves from the tale . . . must be sought, not in the fate
of the characters, and still less in their own comments
on it, but in the kind of atmosphere the telling of their
story creates, the light it casts on questions beyond its
borders." [7] But taking this admonishment literally, it is
impossible not to define the "atmosphere" of *The Valley
of Decision* as one of disillusionment with the possibilities of a human nature freed from the discipline of a
stable social hierarchy and the manners of an established
culture. The general conclusions of the final important
chapter will be reiterated in *French Ways and Their
Meaning, A Motor-Flight through France,* and *A Backward Glance,* and they will be found to occupy the
center of the argument in Mrs. Wharton's subsequent
novels.

Odo Valsecca's contemplated reforms in Pianura are
defeated by the very people they are supposed to benefit.
Following Fulvia's assassination, Odo falls desperately
ill and nearly dies. During his slow return to life, he
reviews the illusions fostered by his devotion to Fulvia's
high-minded aims:

He was beginning to feel the social and political significance
of those old restrictions and barriers against which his early

zeal had tilted. Certainly in the ideal state the rights and obligations of the different classes would be more evenly adjusted. But the ideal state was a figment of the brain. The real one, as Crescenti had long ago pointed out, was the gradual and heterogeneous product of remote social conditions, wherein every seeming inconsistency had its roots in some bygone need, and the character of each class, with its special passions, ignorances, and prejudices, was the sum total of influences so ingrown and inveterate that they had become a law of thought.

The proposed constitution is withdrawn, and for several years Odo governs his duchy apathetically while the old abuses reassert themselves. Then the French Revolution, which prefaces the triumph of Carlo Gamba's liberals and the subsequent annexation of Pianura by Napoleon, forces him to a final revaluation of his humanitarian scheme:

The new year rose in blood and mounted to a bloodier noon. All the old defenses were falling. Religion, monarchy, law, were sucked down into the whirlpool of liberated passions. Across that sanguinary scene passed, like a mocking ghost, the philosopher's vision of the perfectibility of man. Man was free at last—freer than his would-be liberators had ever dreamed of making him—and he used his freedom like a beast.

While Italy is trying futilely to prepare for the French invasion, Odo awakes one morning to find his government overthrown by the people. He is offered a bribe by Gamba to lend his name to the new government, but he refuses. "The ideas he had striven for had triumphed at last, and his surest hold on authority was to share openly in their triumph. A profound horror dragged him back. The new principles were not those for which he had striven. The goddess of the new worship was but a bloody Maenad who had borrowed the attributes of freedom."

Nothing is clearer than that for Edith Wharton, with her conservative, anti-Rousseauistic bias and her preference for gradual, orderly reform within the framework of the existing social structure, the French Revolution was a disaster comparable to the American Civil War and (as we shall see) the First World War, both of which brought about a revolution in manners as deplorable, in her mind, as a revolution in government.

Chapter IV

TOWARD THE NOVEL OF MANNERS

As it turned out, *The Valley of Decision* was a unique performance. In spite of the contemporary frame of reference in which much of its history may be placed, it is a far cry from Odo Valsecca's Italy to the contemporary beau monde of Edith Wharton's second novel, *The House of Mirth*. For all its sentimentality, her first published story, "Mrs. Manstey's View" (1891), with its sordid tenement setting and its unhappy resolution, provided a truer indication of her bent. If we can take seriously one of Mrs. Wharton's earliest recollections, she was destined from the beginning to be a realist. As a child in Paris, she used to sit in a chair, holding in her lap a book she could not read (frequently it was upside down), and make up stories about the only people who were real to her imagination—the grownups with whom she was surrounded almost to the exclusion of company of her own age. Mother Goose and Hans Christian Andersen bored her, but the very mundane domestic crises of the Greek gods roused the future novelist's imagination to a creative boil. Then, as later, she evidently was prolific, but none of her stories was taken down: "All I remember is that my tales were about what I still thought of as 'real people' (that is, grown-up people, resembling in appearance and habits my family and their friends, and caught in the same daily coil of 'things that might have happened')." It is no great descent, after all, from Olympus to the House of Mirth.

Edith Wharton's account of the problems she met and overcame in the writing of her second novel may be found in *A Backward Glance*. Edward Burlingame, to whom the unwritten story was promised, had cut into her leisurely program with the request that she deliver the novel ahead of schedule so that its serial publication in *Scribner's Magazine* could begin immediately. Faced with the task of writing the book in six months, she tied herself for the first time to the professional routine of daily composition. With *The Valley of Decision* the only major work to her credit, she still regarded herself as an apprentice and *The House of Mirth* as the first real test of her powers. "It was not until I wrote 'Ethan Frome,'" she recalled in her memoirs, "that I suddenly felt the artisan's full control of his implements."

She had long since settled on her subject: the pleasure-seeking society of fashionable New York at the turn of the century. But although it was the material she knew best, the question of its "typical human significance" defied her. "In what aspect," she asked herself, "could a society of irresponsible pleasure-seekers be said to have, on the 'old woe of the world,' any deeper bearing than the people composing such a society could guess?" Almost at the same moment, Henry James was recording his renewed impressions of the United States for *The American Scene*. Confronted, in Newport, by "the ivory idol, whose name is leisure," he decided he would hardly choose that idle and luxurious little world, where the social elements, "even in their own kind, are as yet too light and thin," for the materials of a tragedy. "People love and hate and aspire with the greatest intensity when they have to make their time and opportunity." [1] If this was true of Newport, it was no less true of the fashionable New York world of *The House of Mirth.*

It is to Edith Wharton's credit that she recognized the perilous transparency of the human nature she had to deal with—a human nature subject to no stresses that money could not alleviate, and therefore incapable of expressing itself with the greatest intensity. The characterization of Lily Bart was central to the problem; and since Lily, in order to satisfy her function in the novel, had to take her cue from the more worldly of her associates, she remains, so far as the moral significance of her actions is concerned, until almost the end of the novel an essentially lightweight and static protagonist. Nevertheless, she has, if only in embryo, certain qualities which raise her above her associates and make her distinctly worth saving, so that her fate, if not tragic according to any satisfactory definition of the term, at least impresses us with the sense of infinite and avoidable waste. Edith Wharton's own answer to her question was "that a frivolous society can acquire dramatic significance only through what its frivolity destroys. Its tragic implication lies in its power of debasing people and ideals." Change the word "frivolous" to "materialistic," and the story of Lily Bart assumes a larger significance. Edith Wharton was one of the first American novelists to develop the possibilities of a theme which since the turn of the century has permeated our fiction: the waste of human and spiritual resources which in America went hand in hand with the exploitation of the land and forests. *The House*

[1] For notes to chap. iv, see p. 255.

of Mirth belongs in the same category with *Windy McPherson's Son, The Professor's House,* Robert Herrick's *Clark's Field,* and countless other novels which tried to calculate the expense of spirit that a program of material self-conquest entailed.

There is some indication that Mrs. Wharton conceived of her action, perhaps unconsciously, in terms of naturalistic tragedy. In *A Backward Glance* she recalls her introduction to "the wonder-world of nineteenth century science" and the excitement of reading for the first time the works of Darwin, Huxley, Spencer, Haeckel, and other evolutionists. It is impossible, perhaps, to calculate their influence, but it has never been considered. She was perfectly acquainted, moreover, with the French naturalistic tradition beginning with Flaubert, and it is not impossible that Emma Bovary is the spiritual godmother of Lily Bart. But this is at best circumstantial evidence, whereas the novel itself adequately conveys the suggestion. Its theme is the victimizing effect of a particular environment on one of its more helplessly characteristic products. It was the discovery of the nineteenth century, as someone has said, that Society, rather than God or Satan, is the tyrant of the universe; and the society into whose narrow ideal Lily Bart is inducted at birth conspires with her mother's example and training to defeat from the start any chance of effective rebellion. In the naturalistic tradition, the action of *The House of Mirth* is in a sense all denouement, for Lily's conflict with her environment—no more than the feeble and intermittent beating of her wings against the bars of "the great gilt cage"—is mortgaged to defeat. Her vacillation between the claims of the spirit represented by Selden and the prospect of a wealthy marriage is never quite convincing. Beyond Selden's tentative solicitations there is nothing in her life to encourage rebellion. And undermining his influence is the symbolic figure of Gerty · Farish, Lily's cousin, embodying the "dinginess" which above everything else Lily dreads.

Lily, in short, is as completely and typically the product of her heredity, environment, and the historical moment which found American materialism in the ascendant as the protagonist of any recognized naturalistic novel. Like any weak individual—like Clyde Griffiths or Carrie Meeber—she is at the mercy of every suggestion of her immediate environment; she responds to those influences which are most palpably present at a given moment. Although we are asked to believe that two sides of her personality are struggling for possession, there is no possibility of a genuine moral conflict until near the end of the action when as a result of suffering she experiences the self-realization which is the condition of any moral growth. Through no fault of her own, she has—can have—only the loosest theoretical grasp of the principles which enable Selden to preserve his weak idealism from the corroding atmosphere in which they are both immersed.

Inherited tendencies had combined with early training to make her the highly specialized product that she was: an organism as helpless out of its narrow range as the sea-anemone torn from the rock. She had been fashioned to adorn and delight; to what other end does nature round the rose-leaf and paint the humming-bird's breast? And was it her fault that the purely decorative mission is less easily and harmoniously fulfilled among social beings than in the world of nature? That it is apt to be hampered by material necessities or complicated by moral scruples?

The idea, much less happily expressed, might have been taken from Dreiser. It is all there: the deterministic view reinforced by analogies drawn from nature, even the rhetorical form of address. True to the logic imposed by her subject and theme, Mrs. Wharton seems to imply what Dreiser everywhere affirms: that in the struggle for survival the morally scrupulous individual has in effect disarmed himself. Lily's vagrant impulses of generosity and disinterestedness and her antique sense of honor are the weak but fatal grafts on her nature.

I do not want to press the point too far. The impact of the passage is after all still very different from what it would be in Dreiser, for Edith Wharton never rode determinism as a thesis. Her view was conditioned by a faith in moral values that collided head on with the implications of determinism, and it was impossible for her to present a situation without regard to its moral significance. But the day is past when we necessarily see a contradiction if the two views are embraced simultaneously. Naturalism allies itself conveniently—and, if need be, temporarily—with a personal mood of despair, and I think it likely that this is what happened in Mrs. Wharton's case. The mood renews itself periodically, but except in *Summer* (1917) it is never so strong again as in *The House of Mirth*. There is added support for this view, I believe, in the fact that both verbal and dramatic irony are usually active in this novel, helping to establish an unmistakably pessimistic tone.

It should be clear, at any rate, that we are deceiving ourselves if we try to account for the compelling interest of *The House of Mirth* by the nature or intensity of the moral conflict. Besides the reasons I have suggested, the alternatives proposed to Lily Bart in the persons of Selden and Gerty Farish are not at all attractively urged. It was beyond Edith Wharton's powers of sympathy and imagination, and at odds with her distrust of philanthropy, to make Gerty Farish, with her social work, her one-room flat, and the unrelieved dinginess of her life in general, an engaging figure. And what can we say of Selden, who maintains his integrity at the cost of any nourishing human relationship? Like Winterbourne in *Daisy Miller*, he is betrayed by his aloofness, his hesitations, his careful discriminations. He is the least attractive ambassador of his "republic of the spirit," and Mrs. Wharton knows this as well as her readers. In fact, the tragic effect of Lily Bart's fate is jeopardized by an irony directed principally at Selden, for she accidentally takes an overdose of sleeping pills while he is trying to make up his mind to marry her.

The quality in the novel that seizes and holds the reader, and that accounts more than any other for its persistent vitality, is the same which we find in the novels of Dreiser. In the spectacle of a lonely struggle with the hostile forces of environment, there is a particular kind of fascination which is not at all diminished by the certainty of defeat. The individual episodes in Lily Bart's story are moves in a game played against heavy odds, and the fact that the game is conducted according to an elaborate set of rules which are unfamiliar to the general reader gives it an added interest. After her initial success and unexpected reverses, the advantage moves back and forth, but always inclining toward the opponent's side, until Lily is maneuvering frantically to retrieve her position. On the whole, she plays like an amateur, but luck combined with flashes of skill keeps the game from going constantly against her. The episodic structure of the novel, which Mrs. Wharton labored vainly to control,[2] reinforces this impression: the individual moves and countermoves stand out prominently from the action as a whole. In contrast to *The Valley of Decision*, the author treats her subject for the most part scenically, letting the episodes speak for themselves. Moreover, if the interest were centered in the moral conflict instead of the external drama, it would be reasonable to expect a narrower aesthetic distance, as in *The Reef* or *The Fruit of the Tree*. Either that or we must agree with Mrs. Wharton's implication in *A Backward Glance* that she has learned very little from the later Henry James and is still inclined, as the master himself complained, to survey the psychological terrain from too great a height. But the fact seems to be that our attention is directed to a scene of life presented in its broader aspects rather than to a complicated moral dilemma.

For its contemporary interest, the novel relies less heavily than is sometimes assumed on the portrait of a particular society and on the value to the social historian of Mrs. Wharton's authentic delineation of manners. Lily Bart as a type has survived and multiplied, and the society in which she figured is still recognizable, although it has democratized itself to the point where it has lost some of the dramatic possibilities with which a complex gradation of manners once endowed it. Lily is what Justine Brent, in *The Fruit of the Tree*, lives in dread of becoming and what Sophy Viner, in *The Reef*, becomes—"one of those nomadic damsels who form the camp-followers of the great army of pleasure." In return for their hospitality, she serves her wealthy friends —or, rather, is used by them—as social secretary, chauffeur, auxiliary hostess, and, less agreeably, as go-between and scapegoat in their extramarital adventures. The personal freedom of Selden or Gerty Farish seems to her to be purchased at too great a cost. Her compromise is a familiar one in our society; her successors are legion. She is still around, in the person of Susy Lansing of *The Glimpses of the Moon* (1922), when Edith Wharton makes her first survey of postwar manners. Today, every community that can boast the equivalent of a four hundred has its quota of Lily Barts.

If there is a single dominant emphasis in the fiction of the decade and a half preceding the First World War, it is on the drama of social aspiration—a drama managed, I should add, almost entirely by women. *The House of Mirth* joins a trend that had become noticeable in such pioneer treatments of the theme as Henry Blake Fuller's *With the Procession* (1895), Robert Herrick's *The Gospel of Freedom* (1898), and Robert Grant's *Unleavened Bread* (1900). According to these novelists, the moral landscape was being altered by middle-class wives oppressed by too much leisure and by the fact of their husbands' increasing devotion to business. Bored, restless, and conscious as never before of their individuality and their right to a freedom not yet adequately defined, they had begun to exert their powers in the social arena. Although Lily Bart was single and moved in a more inaccessible sphere than the emancipated heroines of Fuller, Herrick, Grant, and David Graham Phillips, her motives were none the less familiar to the public that established *The House of Mirth* among the year's best sellers. Nevertheless, it was in *The Custom of the Country* that Edith Wharton most nearly approximated the type of novel established by her

61

predecessors, and for that reason we will have occasion to look more closely at the "new woman" novel in relation to the career of Undine Spragg.

For present purposes, it is only necessary to remind ourselves that it is the novelist of manners who is able to dramatize most effectively the social-climbing adventure. When Lily Bart, following the debacle on the French Riviera, finds herself reduced to the hospitality of the Gormer set, she is able to measure the extent of her fall by certain unmistakable signs: "The people about her were doing the same things as the Trenors, the Van Osburghs, and the Dorsets: the difference lay in a hundred shades of aspect and manner, from the pattern of the men's waistcoats to the inflexion of the women's voices." In the total context of Mrs. Wharton's fiction, the passage is of the utmost significance, for it emphasizes the importance of manners—the "hundred shades of aspect and manner"—in conditioning the view of reality we get through her novels. Never for a moment was she unaware of the conflict of appearances by means of which the individual and his values, as well as the constant changes within the social structure, are defined. In novel after novel she uses the data resulting from her careful observation and differentiation of manners at various levels of American society not merely to enhance the illusion, but to plot the real undertaking in which most of her characters are engaged: that of determining, fixing, or altering their status in society. In the fulfillment of this purpose, no data is too trivial—not even the pattern of waistcoats. Writing on Balzac, Henry James betrayed his envy of the great French novelist because for him "the old world in which costume had . . . a social meaning" had happily lingered on.

The most personal shell of all, the significant dress of the individual, whether man or woman, is subject to as sharp and as deep a notation—it being no small part of [Balzac's] wealth of luck that the age of dress differentiated and specialized from class to class and character to character, not least moreover among men, could still give him opportunities of choice, still help him to define and intensify, or peculiarly to *place* his apparitions.[3]

The same assumption underlies everything Edith Wharton wrote. When Halo Tarrant, in *Hudson River Bracketed,* is coaching Vance Weston in the writing of his elegiac novel *Instead,* her advice echoes the passage from James: "Don't forget that Alida would always have had her handkerchief in her hand: with a wide lace edge. . . . It's important, because it made them use their hands differently. . . . And their minds, too, perhaps." Edith Wharton's absorption in the minutiae of appearance has such a direct bearing on her intent that we can forgive her the comparatively few occasions when details of dress and decor are elaborated for their own sake.

In his important and suggestive essay "Manners, Morals, and the Novel," Lionel Trilling has defined the novel as "a perpetual quest for reality, the field of its research being always the social world, the material of its analysis being always manners as the indication of the direction of man's soul."[4] He insists that the definition requires the broadest interpretation of the term "manners." To limit it to the forms, gestures, and ceremonies which relieve the friction of social intercourse would be absurd, and to extend it to include the larger notion of "customs" would make the definition only slightly more valid. The term is all but undefinable because it must be used to suggest so much: customs and polite usages, surely—but also language, names, dress, cuisine, the various expressions of religious, moral, political, and aesthetic values— all the signs, tangible and vague, by which a group either comprising or functioning within a culture emphasizes its separateness.

In a long-established, traditionally rich culture the signs will be abundant and generally reliable. Manners will be more or less stabilized and thus provide a surer guide to the novelist. But in a new, amorphous, self-consciously democratic culture the signs will be fewer and more uncertain. Henry James, recognizing this, complained to his friend William Dean Howells that there was little material for the novelist in a rudimentary social order. Howells' reply was characteristic and rather smug: "There is the whole of human nature!" *But,* comments Edith Wharton in relating the exchange, "what does 'human nature' thus denuded consist in, and how much of it is left when it is separated from the web of customs, manners, culture it has elaborately spun about itself?" [5] Howells' remark starts from an assumption that most American novelists have tacitly shared, that a preoccupation with manners is antidemocratic because it admits the existence of class; and the fact that it is addressed to James implies a gentle rebuke. But as Mr. Trilling has observed in another essay: "In fiction, as perhaps in life, the conscious realization of social class produces intention, passion, thought, and what I have called substantiality." [6] Human nature, however we define it, can accommodate itself to a myriad of forms, and these forms in turn provide the data from which we generalize about "human nature." The novelist of manners is above all aware of the importance of these forms as the only reliable index to the passions and ideals of his characters. For Henry James, as for Edith Wharton, human nature could not express itself with any concreteness or dramatic significance except through the medium of manners, and a society that offered a complex field for this kind of scrutiny was more valuable for the novelist's purpose than one that did not. "It is on manners, customs, usages, habits, forms," he wrote to Howells, "upon all these things matured and established, that the novelist lives—they are the very stuff his work is made of." [7] George Frenside, the elderly critic of *Hudson River Bracketed,* speaks with the wisdom of Edith Wharton's three decades as a novelist when he urges Vance Weston to mingle in society: "A novelist ought to, at one time or another. . . . Manners are your true material, after all."

The elegiac tone in Edith Wharton's writing became more pronounced as the opportunities for exercising her particular talent seemed to her to diminish—as manners within her main sphere of observation lost their distinctness and were merged at a dead level of culture. In large part, her fiction is a record of the deterioration of Old World ideals under the impact of industrial democracy. In 1927 she complained that modern America, "inheriting an old social organization which provided for nicely shaded degrees of culture and conduct, . . . has simplified and Taylorized it out of existence." In European fiction, on the other hand, even the novel of provincial life had a "depth of soil" to work in: "This indeed is still true of the dense old European order, all compounded of differences and nuances, all interwoven with intensities and reticences, with passions and privacies, inconceivable to the millions brought up in a safe, shallow, and shadowless world." [8]

There must always have been a great temptation for Edith Wharton to follow James's example and locate her subject in the richer territory of European culture, or, as in *Madame de Treymes, The Age of Innocence, The Buccaneers,* and to some extent in *The Custom of the Country,* to fasten on the conflict between foreign and domestic manners as at once more easily understood and dramatically more distinct. Her values were European, and she found it impossible to conceive of an "American" culture which, in striving toward some sort of integration, would not sacrifice those values and, along with them, the interest which manners imparted to the social scene. Nevertheless, even during the thirty years of her residence abroad, she kept her eye constantly on America, and practically all of her best fiction, including *The House of Mirth, The Custom of the Country, The Age of Innocence,* and even *The Reef,* whose setting for no absolute reason is France, demonstrates that the novel of manners can be domesticated. It was the fault mainly of her experience (certainly not of her reading) that she had such a limited conception of its possibilities. As a whole, the America of her last two decades offered a sharper challenge to the novelist of manners than did the America of her youth; but although she admitted that "the tendency of all growth, animal, human, social, is towards an ever-increasing complexity," [9] she failed to see that tendency confirmed in the development of American society. Even if she had, she probably would have been unable to shift her field of analysis, for she was mainly interested in examining the crisis faced by her own class beginning in the 'eighties and continuing through the opening years of the new century. Her awareness of social change was confined to its impact on the little society to which she belonged. Although she bewailed the increasing standardization of manners in America, it would have been more accurate to admit that they were undergoing a change beyond the range of her notation. She demanded a fixed point of reference, which was provided by the manners of her class but which in the end proved a handicap since it limited her vision. As the manners which defined her world lost their reality and with it their moral significance, the understanding which she brought to bear on her subject, in every novel after *The Age of Innocence,* became more superficial. It was an unfortunate day for the novelist as well as for the daughter of old New York when, as she had foreseen, the Undine Spraggs inherited the earth. In contrast to her subtle differentiation and skillful dramatic use of the manners she knew at first hand, her treatment of the manners of Apex was crude and uncertain.

That she was successful, ultimately, only when diagnosing a partial segment of society seems to me less important than the fact that she made the attempt, unusual at any period in the history of the American novel, to adopt the characteristic interest and method of her great English and continental predecessors—Balzac, Flaubert, Jane Austen, and Thackeray—so far as the resistant nature of her material would permit. Once we have defined her, as she did Henry James, as preëminently a novelist of manners, we are able to estimate her importance in American fiction. It was not by accident that both Sinclair Lewis and Scott Fitzgerald admired her work and that she returned their admiration.

"Manners," wrote Alexis de Tocqueville, "are generally the product of the very basis of character, but they are also sometimes the result of an arbitrary convention between certain men." It seems necessary to make some distinction between manners as an expression of individual character, or what Tocqueville called "natural" manners, and manners as an expression of a particular social ideal, or "acquired" manners. The former are more prominent in any group which is in process of breaking away from one class and forming another, as in the frontier society described by Crèvecoeur or—to bring the example nearer home—in the fast-rising but still indistinct society of *nouveaux riches* who invaded Edith Wharton's New York following the Civil War. Henry James, contemplating the showy mansions, the eternal quest for publicity, and the evanescent values of this group, defined the problem it presented to the restless analyst as one of "manners undiscourageably seeking the superior stable equilibrium." What one noted most of all was the vagueness of its "acquired" manners and, at the same time, the spectacle of its "trying, trying its very hardest, to grow, not yet knowing . . . what to grow *on*." (James merely had a finer sense of the problem's complexity than did E. L. Godkin, whose blunt query in *The Nation*—"Who knows how to be rich in America?"— was prompted by the same observations.)[10] On the other hand, the settled predominance of acquired manners among the mercantile aristocracy of New York was its very hallmark as a class; and since Edith Wharton belonged so wholeheartedly to this class, it is not strange that character in her novels is conceived primarily in terms of acquired manners, the manners which distinguish one class from another, and that she frequently gives us the type only slightly modified by individual traits.

There is another point to be derived from Tocqueville's classification. The conservative individual, whether his name be Newland Archer or George Babbitt —or Edith Wharton—takes refuge, as it were, in the acquired manners of his class. They are a badge of status; they provide evidence of "belonging." The record of Edith Wharton's "motor-flight," some forty years ago, from Rouen to Fontainebleau, contains this pertinent digression:

Never more vividly than in this Seine country does one feel the amenity of French manners, the long process of social adaptation which has produced *so profound and general an intelligence of life.* [Italics mine.] Everyone we passed on our way, from the canal-boatman to the white-capped baker's lad, from the *marchande des quatre saisons* to the white dog curled philosophically under her cart, from the pastry-cook putting a fresh plate of *brioches* in his appetising window to the curé's *bonne* who had just come out to drain the lettuce on the curé's doorstep . . . each had their established niche in life, the frankly avowed interests and preoccupations of their order, their pride in the smartness of the canal-boat, the seductions of the show-window, the glaze of the *brioches,* the crispness of the lettuce. And this admirable *fitting into the pattern,* which seems almost as if it were the moral outcome of the universal French sense of form, has led the race to the happy, the momentous discovery that good manners are a short cut to one's goal, that they lubricate the wheels of life instead of obstructing them.

Not even in the final chapter of *The Valley of Decision* is the conservative viewpoint more complacently expressed. But notice also that the passage proceeds from a consideration of manners in the larger sense to a conclusion about manners in the narrow sense of "good manners," from manners as revealing a "profound and gen-

eral intelligence of life" to manners as administering to
the ease of social intercourse. Even in the novels, one
is never quite sure when Mrs. Wharton is going to make
the transition. Although she apparently means "good"
in the sense of "appropriate," it is clear elsewhere that
merely polite manners had for her a personal value which
led her to exaggerate their importance. Inwardly a shy
person, she used them as a buffer against the impact of
other personalities. According to her friend Mrs. Winthrop Chanler, the formality of French manners was
"comfortable to her," [11] and the accuracy of the observation is implied in Mrs. Wharton's own statement that the
French have a "safeguard against excess in their almost
Chinese reverence for the ritual of manners." [12] Few
people have written about their friendship with Edith
Wharton without commenting on the imposing front she
erected to the world. Most were frankly terrified at their
first encounter with her. "She was one of the few people
I have ever known," recalls Percy Lubbock, "who did
what severe ladies used to do so readily in novels: she
'drew herself up.'" There is little doubt that before she
could confront a large group of people she needed the
assurance that formal manners provided. In the shifting
social panorama, they enabled her to "place" herself—
not necessarily in an invidious sense—in relation to the
people around her.

For the novelist's characters, manners have a similar
value. By defining their relationship to the other characters, they become a means of penetrating to the reality
of the situation. Waythorn, the perplexed husband in
one of Mrs. Wharton's best short stories, "The Other
Two" (1904), is involuntarily thrust into a situation involving his wife's two former husbands, the outcome of

which may be expected to shed some desirable light on
Alice Waythorn's character. Varick, the second husband,
he understands immediately; they "had the same social
habits, spoke the same language, understood the same
allusions." But the first husband, Haskett, is a shabby,
deferential creature, who wears a "made-up tie attached
with an elastic." For Waythorn, the tie becomes the clue
to his wife's remoter past.

He realised suddenly that he knew very little of Haskett's
past or present situation; but from the man's appearance and
manner of speech he could reconstruct with curious precision the surroundings of Alice's first marriage. . . . He could
see her, as Mrs. Haskett, sitting in a "front parlour" furnished
in plush, with a pianola, and a copy of "Ben Hur" on the
centre-table. He could see her going to the theatre with
Haskett—or perhaps even to a "Church Sociable"—she in a
"picture hat" and Haskett in a black frock-coat, a little
creased, with the made-up tie on an elastic. . . . On Sunday
afternoons Haskett would take her for a walk, pushing Lily
ahead of them in a white-enamelled perambulator, and Waythorn had a vision of the people they would stop and talk to.

Waythorn reviews the illusions which surrounded the
first days of his married life: "It was a pity for his peace
of mind that Haskett's very inoffensiveness shed a new
light on the nature of those illusions." To give him his
due, he is ashamed of his snobbery in fastening on the
symbolic detail of the ready-made tie. Nevertheless, the
revelation which it affords him, taken together with
the known fact of Alice Waythorn's callous treatment of
her first two husbands, indicates not only the temporal
progress she has made but the boundless extent of her
ambitions, and in the concluding episode of the story it

helps explain the vulgar ease with which she accommo-
dates herself to the normally embarrassing situation of
having to play hostess simultaneously to her present
husband and two ex-husbands.

There is no better capsule demonstration than in "The
Other Two" of the imaginative use to which Edith Wharton put her interest in manners. By and large, manners
are to the social scene what form is to the physical: both
regulate our sense of the landscape. Absence of manners
in the social scene is likely to be accompanied by absence
of form in the physical. It is significant that Edith Wharton felt most at home in France and Italy, where centuries of civilized living have conferred a recognizable
form on the landscape and architecture as well as on the
manners of the people. In *Fighting France* (1915) she
speaks of "the sober disciplined landscape which the
traveller's memory is apt to invoke as distinctively
French." In *A Motor-Flight through France* she remarks
that the French villages, as opposed to the English, have
"more, perhaps, of outline—certainly of line." The
French discovery, alluded to earlier, that good manners
are a lubricant, "seems to have illuminated not only the
social relation but its outward, concrete expression, producing a finish in the material setting of life, a kind of
conformity in inanimate things."

Here in northern France, where agriculture has mated with
poetry instead of banishing it, one understands the higher
beauty of land developed, humanized, brought into relation
to life and history, as compared with the raw material in
which the greater part of our own hemisphere is still clothed.

In such countries as Germany and Switzerland, but particularly in the America west of the Hudson, Edith

Wharton missed this particular amenity in both the physical scene and the manners of the inhabitants. I have spoken of the "absence" of manners in the social scene and of form in the physical. As a matter of fact, this is hardly permissible, since what is really implied is a lack of distinction—the failure of landscape, architecture, and manners to impress upon the observer any notion of their civilizing value. What accounts for that distinction where it exists? The answer has already been hinted at in an earlier quotation from Mrs. Wharton: it is the "intelligence of life" which landscape, architecture, and manners may, as they do in France, eloquently suggest.

A "profound and general intelligence of life"—it is, after all, the key phrase to an understanding of Edith Wharton's interest in manners. I would refer back for a moment to Mr. Trilling's definition of the novel as a "perpetual quest for reality, the field of its research being always the social world, the material of its analysis being always manners as the indication of the direction of man's soul." Edith Wharton was a realist in the most literal sense of that unreliable term. To her way of thinking, reality was to be sought for in the present and visible, not in the realm of the ideal, in a romantic primitivism, or in the findings of modern psychology. Freud became available to her too late, and then only to be rejected; and the importance of the subconscious she acknowledged only indirectly in her ghost stories and such psychological horror stories as "The Eyes." In the quest for reality, manners were necessarily almost her only guide. She would talk by the hour, Percy Lubbock recalled, "about people, their manners and customs, their scrapes and scandals, so long as these [threw] light upon

the human chase." When she testified, as she did repeatedly, to the true "intelligence of life" which pre-
vailed in France, she was in effect announcing her view
of reality as shadowed forth by a particular system of
manners. That view is comprehensively developed in
her little book *French Ways and Their Meaning* (1919),
but it may be summarized briefly. Throughout the ranks
of French society the diffusion of certain traits is apparent: a reverence for tradition, a sense of continuity with
the past, taste, intellectual honesty, absolute probity in
business, a love of privacy, and a respect for the practical
and intellectual abilities of women. And all of these
traits are embodied equally in the manners which are
apparent at various levels within this rich culture. It
was obvious to Edith Wharton that the French had
solved the art of living in a way which vindicated the
notion of reality fostered by her own background and
training. She found in them a respect for the same traits
that were venerated in the society of her youth, although
she was grateful at the same time that they did not share
her parents' intellectual timidity or their generally low
estimate of women's capabilities.

At any rate, it is in the light of a reality conveniently
implied by French manners that we may view the world
of Edith Wharton's fiction. The manners of the "sham"
society which figures in *The House of Mirth* helped to
generate illusion because they were based largely on
considerations of wealth. "Wages, in the country at
large," commented James in *The American Scene*, "are
largely manners—the only manners, I think it is fair to
say, one mostly encounters," [13] and he stressed the necessity, for those uninterested in making money merely, of
breaking the tie with America. The same objection ap-

plied to the manners of Apex and Euphoria, that mythical hinterland of Edith Wharton's ungenerous imagination: they revealed no "profound and general intelligence of life." Fanny de Malrive, in *Madame de Treymes,* an expatriate who is occasionally nostalgic for America, professes to be enchanted with the idea of John Durham's married sister "spending her summers at—where is it?— the Kittawittany House on Lake Pohunk." But the picture has less appeal for Durham: "A vision of earnest women in Shetland shawls, with spectacles and thin knobs of hair, eating blueberry pie at unwholesome hours in a shingled dining-room on a bare New England hilltop, rose pallidly between Durham and the verdant brightness of the Champs Elysées. . . ." Mrs. Wharton's treatment of provincial America broadens as the geographical distance between herself and her subject increases. By the time she comes to write *Hudson River Bracketed,* she is content with a caricature of Midwestern life so gross that we can take it only as a literary expression of the aversion toward America which came out in the intimate conversation of her later years. Perhaps she was encouraged by younger writers such as Sinclair Lewis and Sherwood Anderson to give free rein to her prejudice, and undoubtedly the tasteful decor of the Pavillon Colombe must have made the living rooms of Euphoria seem more hideous. At any rate, the Midwest of her later novels, with its narrow religion, its go-getting philosophy, and its paramount bad taste in architecture, cookery, and speech, has only the most limited authenticity, and consequently it plays havoc with any serious attention which as a novelist of manners she may have had.

Much earlier in her career, of course, the tendency toward exaggeration and oversimplification had been noticeable—not when she was viewing provincial life and provincial types in isolation, as in *Ethan Frome* and *Summer*, but when she was forcing them into a contrast with the world she admired, as in *The Custom of the Country*. At such times, the children of darkness make an all out attack on the canons of taste. As Alfred Kazin has pointed out, they appear with such names as Mabel Blitch, Ora Prance Chettle, Elmer Moffatt, Indiana Frusk, and Undine Spragg, and their everyday conversation betrays the same degenerative influences at work. "Do you mean to say," Undine asks Mrs. Heeny, her mother's masseuse and confidante, "Mr. Marvell's as swell as Mr. Popple?" "As swell?" replies the other. "Why, Claud Walsingham Popple ain't in the same class with him." Somewhat later, Undine has difficulty keeping her oar in the conversation at a formal dinner party:

. . . She had read no new book but "When the Kissing Had to Stop," of which Mrs. Fairford seemed not to have heard. On the theatre they were equally at odds, for while Undine had seen "Oolaloo" fourteen times, and was "wild" about Ned Norris in "The Soda-Water Fountain," she had not heard of the famous Berlin comedians who were performing Shakespeare at the German Theatre. . . . The conversation was revived for a moment by her recalling that she had seen Sarah Burnhard in a play she called "Leg-long". . . .

Fortunately, it is not often that Edith Wharton overreaches to this extent in the earlier novels. At the same time, she loses no opportunity to enforce the contrast of manners latent in the names, speech, dress, and cultural interests of her characters. In general, it is by such signs, rather than by the explicit commentary, that we establish the tone of her treatment. The names of the men and women in her novels whom we can trust have a certain aristocratic distinction—Lawrence Selden, Ralph Marvell, John Amherst, Justine Brent, Anna Leath—and not only do they speak pure English but they read Montaigne and Shakespeare rather than *Quo Vadis* and *Ben Hur,* and admire Italian primitives rather than "The Light of the World" and the "Mona Lisa." It is not, of course, so simple a matter as these extremes imply, for Edith Wharton has utilized the intervening gradations of taste to differentiate more subtly. If this were not so, her method would be limited always, as in the passages I have just reproduced, to the crudest sort of social satire.

Chapter V

THE REPUBLIC OF THE SPIRIT

Physically, Mrs. Wharton's world was carefully delimited. Although its Western capital was New York, its center—geographically only after 1907 but spiritually always—was Paris, that "great city, so made for peace and art and all the humanest graces." France, England, and the Mediterranean countries together all but defined its extent, with such countries as Germany and Switzerland constituting to her mind a bourgeois hinterland as vulgar in its way as the American Midwest. Anywhere within this sphere one could enjoy life without danger of offending the trained sensibilities, but it was in France particularly that Western civilization was visible at its highest pitch of refinement in the manners and institutions of a people devoted for centuries to an ideal formed of reverence, continuity, taste, and intellectual honesty— qualities which her pioneering countrymen had had, she acknowledged, the least time to acquire.

In a sense Edith Wharton's fiction represents a continuous effort to define the good society; consequently, her series of articles written "with the idea of making France and things French more intelligible to the American soldier" and later collected in the volume *French Ways and Their Meaning* is important because it offers the most concise formulation of her social ideal. What she has to say in this unpretentious little book is echoed in her critical essays, her travel books, and her memoirs, but it is worth summarizing here.

As early as 1908, with the vision of Amiens Cathedral before her, Edith Wharton could write that "reverence is the most precious emotion that such a building inspires: reverence for the accumulated experiences of the past . . . the desire to keep intact as many links as possible between yesterday and tomorrow." From the same trip she preserved an impression of Etampes, "so typical of the average French country town—dry, compact, unsentimental, as if avariciously hoarding a long rich past. . . ." At its worst, she admitted, reverence may be "the wasteful fear of an old taboo." As such it had manifested itself in the New York society of her youth and, consequently, in the more satiric passages of such novels as *The Custom of the Country* and *The Age of Innocence*. But to her adjusted view, and partly as a result of years of residence in France, it seemed a wholly valuable trait because it suggested practically that "whatever survives the close filtering of time is likely to answer some deep racial need, moral or aesthetic."

Basic to the French view of life is the sense of continuity, which helps preserve the vigor and homogeneity of a culture: "France may teach us that, side by side with the qualities of enterprise and innovation that English blood has put in us, we should cultivate the sense of continuity, that sense of the Past which enriches the present and binds us up with the world's great stabilizing traditions of art and poetry and knowledge." Lacking the sense of continuity, a people like the Americans may, for all their energy and daring, allow their inherited tradition in language, art, and manners to deteriorate while they postpone, by constant fresh starts and undisciplined experiments, their cultural coming-of-age. Thus, the two novels in which Edith Wharton tried to diagnose the career of an artist, *Hudson River Bracketed* and its sequel *The Gods Arrive*, are given over in large part to Vance Weston's fitful love affair with the Past. A passage from the first novel, describing Vance at Old Trinity Church in New York, is characteristic: "The idea that there had been people so near his own day who had lived and died under the same roof, and worshipped every Sunday in the same church as their forebears, appealed in an undefinable way to his craving for continuity." Vance, it will be recalled, is a product of the traditionless Midwest —of Euphoria, Illinois—and what impresses him most as he is gently introduced to the Past through the agency of a mellow country house on the Hudson is "the meagreness of his inherited experience." Years later, after he has again committed himself to a rootless, drifting existence, this sense of the past which he has experienced so strongly at the Willows is reawakened by his contact with the English colony at Oubli, which has managed "by sheer continuity of sentiment to fit into the pattern of something big and immemorial."

In more than one context, in her critical essays and reviews as well as in *French Ways and Their Meaning*, Mrs. Wharton reiterates that to perceive is to discriminate, and that by the act of discrimination taste is both formed and measured. Taste is the atmosphere without which art cannot sustain life; it is "the regulating principle of all art, of the art of dress and of manners, and of living in general, as well as of sculpture and music." It demands a perception of scale, proportion, suitability, as essential to its realization. It is as markedly a social as an aesthetic requirement: "I remember being told when I was a young girl: 'If you want to interest the person you are talking to, pitch your voice so that one person will hear you.' " That small axiom of her mother's, Edith Wharton concluded, contained all there was to say about taste.

Now, all of these qualities, along with the intellectual honesty she admired in the French, are most active in an institution which for Edith Wharton epitomized the good society. One need only read the passages in *French Ways and Their Meaning* and *A Backward Glance* in which she describes the *salon* and its place in French life to appreciate its importance to her as a final expression of the social ideal. "Culture in France," she wrote in her memoirs, "is an eminently social quality." In the *salon*, that "best school of talk and of ideas that the modern world has known," those forces which worked for the preservation of culture—*reverence, continuity,* and *taste* —coöperated with the social instinct to produce a general expansion of the individual. In the Anglo-Saxon countries such a fusion of social and cultural aims is hardly conceivable. Mrs. Wharton has exposed at length, in her memoirs and in her fiction, the intellectual sterility of the circles in which her family and that of her husband moved, where a serious interest in literature, music, art, and even politics, was regarded with suspicion or embarrassment as an obstacle to easy social intercourse. It was a society in which the drawing room duet or subdued dinner table comment on the latest polite novel represented the only concession to even the narrowest ideal of culture. But it was also—and this is significant— a society which provided every opportunity for men and

women to meet freely and at regular intervals to play
the social game for what it was worth. The conditions
regulating the encounters between the sexes in older
New York society at least approximated those of the
salon. That this was so was to a large degree the effect
of wealth and leisure, but then Edith Wharton always
found it difficult to imagine any social arrangement that
was not bolstered by at least moderate wealth and moderate leisure. "When I hear," she wrote in *A Backward
Glance,* "that nowadays business life is so strenuous that
men and women never meet socially before the dinner
hour, I remember the delightful week-day luncheons of
my early married years, where the men were as numerous
as the women."

To her mind, the chief recommendation of the *salon*
was that within its charmed circle women were regarded
not merely as ornaments or as objects of conquest but as
the social and intellectual peers of the men who frequented it. Here freedom and tradition met and joined
in the belief "that the most stimulating conversation in
the world is that between intelligent men and women
who see each other often enough to be on terms of frank
and easy friendship." She would have deplored with
Henry James—and, as a matter of fact, did so in her last,
unfinished novel—the social isolation of a Saratoga,
where the women so vastly outnumbered the men that
they were forced to dance together at the balls. John
Durham, in *Madame de Treymes,* discovers in visiting
Paris "that one of the charms of a sophisticated society
is that it lends point and perspective to the slightest contact between the sexes." By far the majority of the
friendships that Edith Wharton commemorated in *A
Backward Glance* were with men. She had, as Percy

Lubbock noted, "a very feminine consciousness and a very masculine mind," and she preferred the company of men as long as she felt perfectly confident of her ability to hold her own in the exchange of ideas.

In *sette-cento* Italy, where young women of Fulvia Vivaldi's station were still limited, as in the Middle Ages, to the alternative of marrying or entering a convent, the heroine of *The Valley of Decision* is as disturbing a prodigy as was Edith Wharton the novelist in the intellectually unfurnished drawing rooms of New York society. Fulvia is one of the "learned ladies" of the eighteenth century, but unlike her fellow bluestockings, "who were forever tripping in the folds of their doctor's gowns, and delivering their most trivial views ex cathedra," she carries her learning lightly and with considerable charm. She first appears as the young Minerva of her father's subversive group, the Honey-Bees, mingling unselfconsciously with the all-male company, joining in the learned conversation, and entertaining the guests with harpsichord performances and poetry recitations. Later, we find her in the Milan household of Count Castiglione, a distinguished naturalist.

In such surroundings her wit and learning could not fail to attract the best company of Milan, and she was become one of the most noted figures of the capital. There had been some talk of offering her the chair of poetry at the Brera; but the report of her liberal views had deterred the faculty. . . . The Signorina Vivaldi became the fashion. The literati celebrated her scholarship, the sonneteers her eloquence and beauty; and no foreigner on the grand tour was content to leave Milan without having beheld the fair prodigy and heard her recite Petrarch's Ode to Italy, or the latest elegy of Pindamonte.

The most interesting thing about the characterization of
Fulvia Vivaldi is the degree to which it projects Edith
Wharton's ideal image of herself against a background
similar to that of her youth and early married years.

Writing of "the new Frenchwoman" in *French Ways
and Their Meaning*, Mrs. Wharton criticized the American women's dependence on the companionship of their
own sex because it developed their individuality in a
void, "without the checks, the stimulus, and the discipline that comes of contact with the stronger masculine
individuality." The "custom of the country," which furnished the title and theme of one of her novels (and, incidentally, furnished a clue to her desire to live abroad),
was the twentieth-century American male's habit of leaving his wife out of things, his failure to take an interest
in women as companions and equals. Charles Bowen,
who figures in that novel as a detached social commentator—like those characters we regularly find in Howells
who arbitrate for the author—puts the case to Laura Fairford:

Why does the European woman interest herself so much
more in what the men are doing? Because she's so important
to them that they make it worth her while! She's not a
parenthesis, as she is here—she's in the very middle of the
picture. . . . Where does the real life of most American men
lie? In some woman's drawing-room or in their offices? The
answer's obvious, isn't it? The emotional centre of gravity's
not the same in the two hemispheres. In the effete societies
it's love, in our new home it's business. In America the real
crime passionnel is a "big steal"—there's more excitement in
wrecking railways than homes.

Struck by the same phenomenon, Henry James wrote
that "the failure of the sexes to keep step socially is to be

noted, in the United States, at every turn, and is perhaps more suggestive of interesting 'drama' . . . than anything else in the country." [1] It was precisely this drama inherent in American social life that Edith Wharton exploited in *The Custom of the Country.*

The Frenchwoman, on the other hand, rules French life in her triple capacity as mother, as her husband's business partner, and as "artist," making her contribution in the home and in the *salon* to the art of living. Given a place in the middle of the picture, she is less a prey to the dissatisfaction, restlessness, and vain material ambitions of her American counterpart. The product of a richer concept of society, she is mature enough to find the answer to her domestic problems outside the divorce court. There is of course a lurking feminism in Mrs. Wharton's brief, which can be detected elsewhere in her implied criticism of the double standard of morality and in the appearance in so many of her stories of the emotionally low-charged, overscrupulous male protagonist (granted that this kind of logic makes Henry James, too, a feminist); but it is not the feminism, either in kind or degree, of Willa Cather or Ellen Glasgow, for she regards men in the abstract neither as junior partners nor as enemies.

The importance of reverence, continuity, and taste in shaping and maintaining the tradition of the *salon* was apparent to Edith Wharton before she had lived a year in Paris. In spite of the regular announcements of its demise, the *salon* had asserted its right to survival because it answered a social, moral, and aesthetic need. Through several profound cataclysms in the social structure, it had continued healthily into the twentieth cen-

---

[1] For notes to chap. v, see p. 255.

tury. Moreover, the permanent nucleus always to be found in the personnel of the older *salons* appealed to the sense of continuity. "When I first went to live in Paris," Mrs. Wharton records, "old ladies with dowdy cashmere 'mantles,' and bonnets tied under their chins, were pointed out to me as still receiving every afternoon or evening, at the same hour, the same five or six men who had been the 'foundation' of their group nearly half a century earlier." For the hostess, the management of a recognized *salon* was a perpetual and demanding exercise of taste: in the selection of its members, in the furnishing of an appropriate setting, in the seating arrangement at the dinner table, in the manipulation of the conversation—in the faultless performance, in short, of a highly complicated ritual. There is little to choose between Edith Wharton's tribute to the genius of a Madame de Fitz-James, whose *salon* "had a prestige which no Parisian hostess since 1918 had succeeded in recovering," and her tribute to the very different genius of a Henry James, whose social aptitudes rate more comment in *A Backward Glance* than do his artistic. "The only completely agreeable society I have ever known," she wrote, "is that wherein the elements are selected and blent by a woman of the world, instinctively alert for every shade of suitability, and whose light hand never suffers the mixture to stiffen or grow heavy." Such a figure, in her own right, was Edith Wharton. We have more than one picture of the great lady holding court, in this country, in England, and in France, "circled," as Percy Lubbock recalls, "by her due of masculine attendance," and reminiscent of Fulvia Vivaldi with Milan at her feet.

From the time she was a small girl she had been conditioned to a social ideal in some ways approaching that

86

of the *salon.* Her mother, who was as final an authority on the New York society of the 'seventies as Sillerton Jackson in *The Age of Innocence,* would, to quote Mr. Lubbock again, "count the names of all the families, in due order of degree, who composed the world to which her daughter was born; and there her world stopped short, it was implied, and no mistake about it." On a smaller scale, the French *salon* was a society as self-contained, as conscious of the fine shadings of degree, as that of Edith Jones's parents; and the influence of her mother's training could be traced, some thirty years later, in Edith Wharton's preoccupation with the seating arrangements at Parisian dinner tables. Always ill at ease in what she called "general society," she began early to seek the equivalent of the *salon.* "My idea of society," she wrote, "was (and still is) the daily companionship of the same five or six friends, and its pleasure is based on continuity." Speaking of the social group which she shyly joined following her debut, she recalled in *A Backward Glance:*

Like all agreeable societies, ours was small, and the people composing it met almost every day, and always sought each other out in any larger company. . . . Our society was, in short, a little "set" with its private catch-words, observances and amusements, and its indifference to anything outside of its charmed circle; and no really entertaining social group has ever been anything else.

Years later, when she and her husband were established at the Mount, in Lenox, she had the opportunity to test her skill as hostess to a mixed and cosmopolitan group. Thanks to her writing, she had by this time broken out of the social shell of her girlhood and early married life, and the new "charmed circle" was more distinguished than the old. The *fondation* of what she called "the inner group" was composed of Walter Berry, George Cabot ("Bay") Lodge, and from England, Gaillard Lapsley (after her death to become her literary executor), Robert Norton, John Hugh Smith, and, as its chief ornament, Henry James. "In this group," she wrote, "an almost immediate sympathy had established itself between the various members, so that our common stock of allusions, cross-references, pleasantries was always increasing. . . ." There is a marked emphasis throughout *A Backward Glance* on the private jokes, private observances, and common interests which, in the successive groups of which Edith Wharton was the center, heightened the sense of "belonging." Henry James's letters to his most intimate friends had, she remembered, to be edited for the general reader to eliminate "long passages of chaff, and recurring references to old heaped-up pyramidal jokes, huge cairns of hoarded nonsense"; otherwise, "the reader could hardly have groped his way without a preparatory course in each correspondent's private history and casual experience." The suggestion of a freemasonry of intelligent, cultured individuals who, regardless of age, sex, or nationality, have the same interests and speak the same language is never absent from Edith Wharton's conception of "society," either in actuality or in her novels. A critic once wrote of the "clever" people in her fiction: "Their minds are formed to the maze of sophistication, and it is a mark of their complexity that they are inseparable. They are like actors who have many times rehearsed a piece together and know each others' roles. . . ." [2] Quite unconsciously, he was also describing Edith Wharton and her intimates.

88

If we look beyond the charmed circle, we find that it is linked with similar groups everywhere. It is not simply that certain regulars at the Mount were also admitted to Howard Sturgis' little company at Queen's Acre or to Madame de Fitz-James's *salon* in Paris. Their passport is not so limited. It is valid anywhere within what Lawrence Selden, in *The House of Mirth*, calls "the republic of the spirit," that international community which embraces all of the charmed circles as well as those isolated individuals who have the qualifications, if not the opportunity, to join one. "Society," explains Ralph Marvell, in his vain attempt to educate Undine, ". . . means the sanction of their own special group and of the corresponding groups elsewhere," whereas the shoddy international set of St. Moritz which she longs to join "isn't 'society' any more than the people in an omnibus are." Durham, in *Madame de Treymes*, learns the same lesson as he observes a gathering of the Malrive clan:

All these amiably chatting visitors, who mostly bore the stamp of personal insignificance on their mildly sloping or aristocratically beaked faces, hung together in a visible closeness of tradition, dress, attitude, and manner, as different as possible from the loose aggregation of a roomful of his own countrymen. Durham felt, as he observed them, that he had never before known what "society" meant; nor understood that, in an organized and inherited system, it exists where two or three of its members are assembled.

Transmuted and refined, this is the distinction which underlies Edith Wharton's concept of the good society. Clearly, there was hardly the stuff for a novel in the relationships which existed within the compact little society of the Mount, or that of Queen's Acre or of 53 Rue

Varenne, where from some time after 1907 to the end of the First World War Edith Wharton conducted her own *salon*. It was not the mere fact of their exclusiveness: Henry James in *The Awkward Age* had found his subject in a similarly self-contained group of intellectuals, complete with catchwords and private jokes. But Edith Wharton's circles were managed on a more impersonal basis. They subsisted on talk and ideas, and she used them as a refuge from more importunate human relationships. The distinction is important because it is from the vantage point of her "republic of the spirit" that she can satirize the societies which lie outside it: that of fashionable old New York; that of the countless Apexes, Euphorias, and Prunevilles, whose manners the invaders brought with them when they began in the 'eighties to lay siege to the citadel of New York society; that of the English colony at Oubli; and that of Bohemia, whose citizens figure more prominently in her later novels.

This is not to say that she freed herself completely from the society in which she grew up. She retained what she thought was best in it: its forms, most—but not all—of its standards, and its awareness of "the subtler shades of taste that civilize humane intercourse." But she rejected its determined innocence, that quality which, as she wrote in *The Age of Innocence,* "seals the mind against imagination and the heart against experience," and like Newland Archer she sought the company of artists and writers (of the more respectable sort), who could provide her with good talk and an atmosphere of intellectual freedom. It was the best of two worlds that she wanted, that of old New York and that of Bohemia; and her republic, like Selden's, embodied the compromise. Newland Archer, attracted by the independent life of his artist and writer friends, comes away from one of his talks with Ned Winsett "with the feeling that if his world was small, so was theirs, and that the only way to enlarge either was to reach a stage of manners where they would naturally merge." It is difficult to believe that Edith Wharton did not have the *salon* in mind when she wrote this. What other civilized institution so clearly gave substance to Newland Archer's vision?

The angle, then, from which Mrs. Wharton surveys life makes it evident that the social ideal expressed in the *salon* is present at least by implication in her fiction. It is present most tangibly in the predicament of her major characters. Few of them can claim full citizenship in her republic—Lawrence Selden, Ellen Olenska, Justine Brent, and the John Amherst who carries a volume of Shakespeare in his pocket to and from his work at the mill, are among them—but the rest are knocking at the gates. Her more characteristic protagonist—Ralph Marvell, Newland Archer, Anna Leath, Vance Weston, Lewis Raycie in *False Dawn* (Undine Spragg is a notable exception) —"belongs" instinctively, but through a conspiracy of circumstances never quite succeeds in being admitted. The men, significantly, outnumber the women. On the spiritual plane the aspiration and the struggle lie rather with them than with the Lily Barts and the Undine Spraggs, who are in fact among the instruments of their defeat. Although it was one of the truisms of American fiction after 1890 that the "new woman" was the chief vessel of the materialism which threatened the values of the older society, the impulse which led Edith Wharton to add her voice to the general indictment was probably personal. Her republic, like her *salon,* is dominated by men—and, judging from the evidence of both her fiction and biography, by single men.

The preponderance of bachelors in her stories is inescapable. Women have no inevitable claims on them, or if they have, they usually remain unsatisfied. They are, most of them, connoisseurs—of books, china, paintings, wine, cigars, and women. The fastidious young narrator of one of her early stories, "The Confessional," may be taken as their prototype. He is willing to answer the demands of the spirit at the sacrifice of basic material satisfactions. The wood fire in his "modest lodgings" brings out "the values of the one or two old prints and Chinese porcelains that accounted for the perennial shabbiness of [his] wardrobe." When Don Egidio visits him, he pours his guest a glass of Marsala and offers him a Havana cigar. Selden, in *The House of Mirth,* has the same taste, which he cannot afford to indulge but does, for the expensive and the rare. He does not, as he tells Lily Bart, underrate "the decorative side of life"—any more, we might add, than does Mrs. Wharton—but he lives at the same time in an atmosphere of books and ideas, and he gives Lily the impression of having "preserved a certain social detachment, a happy air of viewing the show objectively, of having points of contact outside the great gilt cage in which they were all huddled for the mob to gape at."

It is this air of detachment which, more than any other trait, distinguishes Edith Wharton's men. They are, like many of Henry James's protagonists, or like the young men of her girlhood circle who were reluctant to enter politics, too "fine" for the rougher uses of the world. They are born out of their proper time and place. They

are artists *manqués*. They have, many of them, even produced a volume of essays or a thin sheaf of sonnets, and
then abandoned the literary life under the pressures of a
hostile or indifferent environment. You encounter them
from first to last in her fiction, beginning with Danyers,
the young man who figures in the first story of *The
Greater Inclination,* and ending with Chris Churley in
The Gods Arrive. Their counterparts—perhaps their
originals—may be discerned in many of the half-outlined
figures in her memoirs: in that of a Harry Cust, who, like
Ralph Marvell and Newland Archer, was "unhappily too
favoured by a fortune to have canalized his gifts, but a
captivating talker and delightful companion in the small
circle of his intimates"; in that of an Arthur Dexter, introduced as "a finished specimen of the contemplator-
and-appreciator type"; in that of a Geoffrey Scott or a
Howard Sturgis, young men whose personal gifts over-
balanced their creative, and whose accomplishments
never met the expectations of their friends; and, most
important, in that of a Walter Berry, "born with an ex-
ceptionally sensitive literary instinct, but also with a
critical sense so far outweighing his creative gift that he
had early renounced the idea of writing." Remarkable
too the number of them whose endowments were over-
shadowed and finally destroyed by ill health: "Bay"
Lodge, Robert Minturn, Bayard Cutting, Jr., Vernon
Hamilton-Lee, and, again, Geoffrey Scott. By and large,
one is struck by the dilettantism of Mrs. Wharton's circle.
For every Henry James there are a dozen intimates who,
lacking his creative genius and vigor, share his and Edith
Wharton's passion for good company and good talk in
an attractive setting. Not Walter Berry alone, I suspect,
but *all* of these friends must have lent their charm and

their detachment, their idealistic strength and practical weaknesses, to those of her male characters whom Edith Wharton would have us admire. They supplied, in short, the qualities which in her stories are pitted unequally against the practical strength and the capacity for direct, self-interested action of the Simon Rosedales, Elmer Moffatts, and Peter Beauforts. There is a family likeness between Ralph Marvell and George Campton (*A Son at the Front*), who "apparently . . . was fated to be only a delighted spectator and commentator, to enjoy and interpret, not create," and between Campton and George Frenside (*Hudson River Bracketed*), in whom "the critical faculty outweighed all others." And the genealogy can be extended indefinitely.

One of the most remarkable of Edith Wharton's short tales, and one which has been strangely neglected in the anthologies, is "The Eyes" (*Tales of Men and Ghosts*), a Hawthornesque study of egoism, which is worth examining if only for the special light it casts on this familiar personality. Nowhere else in her fiction are the salient traits of a Selden or a George Darrow (*The Reef*) subjected to so merciless an interpretation, as if for the first time Edith Wharton felt impelled to carry her observations to their logical conclusion and to speak more plainly than her usual ironical strategy permitted. The protagonist, an elderly bachelor named Andrew Culwin, represents the least common denominator of the type I have been describing. He is "essentially a spectator, a humorous detached observer of the immense muddled variety show of life." He inhabits the temperate zone of feeling. His plentiful leisure has been devoted "to the cultivation of a fine intelligence and a few judiciously chosen habits; and none of the disturbances common to human experience seemed to have crossed his sky." He had once settled himself in his aunt's library to write a great book, on a subject he can no longer recall. A year later, in Rome, he had planned "another great book—a definitive work on Etruscan influences in Italian art." He is a dilettante, a connoisseur, a world traveler. We first encounter him in his library, "with its oak walls and dark old bindings," on the evening he is to open a revealing chapter of his autobiography to a group of friends who have been matching ghost stories. He does not think highly of the queer, inconclusive tale he is about to relate; he leaves it to his guests, among whom is a young man he has recently adopted as a protégé, to determine its significance.

Many years before, as an idle and bored young man living temporarily with a bookish aunt and writing his first abortive masterpiece, Culwin had been thrown into the society of a cousin, Alice Nowell, a gentle, colorless girl whose inexperience had made her an easy mark for his charms (". . . it interested me to see any woman content to be so uninteresting, and I wanted to find out the secret of her content"). After a brief intimacy, he had decided to abandon the book and light out for Europe, but the girl's disappointment had so flattered his ego that he had impulsively asked her to marry him. That evening, following their interview, he had first seen the eyes. He had gone to bed "bowed under the weight of the first good action I had ever consciously committed," but with his apprehensions tempered by a glow of self-righteousness, and had fallen asleep only to awaken much later to find a pair of eyes staring at him from the foot of the bed. There is an echo from *The Picture of Dorian Gray* in his subsequent confession.

They were the very worst eyes I've ever seen: a man's eyes —but what a man! My first thought was that he must be frightfully old. The orbits were sunk, and the thick red-lined lids hung over the eye-balls like blinds of which the cords are broken. One lid drooped a little lower than the other, with the effect of a crooked leer. . . . But the age of the eyes was not the most unpleasant thing about them. What turned me sick was their expression of vicious security. I don't know how else to describe the fact that they seemed to belong to a man who had done a lot of harm in his life, but had always kept just inside the danger lines. They were not the eyes of a coward, but of some one much too clever to take risks; and my gorge rose at their look of base astute-ness. Yet even that wasn't the worst; for as we continued to scan each other I saw in them a tinge of derision, and felt myself to be its object.

When they reappeared on succeeding nights, Culwin had fled the house, leaving no word for his cousin, and had taken the first steamer for England.

Two years later, while he was settled in Rome, ostensi-bly to write another "great book," a young man had pre-sented himself with a letter of introduction from Alice Nowell begging Culwin to interest himself in her cousin's future—a future predicated like his own on a nonexistent talent for belles-lettres. He had been charmed by the youth's company, had encouraged him to write, had con-scientiously read his pallid stories and poems, and finally, unable to sponsor mediocrity any longer, had determined to sacrifice friendship to truth and give the boy the final hopeless verdict. At the last moment he had reneged, with the result that his protégé was fatally misled by a false profession of confidence. That night the eyes had reappeared.

But it's not enough to say they were as bad as before: they were worse. Worse by just so much as I'd learned of life in the interval; by all the damnable implications my wider experiences read into them. I saw now what I hadn't seen before: that they were eyes which had grown hideous gradually, which had built up their baseness coral-wise, bit by bit, out of a series of small turpitudes slowly accumulated through the industrious years.

By the time Culwin has finished his story, its meaning is apparent to everyone but himself, but particularly to his most recent protégé, who is shocked and depressed by the revelation. Culwin tries to cheer him up. As he does so, he catches sight of his own reflection in a mirror behind the young man—and at long last recognizes the eyes.

The singleness and intensity of effect made possible by this unexpected (as always in Edith Wharton) use of symbolism helps explain why "The Eyes" is more impressive than its many companion stories on the theme of emotional and creative dilettantism. Provided one can accept a necessity of the point of view—that of Culwin's obtuseness, his failure to relate cause and effect, as constituting the essential proof of his egoism—"The Eyes" ranks very close to the pinnacle of Edith Wharton's achievement in the short story. As in *Ethan Frome,* the concluding episode of the framework is skillfully used to apply the last turn of the screw, but it also strengthens the unity of the action as a whole by delegating to itself the climax of Culwin's tale—that belated self-recognition provided by the Hawthornesque device of the mirror. Still, the best touch in the story is Mrs. Wharton's subtle variation on her theme. Ironically, what appeal to Culwin as his most altruistic gestures reveal his egoism most profoundly. It is at the moments when his unconsciously selfish motives are at widest variance with his actions that the eyes appear to accuse him.

Without wishing to imply that all the dilettantes of Edith Wharton's acquaintance were Culwins, I would point out that the Culwins have for her a special and apparently irresistible, although disagreeable, fascination. "The Eyes" gives us her least flattering analysis of a type necessarily prominent in the peculiar world she inhabited, a world suspended, as it were, by equal attraction between the worlds of society and letters, in which the prevalence of leisure, independent means, and a taste for art and letters encouraged the various kinds of dilettantism reflected in her fiction.

Chapter VI

THE TRAPPED SENSIBILITY

The Fruit of the Tree (1907), an earnest, rather dull, and unsuccessful novel, was evidently designed as Mrs. Wharton's contribution to the reform movement which, shortly after the turn of the century, had captured the novelists as well as the journalists, social workers, and general public. She had begun its composition shortly after the publication of *The House of Mirth*. To work up the *mise en scène* of the early chapters, she had conscientiously visited the textile mills at Adams, Massachusetts, an easy distance from the Mount; but her visit had been too brief and the roar of the machines had deafened her, so that the information her guide had shouted into her ear had come out all wrong on paper. A careful reader of the novel during its serialization in *Scribner's Magazine* had written to point out her technical errors, and these had been corrected before the story appeared in book form.[1]

Assuming that the distrust of organized reform which colors the final chapters of *The Valley of Decision* and finds its way via occasional remarks into many other stories was genuine, it is difficult to understand why she permitted the impulse to mislead her in the first place.

---

[1] For notes to chap. vi, see p. 255.

Her investigation of one of the basic social problems of the day, the responsibility of the factory owner for the physical and moral welfare of his employees, is conducted halfheartedly at best; and it is apparent, before the novel gets well under way, that the author's real sympathies and interests are going to run away with her original intention. This is precisely what happens. The story is diverted from its muckraking pretensions by the complicated moral problem which arises out of the relations of the four principal characters; and as this interest usurps the center of attention, Justine Brent takes over from John Amherst as protagonist. As a result, *The Fruit of the Tree* is successful neither as a novel nor as a tract.

The story, rather brutally simplified, is this: John Amherst, a foreman in a large New England textile factory, convinces its absentee owner, a widow named Bessy Westmore, that basic reforms in the policy and conditions at the plant are needed. Essentially a frivolous person, she is for a time absorbed in his vision, marries him, and then loses interest in his plans. The marriage goes rapidly downhill. In defiance of Amherst's wishes, Bessy takes an intractable mare for a gallop over the icy winter roads, is thrown and injures her spine. A long ordeal of pain, which can end only in death, is cut short when Justine Brent, a former schoolmate who is serving as emergency nurse, deliberately administers a fatal dose of morphine. In due course, Amherst and Justine are married. Inevitably, the latter's complicity in Bessy's death is revealed by the doctor in charge of the case, who happens to be a disappointed suitor of Justine's. Amherst, shocked and, as it develops, unexpectedly obtuse, fails to rise to the occasion, and the hitherto singularly happy marriage is jeopardized. Justine performs the usual expiation without which few novels of the period were complete, and the story concludes with a reconciliation on a somewhat lower level of mutual confidence.

What seems at first glance to be a fault in the management of the plot may well be intentional. Mrs. Wharton has attempted the difficult feat of introducing two centers of revelation, but unfortunately they are not expanded simultaneously, and this helps account for the broken-backed structure of the novel. Nevertheless, there is a repetition of the thematic pattern which provides a certain formal unity as well as a major stroke of dramatic irony. Amherst's failure to raise his first wife, Bessy, to his level of moral insight and conviction is followed by Justine's near failure to raise Amherst to hers; the disaster which concludes the first experiment is narrowly averted in the second.

The structural weakness of the novel cannot be easily extenuated, however, and it seems likely that it is bound up with Edith Wharton's method of composition. In *A Backward Glance* she relates how Walter Berry came to her rescue when she bogged down in the early chapters of *The Valley of Decision.*

He looked through what I had written, handed it back, and said simply: "Don't worry about how you're to go on. Just write down everything you feel like telling." The advice freed me once for all from the incubus of an artificially predesigned plan, and sent me rushing ahead with my tale, letting each incident create the next, and keeping in sight only the novelist's essential sign-post, the inner significance of the "case" selected.

In a later chapter she spoke of Henry James's tendency to sacrifice to his technical experiments "that spontaneity which is the life of fiction." It is one of the statements that helps to modify the view that she was merely his disciple. "Everything, in the latest novels," she continued, "had to be fitted into a predestined design, and design, in his strict geometrical sense, is to me one of the least important things in fiction." With another good friend and fellow novelist, Paul Bourget, she took issue on the same point:

Nous parlions souvent de l'art du roman, car la technique de notre métier nous passionait tous deux; et bientôt je me rendis compte que les idées de Bourget étaient tout à fait opposées aux miennes. Dès qu'il commençait un roman, Bourget montait en chaire; il fallait que chaque personnage fût un pion dans un jeu savamment combiné d'avance, et d'où l'imprévu déconcertant de la vie était totalement banni.[2]

These admissions, together with her subsequent complaint that James's design left insufficient room for "the irregular and irrelevant movements of life," may be placed beside her remarks in *A Motor-Flight through France* on the general method of Gothic art. It is not without significance, I think, that she was so captivated by the west front of Amiens Cathedral. "So steadily, so clearly was this great thing willed and foreseen, that it holds the mind too deeply subject to its general conception to be immediately free for the delighted investigation of detail." But both the exterior and the interior of the great structure are decorated with a prodigality of sculptured detail—bas-reliefs "full of crowded expressive incidents . . . with a Burgundian richness and elaborateness of costume, and a quite charming, childish insistence on irrelevant episode and detail. . . ."

Of composition there is none: it is necessarily sacrificed to the desire to stop and tell everything. . . . And thus one is brought back to the perpetually recurring fact that all northern art is anecdotic, and has always been so. . . .

In all of Edith Wharton's early novels one is aware of the conflict between form and subject, between the author's recognition of the need for a measure of control and her desire to "write down everything you feel like telling." In writing *The House of Mirth*, she tells us, "my trouble was that the story kept drawing into its web so many subordinate themes that to show their organic connection with the main issue, yet keep them from crowding to the front, was a heavy task for a beginner." That she could discipline herself in her longer fiction to the demands of form, she more than once proved, notably in *Ethan Frome, The Reef,* and *The Age of Innocence;* but her impatience with the restrictions of design was again apparent in *The Custom of the Country* and, much later, in *Hudson River Bracketed.* In general, she relied on the control exerted by the deeply felt "inner significance" of her action to insure the general outline of her structure and, in doing so, tried to free herself of the responsibility for an absolute agreement between form and subject. The method breaks down, of course, as it does in *The Valley of Decision* and *The Fruit of the Tree,* when the theme is not clearly defined or adequately felt—when the "essential sign-post" is missed, with the result that the structure is largely improvised.

From the time its earliest reviewers disputed its merits, there has never been much critical accord on *The Fruit of the Tree.* Robert Morss Lovett describes Mrs. Wharton's account of the industrial situation at Westmore as "amusingly vague," but Edmund Wilson finds it "ably handled." Edith Wharton herself gave the signal for the confusion when, possibly bored by an uncongenial subject, she slackened her hold on her original theme. But like so many second-rate productions, *The Fruit of the Tree* is to a high degree characteristic and revealing of its author. None of Edith Wharton's heroines, I think it can be said, contains so much of herself as does Justine Brent. She stands in relation to her creator as Maggie Tulliver does to George Eliot, and for that reason, undoubtedly, she is more sympathetically presented than any other woman in Edith Wharton's novels, not excepting Anna Leath. She defines herself for us reluctantly at first, but emerges gradually by means of contrast with Bessy Westmore, who is a composite portrait of everything that Edith Wharton disliked in her own sex. Vain, shallow, and self-centered, Bessy is one of the "most harrowing victims," as Mrs. Ansell remarks, "of the plan of bringing up our girls in the double bondage of expedience and unreality, corrupting their bodies with luxury and their brains with sentiment." Note particularly that, as in the characterization of Lily Bart, Undine Spragg, and Mrs. Waythorn in "The Other Two," Edith Wharton stresses her "chameleon-like" nature, her inability to conceive any image of herself save the most flattering of those which her friends supply—her lack, in other words, of any power of accurate self-appraisal.

Justine, on the other hand, is singularly aware of herself both as she is in fact and as she appears to others; she provides her own firm center of belief. She has, I repeat, all the traits which are apparent to a marked degree in her creator. She confronts life stoically and expresses her view of it ironically. We are told that she "felt with her brain," and this is the objection most frequently voiced by critics of Mrs. Wharton. She has the same independent spirit that enabled Edith Wharton to make a career for herself in opposition to her family and her class. Condemned to the frivolous society of Lynbrook, where "all sense of that vaster human consciousness" is excluded, she longs, as Edith Wharton did until the age of thirty-five, for "a life in which the high chances of doing should be mated with the finer forms of enjoyment." Nevertheless, one aspect of the life at Lynbrook attracts her: she is "sensitive to the finer graces of luxurious living, to the warm lights on old pictures and bronzes, the soft mingling of tints in faded rugs and panellings of time-warmed oak." Forced as a nurse to participate in the ugliness, pain, and drudgery of the submerged lives that she touches in her work, she finds that life "recovers its meaning under the aspect of a graceful leisure." No more than Mrs. Wharton can she willingly embrace a life of self-denial and sacrifice, and for the same reason: she has a horror of the sentimentality which so often provides the only motive in that decision. At the same time, the high valuation she places on the decorative side of life is modified, as in Lawrence Selden's case, by the realization that the setting furnished by wealth and leisure is worth nothing without the graces of mind and spirit which help to create "the freer world of ideas." It is one of the central ironies of the human situation in the novel that, with all her intelligence and taste, Justine is confined by circumstances to a narrow scope, while the rattle-brained Bessy has all the material, if none of the spiritual aids to freedom.

Possibly it is Edith Wharton's self-identification with her heroine that accounts, at the same time, for the most

ludicrous and amusing touch in the novel. Justine is provided with a set of impeccable antecedents which are
evidently supposed to belie her rather humble role in
life. As a girl she had attended boarding school in Paris
with Bessy Langhope, and she cherishes "memories of a
childhood nestled in beauty and gentle ways, before her
handsome prodigal father had died, and her mother's
face had grown pinched in the long struggle with poverty." But then John Amherst, who is comparably placed
in life, derives from similar stock. His father had been
rather well off, and his mother is a friend of Mrs. Ansell's,
who solves the question of his social acceptability by
identifying him as "one of the Amhersts of Albany." The
social prejudice which these details imply is not so awk-
wardly introduced in the other novels, but it is nonetheless present. Mrs. Wharton was never able to dissociate
good breeding from the other desirable badges of distinction—character, sensibility, a high degree of cultural
awareness, and even good looks—and the disconcerting
effect of this prejudice is particularly evident, as we shall
see, in her ambiguous treatment of Vance Weston in
Hudson River Bracketed and *The Gods Arrive*.

I have dwelt on the marked resemblance of Justine
Brent's personality to that of Edith Wharton because
it may help to explain why her "case" in the end proves
the more interesting of the two which the novel sets itself to examine. Amherst disappoints us. In the domestic impasse with Justine he reveals the inadequacy of his
moral sensibility when it is not being applied to broad
abstract social problems. At the same time, although his
character is in no way inconsistent, he is a victim of the
alteration of tone which sometimes marks Edith Wharton's transactions with her characters. She is easily capti-

vated or repelled by her creations as they develop under her hand. Undine Spragg becomes an inhuman abstraction, whereas Newland Archer, who is subjected to some of Mrs. Wharton's finest irony in the opening chapters of *The Age of Innocence,* manages to win a more sympathetic hearing as his difficulties multiply. With the reappearance of Justine Brent, at any rate, Amherst's stature begins to diminish and a characteristic suggestion of futility touches his welfare aims. Mrs. Wharton has by this time fairly shed her pose and, in the person of Justine, acknowledged her real sympathies.

Beginning with *The Fruit of the Tree,* the argument of Edith Wharton's novels focuses with varying depth but remarkable consistency on a single theme, which she once defined as "the immersion of the larger in the smaller nature which is one of the mysteries of the moral life." [3] It is a mystery that many novelists have explored intermittently, but it had a striking and permanent attraction for the three most readily identifiable masters of Edith Wharton's art, Balzac, George Eliot, and Henry James, as well as for Marcel Proust, the chief enthusiasm of her later years, whose central theme as she defined it was "the hopeless passion of a sensitive man for a stupid uncomprehending woman." [4] And yet none of them exploited it as persistently as she did. Although it is prefigured in her long tales *The Touchstone* and *Sanctuary,* it is not until we are confronted in succession by *The Fruit of the Tree, Ethan Frome,* and *The Reef* that we are able to appreciate its centrality.

A glance at the principal relationships in some of the novels may help confirm my point. In each case the emphasis falls on the baffling, wasteful submission of a superior nature to an inferior. It is a phenomenon which Edith Wharton no more than her predecessors was able to explain, but it presented intriguing possibilities to the novelist who believed that it was moral issues principally that guaranteed the life of fiction. Looking back, we can see that the whole of her subsequent thematic development is implied in *The Fruit of the Tree,* in which John Amherst's humanitarian program is hampered by the petty social aims of his first wife Bessy and then, by an ironic inversion, the happiness of his second wife, Justine, is threatened by the limitations of his own moral vision. In later stories, Ethan Frome is morally victimized by Zeena, Ralph Marvell by Undine Spragg, Ann Eliza Bunner ("Bunner Sisters") by her sister Evelina. Lawyer Royall, in *Summer,* a man of Ethan Frome's dignified stature, is thwarted and humiliated by his passion for his self-centered ward Charity. Two of Edith Wharton's rarest spirits, Halo Tarrant (*Hudson River Bracketed* and *The Gods Arrive*) and Anna Leath (*The Reef*), having blundered in their first marriages, find illusory compensation in Vance Weston and George Darrow. Martin Boyne, in *The Children,* foregoes his chance of happiness with Rose Sellars to rescue the Wheater children—a quixotic effort born of his hopeless middle-aged passion for the girl Judith Wheater, who can neither appreciate his sacrifice nor return his love. The examples can be multiplied to include every novel Edith Wharton wrote after *The House of Mirth* with the exception of *A Son at the Front,* in which the usual relationship is reversed.

How do these unequal partnerships originate? Invariably in a sentimental error on the part of the destined victim. Amherst, in love with Bessy Westmore, is deluded into thinking that she shares his interest in reform. Ethan Frome is led astray by his gratitude for Zeena's devoted nursing of his parents. Ralph Marvell, naïvely fancying himself a Perseus, rescues his corn-belt Andromeda from the clutches of rich, lecherous, popeyed Peter Van Degen. Anna Leath, impatient of the restraints which the sheltered life has imposed on her, is somewhat too anxious to extenuate Darrow's conduct in the affair with Sophy Viner. Halo Spear marries Lewis Tarrant because she is grateful to him for rescuing her brother from a scandal and for underwriting her parents' financial future. Newland Archer (*The Age of Innocence*) is trapped by his own futile logic into giving up Ellen Olenska for the duller and more respectable charms of May Welland. The motive in each case is high-minded, and the act calls for a generous, if vain, display of altruism.

One is tempted to trace the motive for her preoccupation with this theme to her confessedly unsatisfactory relationship with Edward Wharton—a relationship that, so far as we can gather, had become critically strained by the time she wrote *The Fruit of the Tree*. But the fact that the theme persists in her fiction long after their divorce suggests that her interest in it was fed from still another source. Mrs. Wharton's future biographer, encouraged by certain remarks in Percy Lubbock's book, may depend on the at present shadowy figure of Walter Berry to furnish the explanation. Lubbock has described the latter as a man, "I am ready to believe, of strong intelligence and ability—but also, I certainly know, of a dry and narrow and supercilious temper," and has spoken of the disastrous influence of his rationalism on Edith Wharton's creative life. Dogmatist, egotist, and snob though he seems to have been (and there has been some objection to Lubbock's estimate), there is no question of Edith Wharton's devotion to him; there is no doubt, even on the basis of her own cautious testimony in *A Backward Glance,* that for over forty years he made himself felt through the medium of her fiction. It is difficult to believe, moreover, that she could remain determinedly unaware of her friends' view of the relationship and that her novels do not reflect her own troubled probing of its various aspects. Those who have discerned the lineaments of Walter Berry's personality in a succession of Edith Wharton's heroes would probably agree that his relationship with the novelist is also reflected in the nature and treatment of the moral problems in her stories.

In the antiromantic tradition, none of the love affairs in Edith Wharton's novels acquires interest or significance until one or both of the partners is married. Once she has her characters ensnared as a result of their sentimental miscalculations, she is able to introduce a second, contingent theme. In all of the stories I have mentioned, she proceeds directly to the question: What is the extent of one's moral obligation to those individuals who, legally or within the framework of existing manners, conventions, taboos, apparently have the strictest claim on one's loyalty? This question occupies the center of Edith Wharton's moral consciousness as it reveals itself in her fiction. There is no doubt in her mind regarding the prior assumption that a sense of individual responsibility is the only basis of social order and development. But she is seeking the most liberal interpretation of that axiom consistent with her inherited notions of fair play and respectability. In all of these novels she is trying to determine the limits of responsibility.

As might be expected, the moral implications of divorce are debated endlessly in her fiction. The traditional prejudice of her class outlawed it. It was one of the convenient arrangements introduced by the invaders of her old New York, and partly because of her instinctive hostility to this group she rejected it, in her fiction at least, as a solution. From first to last, the tone which she adopts in discussing the matter suggests that inherited scruples have conquered after all and that, like Mrs. Lidcote in her story "Autres Temps," she has been forced to admit that "traditions that have lost their meaning are the hardest of all to destroy." In spite of the latitude with which she treats certain moral problems, she generally rests her case on the status quo. There is a pronounced straining at the seams of conventional morality, and an occasional triumph of open-mindedness, as in the treatment of euthanasia in *The Fruit of the Tree;* but in her fiction, as in her life, flat rebellion is usually disparaged or at least shown to be futile.

There is of course a reason for this, which is rooted in the Puritan subsoil of Edith Wharton's nature. The morality of an act is evaluated in terms of its cost to others. When Mr. Langhope, Amherst's father-in-law, proposes divorce as the solution to his daughter's difficulties, Mrs. Ansell protests:

"Bessy will never be happy in the new way."
"What do you call the new way?"
"Launching one's boat over a human body—or several, as the case may be."

Given the notion of individual responsibility, no human destiny can be detached from those it touches, directly or indirectly, and the ramifications of a selfish or thought-

less act are indefinitely extended. The individual justification is forced to yield to the larger question of the act's
effect on the social structure as a whole. "Don't you understand," Halo Tarrant asks Vance Weston at the close
of *Hudson River Bracketed*, "that what I want is all you
can give me without having to hurt anybody else?"

Taken in this light, one of Edith Wharton's comments
in her review of Leslie Stephen's *George Eliot* not only
betrays the characteristic bent of her interests, but may
go a long way in explaining to her biographer (when he
is permitted to appear) her own position:

All of George Eliot's characters shrink with a peculiar dread
from any personal happiness acquired at the cost of the
social organism; yet her own happiness was acquired at such
cost. That she felt herself justified by special circumstances
her letters assert, and those who know her best have repeatedly affirmed. She wrote, *in a moment of profound
insight* [italics mine], that "the great problem of the shifting relation between passion and duty is clear to no man who
is capable of apprehending it"; but she never ceased to
revere the law she transgressed. . . .[5]

The "shifting relation between passion and duty" is
merely another way of formulating the second problem
I have been discussing. Edith Wharton's attempt to define the limits of responsibility is an act of mediation, as
uncertain as George Eliot's, between the claims of passion and duty. She is not a problem novelist. Except in
some of the early short stories, her themes never become
merely problems, demonstrations, propositions. The dilemmas of her characters, however much light they may
shed on the nature of the conflict, are never resolved—

except, as I have remarked, by a return to the status quo, as for example in *Ethan Frome*, *The Reef*, and *The Age of Innocence*. Her own experience, we must believe, was a perpetual testing ground for her situations, but it provided no final answers. Her separation and divorce from Edward Wharton were not followed, as might have been anticipated, by a rationalization of the act in fiction: there is no discernible compromise in her attitude toward divorce.

On the contrary, there is a tendency in her later novels and short stories toward an almost ironclad rectitude in the treatment of ethical questions—a tendency in which a certain hardness and even a certain cruelty are involved, and which is likely to outrage the sensibilities of a later, more tolerant generation. It is, we sometimes feel, a rectitude which compromises itself temporarily in open discussion of the issues only to emerge triumphant in the tone of her conclusions. It is noticeable as early as *The Reef* (1912), with its regrettable final chapter, and it frequently weakens her later novels by encouraging the impression of a dowager-like severity.

It is necessary at this point to take another long look at *The Fruit of the Tree*. Clearly, it is Justine's "case" which is the pivotal one. Her dilemma, which I have mentioned only in passing, involves the question of her responsibility to the other three main characters, whose moral sensibilities are far less acute than her own. At one time or another, the individual fates of Amherst, Bessy, and the young doctor Stephen Wyant pass into her unwilling control. By the time Bessy Amherst injures her spine in a fall from her horse, the Amherst marriage is on the rocks. Justine, thrust into the un-grateful role of mediator, has already established—however involuntarily—a certain influence over John Amherst. In the emergency she serves as head nurse. Dr. Wyant, her former suitor, who has been slipping downhill morally and physically since she rejected him, is in charge of the case. There is one chance in a thou-sand that Bessy can survive. In frightful pain, she lin-gers between life and death, her ordeal prolonged by the skill of Wyant, who to retrieve his reputation is de-termined to keep her alive as long as possible. Justine, unsentimental and at the same time deeply humane, is convinced that her friend will not recover, and unable any longer to watch her suffer she decides to end the senseless torture. By chance, she is helped to her deci-sion by some marginal annotations in a copy of Bacon in Amherst's library, and particularly by the sentiment, which she assumes he endorses, "La vraie morale se moque de la morale." She gives Bessy an overdose of morphine. When Wyant returns to find his patient dead, he suspects, but refrains from announcing, the truth.

The dilemma has been established with some skill, and in such a way as to introduce the utmost complexity into the question of Justine's guilt and her responsibility. The nature of her liaison with Amherst, although ap-parently innocent, has been left deliberately uncertain, in her own mind, in Amherst's, and above all in Wyant's. But Wyant is inclined to suspect the worst: that she has eliminated Bessy in order to secure Amherst for herself. Two years after her marriage he reappears. He has succumbed to the drug habit, lost his job, and cannot support his family. He threatens to expose Justine un-less she comes to his aid. Under the circumstances, and in spite of her conviction that her action is morally defensible, she falls an easy victim to blackmail, not merely because she is terrified of exposure but because she feels obscurely responsible for Wyant's predicament. After all, she had temporized with him following Amherst's reappearance on her horizon, and she had spoiled the case by which he had hoped to reinstate himself in his profession. She responds to his periodic appeals for money until she has thoroughly implicated herself and in the eyes of the world underlined the circumstances pointing to her guilt. Finally, when he demands that she use her influence with Amherst's former father-in-law to secure him the post of house physician at a well-known hospital, she balks. Amherst learns the story of Bessy's death from the baffled and vindictive Wyant, and the hitherto idyllic partnership between husband and wife is suddenly dissolved. Amherst accepts Justine's explanation, they continue on an apparently unchanged domestic footing, but before long it is clear to Justine that her presence is an embarrassment to her husband, who is still linked, through his work at the mill and through his affection for his stepdaughter Cicely, to Bessy's family. When they learn that Wyant has secured the hospital post after all, it becomes imperative to lay Justine's case before Mr. Langhope, Bessy's father, who has always regarded Justine as an interloper.

With this development, Justine is confronted by the difficult and by now hopelessly complex question of her responsibility toward Amherst. By repudiating the sentiment inscribed in his copy of Bacon—or at least the practical application of it—he has withdrawn his moral support. He must not be implicated in a deed for which she must assume the responsibility.

Justine had paid, yes—paid to the utmost limit of whatever debt toward society she had contracted by overstepping its laws. And her resolve to discharge the debt had been taken in a flash, as soon as she had seen that man can commit no act alone, whether for good or evil.

Although Amherst is willing to perform the disagreeable task of explaining matters to Mr. Langhope, Justine, hoping to preserve the latter's regard for her husband, beats him to the interview. She reveals her guilt in the worst possible light, clears Amherst of any suspicion of complicity, and then agrees to Langhope's demand that she be ready at a signal from him to drop out of her husband's and Cicely's lives.

By this time it is apparent that the larger nature of Justine, which has argued consistently for the freedom to act on its most generous impulses, has been betrayed by the smaller natures surrounding it—by Wyant, Bessy, Mr. Langhope, but particularly by Amherst, who cannot penetrate to the clear moral atmosphere in which her decisions are formed. What follows, for Justine, is the usual expiation. There is the long separation, then Amherst's discovery of the pact between his wife and Mr. Langhope, followed by forgiveness on all sides and a reunion, in which, however, "nothing was left of that secret inner union which had so enriched and beautified their outward lives." The novel ends on a familiar note of irony. At the dedication of a workers' recreation project at Westmore, Amherst shows the audience the original plan for the building, a testimony, he tells them, of his first wife's devotion to their welfare. Justine alone knows that it is Bessy's blueprint for a private swimming pool and gymnasium at Lynbrook, her final extravagant gesture of defiance at Amherst. Although bitterly resentful at being supplanted by Bessy's shadow, she allows Amherst to retain his illusion.

She accepted the last condition as she had accepted the other, pledged to the perpetual expiation of an act for which, in the abstract, she still refused to hold herself to blame. But life is not a matter of abstract principles, but a succession of pitiful compromises with fate, of concessions to old tradition, old beliefs, old charities and old frailties.

There is never any doubt in Justine's mind as to the moral justification of euthanasia under the particular circumstances that compelled her to act. The purity of her motive is undeniable. But the step is taken with little thought of its possible consequences, and it is only after its exposure threatens the happiness of several people that the moral issue loses its original simplicity and becomes compromised with questions outside the abstract realm. Too late, Justine learns what Delia Ralston in *The Old Maid* is to learn, that it is "a terrible thing, a sacrilegious thing to interfere with another's destiny, to lay the tenderest touch upon any human being's right to love and suffer after his own fashion," and that her responsibility is limited, practically if not ideally, by the complexity of the human situation and the fact that the gods are jealous of their prerogatives.

The theme is renewed in Edith Wharton's next important work, *Ethan Frome* (1911). Although much has been made of this minor classic of our literature as a picture of New England life and a triumph of style and construction, its relation to Mrs. Wharton's more characteristic and important stories has never been clearly established. *Ethan Frome* is not a "sport." It belongs to the main tradition of Mrs. Wharton's fiction, and it has a value, independent of its subject and technique, in helping us to define that tradition. Alfred Kazin has linked it to *The House of Mirth* as a demonstration of the spiritual value of failure, but although this is a recurrent theme in Edith Wharton, particularly in the novels she wrote in the 'twenties, and is inescapable in the conclusion of *The House of Mirth*, it is no mean feat, I think, to reconcile it with the episode which forms the narrative framework of *Ethan Frome*. She was by no means convinced of its soundness, and it is possible, as I intend to suggest, that the spectacle of Ethan's prolonged and hopeless defeat, reinforced by the glimpses of his spiritual isolation, his scarred and twisted body, and his querulous, demanding womenfolk, is intended to convey quite the opposite of what Mr. Kazin finds in the story.

The final, lingering note of the story, it seems to me, is one of despair arising from the contemplation of spiritual waste. So emphatic is it that it drowns out the conventional notion of the value of suffering and defeat. Ethan himself sounds it just before his last, abortive effort to escape his destiny:

Other possibilities had been in him, possibilities sacrificed, one by one, to Zeena's narrow-mindedness and ignorance. And what good had come of it? She was a hundred times bitterer and more discontented than when he had married her: the one pleasure left her was to inflict pain on him. All the healthy instincts of self-defence rose up in him against such waste. . . .

And taking Mrs. Wharton's novels as a whole, that note swells into a refrain whose burden, as George Darrow in *The Reef* formulates it, is "the monstrousness of use-less sacrifices." Here is the ultimate result of that "im-mersion of the larger in the smaller nature which is one of the mysteries of the moral life." As a theme, the vanity of self-sacrifice is merged repeatedly with the primary theme of the limits of individual responsibility. A realization of "the monstrousness of useless sacrifices" encourages the characters' selfish, passional bent, which is curbed in turn by the puritanical assertion of respon-sibility. For Ethan as for most of Edith Wharton's pro-tagonists who are confronted by the same alternatives— Ann Eliza Bunner, Newland Archer, Charlotte Lovell, Kate Clephane, Nona Manford, Martin Boyne—the in-herited sense of duty is strong enough to conquer, but the victory leaves in its wake the sense of futility which self-sacrifice entails. Their moral transactions are such as to preclude a satisfactory balancing of accounts.

How and to what degree does the situation in *Ethan Frome* embody this conflict? No element in the charac-terization of Ethan is more carefully brought out than the suggestion of his useful, even heroic possibilities. He had longed to become an engineer, had acquired some technical training, and is still reading desultorily in the field when the narrator encounters him. This is one aspect of his personality. There is still another which helps explain why Edith Wharton, who was deeply drawn to nature, is predisposed to treat his case with the utmost sympathy: "He had always been more sensitive than people about him to the appeal of natural beauty. His unfinished studies had given form to this sensibility and even in his unhappiest moments field and sky spoke to him with a deep and powerful persuasion." Add to these qualities his superior gifts of kindness, generosity, and sociability, and his impressive physical appearance ("Even then he was the most striking figure in Stark-field, though he was but the ruin of a man"), and it is evident that Edith Wharton set about, as Melville did with Ahab, to invest her rather unpromising human material with a tragic dignity.

It is in view of his potentialities that Ethan's marriage to Zeena is a catastrophe. By the time Mattie Silver appears on the scene, he is only twenty-eight but already trapped by circumstances and unable to extend the horizon of his future beyond the family graveyard. Mattie, once she has become the victim of Zeena's jealousy, offers a way out which Ethan is quick to follow. But immediately his plans are set afoot, things begin to close in on him again: farm and mill are mortgaged, he has no credit, and time is against him. Moreover, even in the heat of his resentment he cannot disregard Zeena's plight: "It was only by incessant labour and personal supervision that Ethan drew a meagre living from the land, and his wife, even if she were in better health than she imagined, could never carry such a burden alone." His rebellion dies out, but only to be rekindled the next morning as Mattie is about to leave. Suddenly it occurs to him that if he pleads Zeena's illness and the need of a servant, Andrew Hale may give him an advance on some lumber. He starts on foot for Starkfield, meets Mrs. Hale en route, is touched by her expression of sympathy ("You've had an awful mean time, Ethan Frome"), continues toward his rendezvous—and is suddenly pulled up short by the realization that he is planning to appeal to the Hales' sympathy to obtain money from them on false pretenses. It is the turning point of the action:

With the sudden perception of the point to which his madness had carried him, the madness fell and he saw his life before him as it was. He was a poor man, the husband of a sickly woman, whom his desertion would leave alone and destitute; and even if he had the heart to desert her he could have done so only by deceiving two kindly people who had pitied him.

Although he is neatly hemmed in by circumstances, it is Ethan's own sense of responsibility that blocks the last avenue of escape and condemns him to a life of sterile expiation.

In *Ethan Frome* all the themes I have mentioned are developed without the complexity that the more sophisticated characters and setting of *The Fruit of the Tree* and (as we shall see) *The Reef* require; they are reduced to the barest statement of their possibilities. To a person of Ethan's limited experience and his capacity for straightforward judgments, the issues present themselves with the least ambiguity or encouragement to evasion; and in this, I believe, we have the measure of the subject's value for Mrs. Wharton. As her characters approach her own sphere, their motives are disentangled with increasing difficulty from her own, and their actions are regulated by a closer censure; they become more complex and are apt to lose their way amid fine distinctions and tentative judgments. They are aware, like Woburn in the short story "A Cup of Cold Water," of the impossibility of basing a decision upon absolutes:

Was not all morality based on a convention? What was the stanchest code of ethics but a trunk with a series of false bottoms? Now and then one had the illusion of getting down to absolute right or wrong, but it was only a false bottom—a removable hypothesis—with another false bottom underneath. There was no getting beyond the relative.

Ethan Frome is closer than any of her other characters to the source of the ideas that underlie Edith Wharton's ethical judgments. Puritanism has lost very little of its hold on that portion of the New England mind which he represents and its ideas have not been weakened, as they have in the more populous industrial and commercial centers, by two centuries of enlightenment based on what Bernard Shaw called the Mercanto-Christian doctrine of morality. It is not surprising that many persons unacquainted with Edith Wharton's biography associate her—and not wholly on the strength of *Ethan Frome*—with Boston or with New England as a whole. Whatever the influences exerted by her New York origin and background and her long career abroad, it is the moral order of Ethan Frome's world that governs the view of reality in all her novels.

For this reason, and for others I will suggest, I am unable to appreciate John Crowe Ransom's objections to Mrs. Wharton's handling of point of view in *Ethan Frome*, a problem he assumes to have bothered her more than I suspect it really did.[6] In trying to reconstruct her approach to a solution, he writes that "if Ethan should tell it himself, it would not be identifiable with the main body of Mrs. Wharton's fiction." I am not sure why it is absolutely desirable that it *should* be, but, at any rate, the difficulty does not seem to have bothered the author of either "Bunner Sisters" or *Summer*, which are no more readily identifiable than *Ethan Frome* with her usual subjects. "But if she should tell it," Ransom continues, "it would very likely be the story of a rather metamorphosed Ethan." Her "trained and sophisticated sensibility . . . would have falsified the whole." To this last suggestion, one can only reply that it would have in any case, whatever point of view she might have chosen. Nevertheless, Ransom concludes that she "temporized": "She invented a special reporter for Ethan in the person of a young man of sensibility and education very like her own. In theory it gained for her this, that the reporter became a man; and this, that not being herself he need not render quite the complete spiritual history of events associated with her name as an author. In effect, it gained her very little."

This is raising difficulties where they do not necessarily exist. In the first place, Edith Wharton was simply following the structural method of Balzac's "La Grand Bretèche," as her hint in the preface and a comparison of the stories will confirm. She did not apply it with Balzac's success, however, for, as Ransom has correctly noted, her narrator's "vision" of Ethan's story (not "version," as Ransom misquotes) is based in large part on data that we cannot imagine any of the principals supplying, so that the story *is* in reality a "vision" rather than a "version." In the second place, the narrators employed in the framework of Edith Wharton's early stories are *always* men—whether because she had, as her contemporaries claimed, a masculine mind or because this refinement of the point of view allowed her greater freedom, I am not sure. But the choice is particularly defensible in *Ethan Frome*, first, because the narrator must have a pretext for visiting Starkfield, and this is more easily supplied for an engineer than for a woman with the requisite "sensibility and education," and second, because there must be some probability established for Ethan's inviting the narrator into his home—over and above, that is, the accident of the storm. Finally, I am not so willing to assume, as Ransom and many others have, that ten years' residence in the Berkshires (even allowing for the annual jaunts to Europe) was not enough to give Mrs. Wharton the needed understanding of the lives of her poorer neighbors. "When the mind is imaginative," writes Henry James in "The Art of Fiction," ". . . it takes to itself the faintest hints of life, it converts the very pulses of the air into revelations." In *The Valley of Decision* Edith Wharton had already demonstrated that she could do this with the materials of history. Why not, then, with the life just beyond her doorstep?

In connection with *Ethan Frome,* it is anticipating the chronology only slightly to bring in another long tale, "Bunner Sisters" (1916), not merely because it again illustrates Edith Wharton's surprising success in imagining the lives of the poor and the desperate, but because the subject in both stories is seen, felt, and interpreted from the same angle. Although it dates back to 1891–1892 in its original version and retains some of the melodramatic appeal of the tenement tales so popular in that decade, it evidently was rewritten shortly before publication, so that it belongs in part at least to the *Ethan Frome* period. Ann Eliza and Evelina Bunner are spinster sisters who manage an unprosperous notions and dressmaking shop off Stuyvesant Square, New York, in what seems to be the 1870's. The elder, Ann Eliza, is a wrenlike creature, dressed permanently in black silk, and presenting to the world an "habitually anxious face"; the younger is a peevish, self-centered woman with "a thin voice pitched to chronic fretfulness," reminiscent of Zeena Frome's. Their lives unroll monotonously, until one day Ann Eliza purchases a clock for Evelina's birthday at the shop of Hermann Ramy, a German, fortyish and unmarried. The unprepossessing jeweler manages to stir the dead embers of romance in his client's soul. But Evelina, taking the clock one day to be repaired, also notices him, and later, when he comes to call, she is obviously fluttered. Before a rivalry can develop, Ann Eliza quietly gives over her dream and embarks on a long career of self-sacrifice. Although Mr. Ramy prefers her to Evelina, she encourages his attentions to her sister. When they are married, she gives the bride half of their savings so that the jeweler, who by now has failed in business, can take a job in St. Louis. For some months Evelina's letters are progressively glummer and then they cease altogether. Ann Eliza, oppressed by loneliness and forced to watch her little business dwindle away, keeps a frightened vigil until her sister returns, ill and deserted by her husband, who, it turns out, is a drug addict. The tale is marred from this point by the author's determination to wring the last drop of pathos from her situation. Evelina has been beaten, forced into menial work, and later confined to a hospital with brain fever after losing her baby. On her release, she has had to beg in the streets for train fare to New York. By the time she arrives she has pneumonia, which quickly ripens into consumption. Ann Eliza nurses her devotedly. Months later, Evelina dies, and her sister, after having spent her last penny on medical bills, is dispossessed from her shop. When we last see her, she is looking for work and being turned away because she is too old.

The weakness of a synopsis is that it emphasizes

mainly the rather trite situation involving the long-suffering older sister and the selfish younger sister who later, with all the lugubrious detail of the popular ballad, turns into the deserted wife. But Edith Wharton is, in tone at least, the most unsentimental of novelists, and her treatment of this unrelievedly pathetic subject secures for it a kind of dignity. The story is far from being another *Ethan Frome,* but it depends on a similar situation. By now Edith Wharton has available a set of clearly defined and interrelated themes. Like Ethan, Ann Eliza Bunner is tied to an inferior partner and has a strong sense of personal responsibility, although her impulse toward freedom, unlike Ethan's, is immediately suppressed. Moreover, if we look for the clue to Mrs. Wharton's intention in the story, it reveals itself most conspicuously in Ann Eliza's meditation following her sister's return.

For the first time in her life she dimly faced the awful problem of the inutility of self-sacrifice. Hitherto she had never thought of questioning the inherited principles which had guided her life. Self-effacement for the good of others had always seemed to her both natural and necessary; but then she had taken it for granted that it implied the securing of that good. Now she perceived that to refuse the gifts of life does not insure their transmission to those for whom they have been surrendered; and her familiar heaven was unpeopled.

It is the revelation forced upon Justine and Ethan, and later with equal conviction upon an almost unbroken succession of Edith Wharton's protagonists.

Chapter VII

THE REMOTER IMAGINATIVE ISSUES

Ethan Frome marks a gain in artistry that was to be consolidated later in *The Reef* and *The Age of Innocence*.
The first important work to appear after Edith Wharton
had established her permanent residence abroad, it had
been undertaken as an exercise in French to modernize
her idioms, but had been abandoned after a few weeks.
A sojourn at the Mount, some years later, had revived
the story in her mind, and it had been written in Paris
during the following winter. From the directness and
simplicity of the style of the final version, one might suppose that it had been composed entirely in French and
then translated, but it was in fact an independent growth
from the original seed. She and Walter Berry had
"talked the tale over page by page," and the results of
their collaboration may be glimpsed in the fragment
of a working version preserved among the manuscripts
at Yale. Berry was a rigorous taskmaster. "With each
book," Edith Wharton acknowledged gratefully, "he
exacted a higher standard in economy of expression, in
purity of language, in the avoidance of the hackneyed
and precious." The stylistic restraint of the final version,
unusual even for Mrs. Wharton, may in part be a tribute
to his discipline. How many revisions the tale underwent

may never be known, but a comparison of the manuscript fragment with the corresponding portion of the printed text indicates that Edith Wharton worked hard to meet Berry's standards and to eliminate redundancies, circumlocutions, and ambiguous or misleading expressions, realizing that the language as well as the theme of *Ethan Frome* had to be treated "starkly and summarily." [1]

Enough has been said, by Mrs. Wharton among others, about the technical resourcefulness brought into play by the peculiar difficulties of telling Ethan's story; but in view of the widespread feeling that the author's human sympathies were hobbled by her rationalism, it should be stressed that the best touches in the story are there because she felt her subject deeply enough to be able to charge it with conviction at every point. The details are few but impressive; they arise directly and easily, and always with the sharpest pertinence, from the significant grounds of character and situation; they are, as Percy Lubbock suggests, "the natural and sufficient channels of great emotion." [2] Every reader will recall some of them: Mattie's tribute to the winter sunset—"It looks just as if it was painted"; Ethan's reluctance to have Mattie see him follow Zeena into their bedroom; the removal of Mattie's trunk; the watchful, sinister presence of Zeena's cat disturbing the intimacy of the lovers' evening together by appropriating her mistress' place at the table, breaking the pickle dish, and later setting Zeena's rocking chair in motion. Zeena may not be a sympathetic character, but there is a moment when she makes us forget everything but her wronged humanity. As she confronts the guilty lovers, holding the fragments of her

---

[1] For notes to chap. vii, see p. 256.

beloved pickle dish, her face streaming with tears, we have a sudden and terrible glimpse of the starved emotional life that has made her what she is. The novelist's compassion can reach no further.

Although it functioned generally at a mundane level, Edith Wharton's imagination could occasionally be roused to symbol-making activity by the conjunction of a theme and a setting both deeply cherished and understood. In *Ethan Frome* her theme is enhanced by every feature of the landscape: by the "orchard of starved appletrees writhing over a hillside among outcroppings of slate," the crazily slanted headstones in the Frome graveyard, the truncated "L" of Ethan's farmhouse in which one saw "the image of his own shrunken body," but predominantly by the landscape as a whole, buried under snow, silent and incommunicative as the characters. The method looks ahead to *Summer*, with its naturalistic symbol of the Mountain and its subtle accommodation of the human drama to the rhythm of the changing seasons; to the moment in *The Reef* when Darrow recalls his vision of Anna Summers advancing toward him slowly down an avenue of trees, now transformed in his imagination to the passing years, with the "light and shade of old memories and new hopes playing variously on her"; and to *Hudson River Bracketed*, with its dominating symbol of the Willows, equated in Vance Weston's mind with the Past he is struggling to recapture in his first novel. Only in *Ethan Frome*, however, is the symbolism sustained by every element in the setting. It is the one occasion in her longer fiction when her imagination worked freely and without faltering in this extra dimension.

Recalling the abortive French version of *Ethan Frome*,

Edith Wharton remarked in *A Backward Glance* that
after the lessons were concluded "the copy-book containing my 'exercise' vanished forever." Fortunately, it
did not. It is preserved among the manuscripts in the
Yale collection,[3] and it is interesting because, along with
the manuscripts of *The House of Mirth* and *The Reef,*
it helps to belie one of Mrs. Wharton's most emphatic
generalizations about her method as a novelist. In her
memoirs, as in *The Writing of Fiction,* she revives the
hackneyed discussion of the novel of situation versus the
novel of character, concludes that any novel worth its
salt is a combination of the two, and then adds: "In my
own case a situation sometimes occurs to me first, and
sometimes a single figure suddenly walks into my mind."
But regardless of which comes first, there is an "odd feature" of her creative experience that she has not heard
of elsewhere: ". . . My characters always appear with
their names."

Sometimes these names seem to be affected, sometimes almost ridiculous; but I am obliged to own that they are never
fundamentally unsuitable. And the proof that they are not,
that they really belong to the people, is the difficulty I have
in trying to substitute other names. For many years the
attempt always ended fatally; any character I unchristened
instantly died on my hands. . . .

The ideal statements that writers make about their
method are frequently untrustworthy, and I have often
wondered to what extent Edith Wharton may have been
influenced *ex post facto* by Henry James's remarks, in
person or in his preface to *The Portrait of a Lady,* about
"the intensity of suggestion that may reside in the stray
figure, the unattached character, the image *en dispo-*

nibilité." Turgenev's stories, James recalled, "began for him almost always with the vision of some person or persons, who hovered before him, soliciting him, as the active or passive figure, interesting him and appealing to him just as they were and by what they were." And echoing these remarks at the close of the long discussion of her own characters as *disponibles,* Edith Wharton adds that "what I want to try to capture is an impression of the elusive moment when these people who haunt my brain actually begin to speak within me with their own voices."

One would be hard put to find anywhere in her fiction more oddly appropriate names than Ethan and Zeena Frome, and yet this unhappy couple appears in the French version with the characterless names of Ethan and Anna Hart. In the extant fragment of the later, English version they go by the names that are familiar to us, but Harmon Gow appears variously as Harmon Eddy or Hosea Eddy. The same quest for the right name is apparent in other manuscripts. Darrow in *The Reef* was once Caringdon. The heroine of *The House of Mirth* was Juliet Hurst then Lily Hurst before she became Lily Bart; Selden had the original surname of Hensley; Gerty Farish was Nelly Varick, Rosedale was Rosendale, and so on. The examples, taken at random, should be sufficient to throw at least some doubt on Mrs. Wharton's remarks, although on such evidence it would be presumptuous to deny the general accuracy of her account.

Ethan Frome was Mrs. Wharton's fourth experiment with the long tale and was destined to remain her most successful. It is a far cry from *The Touchstone* (1900), *Sanctuary* (1903), and *Madame de Treymes* (1907), in which the characters are people who react in a complicated way to the moral issues confronting them, both the situations and motives are frequently stretched to the limits of credibility, and the handling of structure and point of view is wholly conventional. By the time she came to write *Ethan Frome* she had passed beyond both the excessive verbal irony of *The Touchstone* and the sentimentality transiently apparent in *Sanctuary* and the stories composing *Crucial Instances,* but even if she had not, she would have been barred from these two refuges by the inescapably tragic nature of Ethan's case.

A number of critics have referred to these pieces as "novelettes." I have purposely avoided the term because I cannot recall its ever having been used by Mrs. Wharton and because it implies just the opposite of what she understood to be the inherent qualities of this type of fiction. Her single remark on the subject, in *The Writing of Fiction,* is a sufficient guide. Differentiating between the functions of the novel and the short story, she remarks parenthetically: "Meanwhile, it may be pointed out that a third, and intermediate, form of tale—the *long* short-story—is available for any subject too spreading for conciseness yet too light in texture to be stretched into a novel." This definition, plus the fact that she nowhere develops a separate rationale of the long tale, implies that the form is governed by the same general considerations that apply to the short story. But with this difference, relating it to the novel: the subject of the long tale, containing as always its own dimensions, demands a more extended development, because the inner life of the characters must be revealed to us gradually and because the reader must obtain a sense of the lapse of time.

On these grounds, the long tale is better adapted than the short story to the unfolding of the complicated (and sometimes rather tenuous) moral issues that were the hallmark of Mrs. Wharton's early fiction. Moral dramas, she wrote, "usually have their roots deep in the soul, their rise far back in time; and the suddenest-seeming clash in which they culminate should be led up to step by step if it is to explain and justify itself." The short story can invade this province only when its situation can be illuminated by " a single retrospective flash"—a condition that never prevented Edith Wharton from finding many such situations.

The subjects of all the long tales preceding *Ethan Frome* require this more leisurely development. The sources of Glennard's dilemma (*The Touchstone*) lie deep in the past, in his one-sided affair with the late Margaret Aubyn, the most famous woman writer of her day, whose pathetic letters—testimonials of her un-requited love—he publishes anonymously in order to finance his marriage. It is a situation rich in possibilities if somewhat unconvincing, and there are enough unex-ploited suggestions in Edith Wharton's treatment of it to warrant its expansion to novel length. The moral drama of *Sanctuary*, the weakest of these tales, requires the juxtaposition of two episodes separated in time by twenty-odd years; moreover, it depends on the most fantastic and, when all is said and done, the most inex-plicable of motives: Kate Orme's conviction that she must marry Denis Peyton in order to save the child he will someday have from what she regards as an heredi-tary moral taint. Only *Madame de Treymes*, with its moral issue rigorously defined and expressed through a simple opposition of manners, is able to tailor its development to the dimensions of the long tale in such a way that there are no stresses at the seams, as in its predecessors. And the theme of *Ethan Frome* had the inherent advantage of being one on which, as Edith Wharton put it, only a few variations could be played.

Surveying Edith Wharton's development as a whole, it is apparent that her next novel, *The Reef* (1912), is a crucial one. Having tried her hand at the themes we noted in *The Fruit of the Tree* and *Ethan Frome,* she put them, and herself, to a severer test in the novel that Henry James and, following him, Percy Lubbock described as her masterpiece. It is the one of her novels that on the technical side reminds us strongly of James, in the degree to which the "case" is isolated and scrutinized, in its reluctant and shaded avowals, in its carefully controlled point of view, and even in its metaphors. It is, again, the only one of her novels that James might have been willing to exempt from his general complaint that she surveyed the psychological terrain from too great a height, for the play of forces which constitutes the inner life of George Darrow and Anna Leath is analyzed with a sustained closeness of attention. The formal design is achieved with the economy of French classical drama. As a vehicle for her maturest style, *The Reef* is on a level with *Ethan Frome* and *The Age of Innocence,* and, ranged alongside those masterpieces, it is a tribute to her versatility in adapting style to subject. Anna Leath is the most completely represented and, along with Justine Brent, the most sympathetic of her heroines, and the characterization of Sophy Viner, although refracted through the consciousness of Darrow and Anna, is striking in its definiteness and individuality of outline.

In fact, *The Reef* is such a good novel that one wishes it were better. As it stands, however, its tone is uncertain. If we could define satisfactorily Edith Wharton's attitude toward George Darrow, the difficulty might resolve itself; but this is unlikely, for it seems probable that *The Reef* not only shaped itself in deference to certain questions posed insistently by her private experience, but that more than any other of her novels it bases its answers on moral conventions whose force is to a large degree lost upon the present-day audience. It is difficult always, but particularly in *The Reef,* to get the right perspective on Mrs. Wharton's world, and there is always the danger of passing the kind of judgments on Darrow's conduct that can be defended only by appealing to a morality lying outside the novel. But nothing will ever prevent the reader from doing just that, and the permanent value of *The Reef* therefore remains an uncertain quantity. That the reader is repelled, however unjustifiably from the standpoint of things as they are, by the two very different kinds of justice accorded to Darrow and Sophy Viner, I feel certain. A strong personal bias is evident in the lenient treatment of Darrow's case as opposed to that of Sophy. Regardless of the logic of the particular circumstances governing the action as a whole, one is struck, for instance, by the gross unfairness—even inconsistency—of the concluding chapter, in which Sophy Viner's future is foreshadowed in the vulgar outlines of her sister's career. The factors which in Mrs. Wharton's view weigh so heavily in Sophy's disfavor—her shabby antecedents, her pathetic liaison with Darrow, her little social blunders, the fact that she powders her face—are apt to count negligibly in directing the sympathies of a more tolerant latter-day audience.

The question might intrude itself less clamorously if the novel did not encourage the comparison with James. For in addition to the similarities of technique, the situation is one which the master would have found attractive, and Anna Leath is a Jamesian heroine in a Jamesian predicament. But James's treatment of moral problems is freer than Edith Wharton's, because he deals more consistently with what, for lack of a better term, might be called moral universals. Moreover, his tone is seldom ambiguous. Even when the irony is turned back upon the fictional narrator, it reaches us unmistakably. The confusion of tone in *The Reef* may be partly ascribed to the limitations in the point of view. The entire situation is revealed alternately through the consciousness of George Darrow and Anna Leath, who share the same background and prejudices and are liable to the same failures of perception. In the absence of the usual fictional referee, the reader comes to depend on the more admirable of the two principals, Anna Leath, for his final appraisal of Darrow. But her judgment is not to be trusted casually. Her acceptance of Darrow is strongly conditioned by her eagerness for a larger kind of experience than she has known and by an impatience with the restraints, timidities, and evasions that until now have distinguished her conduct. In her quest for emotional freedom, she has abandoned her former guides and stands uncertainly on the threshold of an unfamiliar moral realm.

Mrs. Wharton's task might have been easier if she had been able to multiply her centers of consciousness to include Sophy Viner, Owen Leath, and perhaps Adelaide Painter. From one standpoint, Sophy is the best qualified of the three, for she alone is fully aware of the situation. But there are two good reasons why she could not be employed for this purpose. In the first place, the unity of effect would have been imperiled by a third center of consciousness. It must find its source either in the private drama enacted between Darrow and Anna, to which Sophy is the accessory, or—much less conceivably—in that enacted between Sophy and Owen Leath, to which Darrow is the accessory. Given one or the other, all the relationships must be made to converge on that single center of interest; and since Mrs. Wharton chose the first, it would have been fatal to have concentrated disproportionately on Sophy Viner's dilemma. In the second place, Sophy fails to suggest that she is the "fine central intelligence" demanded by the complexity of the situation. This is evident early in the novel as Darrow contemplates her "ingenuous absorption" in the performance at the Theatre Français: "It was on 'the story' that her mind was fixed, and in life also, he suspected, it would always be 'the story,' rather than its remoter imaginative issues, that would hold her. He did not believe there were ever any echoes in her soul . . ." Edith Wharton's fiction, concerned like that of Henry James with the "remoter imaginative issues," requires the aid supplied by a fine sensibility interposed between the felt experience of the novel and the reader. In *Ethan Frome* and in many of the short stories the demand is met by a narrator whom we accept as qualified but who is never so individualized that he makes us question the reliability of his judgments or impressions. Alone among Edith Wharton's novels, *The Reef* represents the experience of its characters directly throughout, imposing a condition that makes Sophy Viner unacceptable as a center of consciousness.

I started by speaking of the confusion of tone which the point of view helps to introduce. I should add that the question has nothing to do with the resolution of the novel's situation. The dubious morality of *The Reef* is unrelated to the fact that the dice are loaded against Sophy and in favor of Darrow and that Darrow comes off better than he deserves—or, rather, it is unrelated so long as we are convinced that, given these characters and the particular circumstances in which they are brought together, this is what must inevitably happen. It derives from the suspicion that Edith Wharton unconsciously condones this sort of justice, and the grounds for suspicion are by no means confined to *The Reef*. She once referred to moral sensibility as "that *tuning-fork* of the novelist's art" and criticized Proust for his lack of it. "When he is unaware of the meanness of an act committed by one of his characters, that character loses by so much of its life-likeness, and, reversing Pygmalion's gesture, the author turns living beings back into stone." [4] In the light of her own professed convictions, the problem of determining the quality of Edith Wharton's moral sensibility, especially as it manifests itself in the tone of *The Reef*, assumes a real importance.

In dealing with characters whose social orbits lie outside her own, she is able to preserve her detachment only so long as their actions in no way threaten the values, standards, manners that she cherishes. From the moment they present themselves to her imagination in a subversive guise, they can expect no sympathy. She can make the effort to understand an Ethan Frome, an Abner Spragg, or an Ann Eliza Bunner because—and it comes down to this—they are content with the role to which their birth, training, and sensibility assign them.

But when she is confronted by a Sophy Viner or an Undine Spragg, her reaction is instinctively hostile, she loses her detachment, and the characterization that results is at the best reluctantly sympathetic, at the worst a caricature. In the early episodes of *The Reef* Sophy Viner, helpless and adrift, and starved for the kind of emotional experience that Paris and intimacy with a man like Darrow can give her, is an appealing and totally sympathetic figure. Her role as the casual partner in a sentimental interlude in Darrow's career is one for which, we must assume, her background and experience qualify her, and so long as she adheres to it she runs no risk of alienating the sympathy that her situation naturally calls forth. But when she appears at Givré as Owen Leath's fiancée, it is under different circumstances, and we are compelled to view her in a different light, as a pretender. Because of her guilty secret, she is not only frightened, but a little hard, a little obstinate; and there is a corresponding hardness in Mrs. Wharton's attitude toward her (so far as this can be disengaged from the point of view) that is not easy to comply with. The novelist's experience has provided her with little real compassion for the "wronged" women in her fiction—the Sophy Viners, Charity Royalls, and Evelina Bunners—so it is not surprising that their destinies are charted with a certain ruthlessness. Sophy Viner's status is fixed as unalterably as that of Aunt Agatha, the "ruined" southern gentlewoman of Ellen Glasgow's *They Stooped to Folly:* however much we may understand and sympathize with the circumstances of her fall, she is irrevocably beyond the pale. "You had no right to let Owen love you," Anna Leath tells her, disposing of the question once and for all.

I have mentioned the concluding chapter, which contains the last word on Sophy in Anna Leath's glimpse of her blowsy elder sister Laura installed in a cheap hotel room and receiving her guests in bed, surrounded by her lover, her masseur, and her poodle:

In the roseate penumbra of the bed-curtains she presented to Anna's startled gaze an odd chromo-like resemblance to Sophy Viner, or a suggestion, rather, of what Sophy Viner might, with the years and in spite of the powder-puff, become. . . . As she stretched her bare plump arm across the bed she seemed to be pulling back the veil from dingy distances of family history.

The adjective "dingy" gives the show away, for by now it has acquired a peculiar significance in Edith Wharton's vocabulary: it connotes everything in Sophy Viner's world from which she, like Lily Bart and Justine Brent, instinctively shrinks—the ugliness, the vulgarity, the absence of protective manners, the constant economic struggle. By the time Anna Leath's visit occurs, Sophy has set off for India with Mrs. Murrett, a notorious London hostess from whose service she had originally fled. Blood will tell. Water will seek its own level. Nothing has quite prepared us for the shock of this final revelation and the judgment it implies. With its depressingly narrow sense of human values, it is one of the most regrettable passages in Edith Wharton's fiction.

At the same time, it has the function of seeming to justify Darrow in his denial of any genuine responsibility for Sophy's plight. When I spoke of *The Reef* as a crucial novel, it was with the thought that in the handling of the problem she has set herself Edith Wharton may for the first time be accused of begging the question.

The "remoter imaginative issues" of *The Reef* are those
we have isolated in *Ethan Frome* and *The Fruit of the
Tree,* and, as before, they come to rest ultimately on the
single issue of the limits of individual responsibility. But
they are not handled with the same conviction, the same
equity, and although they will continue to solicit Edith
Wharton's imagination long after *The Reef,* they will receive the same uncertain and somewhat slanted treatment in such novels as *The Mother's Recompense, Hudson River Bracketed,* and *The Gods Arrive.* With such
rare exceptions as *The Age of Innocence,* her tuning fork
will be applied less reliably.

What *is* Darrow's position in relation to these familiar
issues? When we first encounter him, he is nursing his
resentment at Anna Leath's seemingly capricious action
in deferring the meeting on which he has pinned his
hopes of making her marry him. By the time her mes-
sage reaches him, he has already embarked for France
and their rendezvous at Givré. On the channel boat he
meets Sophy Viner, fleeing from her compromising position in the London household of Mrs. Murrett as once
before she had fled the unwelcome attentions of the
valet of another employer, motivated on both occasions
by "the urgent need of gaining, at any cost, a name for
stability." Darrow is attracted by her inexperience, her
helplessness, and her invincibly cheerful outlook. While
she is trying to get in touch with her friends, they do
Paris together. Darrow's attitude is at first paternal; he
finds a novel kind of pleasure in contributing to the girl's
first experience of Paris. But he is still annoyed with
Anna Leath, and before long he is seeking balm for his
wounded vanity in Sophy's grateful dependence on him.
When she proposes to join her friends, he pleads with

her to remain in Paris. He has nothing to lose by following up this clandestine affair (". . . the women he had frequented had either been pronouncedly 'ladies' or they had not"), whereas Sophy, whose reputation for respectability is precariously maintained, risks her whole future. They become intimate before Darrow, in a sudden revulsion of feeling, returns to London.

Several months later, after he has been summoned belatedly to Givré and has reached an understanding with Mrs. Leath, he learns that her son Owen has become engaged to a girl of inferior social standing and that his mother is unwilling to marry until she has ensured Owen's happiness by clearing the difficult way through family objections. The success of Darrow's venture, it is clear, depends on the success of Owen's. It is Anna Leath who early introduces the theme of responsibility. "You see," she tells Darrow, "I couldn't bear it if the least fraction of my happiness seemed to be stolen from his." With the discovery that Sophy is present at Givré as governess to the youngest Leath child and, later, that she is Owen's fiancée, the whole question of Darrow's conflicting responsibilities toward Sophy and Anna is brought sharply to a head. Thanks to his diplomatic training, Darrow is able to confront his dilemma with extraordinary self-possession. He waits for Sophy to make the first move. When she seeks him out, he finds her thin and pale, and tragically subdued. On *her* at least the Paris adventure has left its mark. At the outset, she puts the responsibility for her fate squarely on his shoulders: "I suppose it depends on you whether I go or stay." Darrow is shocked by the challenge. "Good God," he replies, "what can you think of me, to say that?"

Temporarily, he is unable to act. In a subsequent interview with Sophy he learns that she has broken her engagement—not because of any tardy scruples, but because she loves *him* and cannot face the prospect of living with Owen at Givré. For a moment it seems as if Mrs. Wharton is seeking a way out by relieving Darrow of his responsibility in at least one direction. Earlier, during the Paris episode, she has covered for him by having Sophy announce her intention not to marry: "You see, I'm all for self-development and the chance to live one's life. I'm awfully modern, you know." In the meantime, however, Sophy has been changed by her experience to a degree not immediately apparent to Darrow. In recognition of her suffering, and its possible value, Edith Wharton gives her—inexplicably, I think—a moment which throws the characterization out of focus and provides an irrevocable commentary on the shifts and evasions of the other characters. "I'd always wanted adventures," she tells Darrow, "and you'd given me one, and I tried to take your attitude about it, to 'play the game' and convince myself that I hadn't risked any more on it than you. Then, when I met you again, I suddenly saw that I *had* risked more, but that I'd won more, too —such worlds!" This is the one glimpse we are allowed into the passionate depths of Sophy's being, but it is sufficient to discredit Darrow's motives and his whole course of conduct. Although ostensibly they are quits, the interview forces him disagreeably to confront his conscience. "Was it he, then, who, in the sequel, had grown impatient of the bounds he had set himself? Was it his wounded vanity that, seeking balm for his hurt, yearned to dip deeper into the healing pool of her compassion? In his confused memory of the situation

he seemed not to have been guiltless of such yearn-
ings. . . ."

Yet when the crash comes—when Darrow can no
longer maintain his deception—he manages to shift the
blame on Sophy ("She didn't wish it known that I'd met
her"). He has rationalized his way out of his dilemma,
but with Anna's discovery of the liaison, the situation has
passed beyond his control. The problem of finding a
solution is inevitably transferred to Anna, and her decision must present itself as throwing some light on the
moral complications. By now the emphasis is misplaced
so long as it is on Darrow's static, helpless view of the
situation, and already it has lingered there too long.

Anna is at first angry, hurt, and uncharitable. With
sudden magnanimity, Darrow pleads Sophy's case—and
Sophy counters by pleading Darrow's. But Anna's cloistered experience prevents her from being an altogether
satisfactory tribunal: "There were certain dishonours
with which she had never dreamed any pact could be
made: she had an incorruptible passion for good faith
and fairness." Sophy, without a word to Owen, leaves
for Paris, but he follows her. When Darrow departs,
Anna, in a blind fear of losing him but without any plan
of action, takes the next train to Paris. There, at Adelaide
Painter's flat, she again listens to Sophy extenuate Darrow's part in the affair ("I wanted to be happy just once—
and I didn't dream of the harm I might be doing him"),
and later, in her own apartment, she gives Darrow another hearing. He dismisses her unimaginative suggestion that he make Sophy an honest woman: "We've often
talked of such things: of the monstrousness of useless
sacrifices. If I'm to expiate, it's not in that way." The

144

argument proves to be his trump card. If it does not halt Anna's vacillations immediately, it finally recurs to her with enough force to bring about her capitulation in time to prevent Darrow's departure for England. Sophy, in the meantime, has acted on her promise never to see Owen again, and Owen has sought the conventional solace in travel. They are the only victims of the event. In a curious way, Anna Leath's devotion to an abstract concept of duty, her determination to gain no smallest fraction of happiness at someone else's expense, has given way to a profounder realization (reminiscent of Justine Brent's) of the necessity of compromise.

There is no conceivable ending for *The Reef* that will satisfy both the logic of the situation and any absolute notion of justice. To have Anna Leath abandon Darrow, in the high-minded tradition of many serious novels of the day, would have violated the propensities of the character as well as the principle of growth that governs her function as the protagonist. She must be able to accept him finally for reasons that earlier would have been incomprehensible to her. There is of course no accounting for the submission of a nature such as hers to the meaner nature of a Darrow unless we regard it as the tribute that inexperience usually pays to what passes for sophistication. But, as in Edith Wharton's other novels, once we have accepted the phenomenon, we are prepared for a view of its consequences in which the by now familiar themes will be again rehearsed. From this standpoint, *The Reef* is less conclusive than *Ethan Frome*. Ethan sacrifices his and Mattie's chance of happiness to the performance of his duty to Zeena and the community, and, in doing so, brings on the long denoue-

ment of wasted years. With Anna Leath the ideal of duty
gradually succumbs to her passion for Darrow, and we
are spared the futile sequel that self-sacrifice would entail. But the irony of Anna's situation at the close is that
she looks for guidance to Sophy Viner, whose moral
sensibility she has been accustomed to regard as inferior
to her own: "It was Sophy Viner only who could save her
—Sophy Viner only who could give her back her lost
serenity. She would seek the girl out and tell her that
she had given Darrow up; and that step once taken there
would be no retracing it, and she would perforce have
to go forward alone." But Sophy has already carried out
her part of the bargain: she has fled Paris without leaving
Owen her address. "She's kept faith with herself," Anna
realizes, "and I haven't." The price she has to pay for
Darrow is a shrinkage of her moral nature to a point
where it can accommodate itself to his. And this view
of her decision does not reckon the cost to Owen and
Sophy or take into account the fact that Sophy has paid
solely with the currency of her own happiness. The significance of the transaction, so far as it can be determined, seems to reside there.

So much for the "remoter imaginative issues" of *The
Reef*. They can be extended almost indefinitely, so rich
in suggestions are the central problem and the paradoxes
of Anna Leath's character ("I'm not sure," Henry James
wrote the author, "that her oscillations are not beyond
our notation").[5] Perhaps no satisfactory interpretation of
the novel is possible. Edith Wharton once recorded a
dictum of Flaubert's, that "there is nothing real but the
relation of things, that is to say, the connection in which
we perceive them," and added: "In this phrase, which
confesses the predominance of the personal equation, he

has supplied the touchstone of good fiction." [6] The personal equation is certainly present in *The Reef*, but it is so hopelessly embedded in the point of view that we cannot confidently extract it.

Chapter VIII

THE WIDENING GYRE

With her next novel, *The Custom of the Country* (1913), Edith Wharton belatedly joined the discussion of the "new woman" which had been carried on for years by certain of her fellow novelists. Although Robert Grant's thoroughly second-rate novel *Unleavened Bread* (1900), by the accident of having become a best seller, undoubtedly expanded the vogue, the type was already established in the early 'nineties. Later, the enormous popularity of the romantic costume novel, by reinforcing the tradition of the insipid heroine, made it difficult to conduct an open forum on the woman question. The determination of such novelists as Grant, Robert Herrick, David Graham Phillips, and Theodore Dreiser to portray the American woman realistically collided headlong with the equal determination of the vast audience of women who underwrote the fiction of the day to see themselves idealized in print.

By the time Edith Wharton entered the lists the realists had won, and the public was conditioned to meet the most egocentric and dehumanized female in American fiction. Undine Spragg is the perfect flowering of the new materialism. Rootless, vain, and crudely opportunistic, she has all the worst traits of her fictional predecessors. Like Selma Babcock in *Unleavened Bread* and most of Herrick's women, she lacks the instinct of motherhood and rebels at her confinement during pregnancy, complaining that it spoils her freedom. Adela Anthon in Herrick's *The Gospel of Freedom* speaks for the sisterhood: "We are all striving for some kind of freedom, for some escape. . . ." The partial emancipation of women has aggravated Undine's restlessness and widened the scope for her blind ambition. A female Cowperwood but without his redeeming sense of beauty, she has the practical advantage of being completely amoral, unsentimental, and without conscience. With society constituted as it is, she holds all the cards.

For the most part she is cut to the familiar pattern, but not entirely. In their frantic search for self-expression, and incidentally to get the money to refurbish their wardrobes, the heroines of Grant, Herrick, and Phillips frequently devote themselves to pushing their husbands' careers. Undine is incapable of even this degree of altruism. Again, in the majority of "new woman" novels the heroine is strenuously aesthetic, strenuously philanthropic, or both; she seeks an outlet for her individuality in reading papers on Ruskin before women's clubs or in organizing recreation centers for office girls. Neither of these impulses diverts Undine. Finally, the "new woman" is very likely to be neurotic, and as such an easy prey for quacks and faith healers. Undine's nerves are perfect (it was not until the 'twenties, in such novels as *Twilight Sleep* and *The Children*, that jangled nerves began to take their toll of Mrs. Wharton's women). Psychologically, she is the most uncomplicated heroine in Edith Wharton's gallery. Like Dreiser's Carrie Meeber, she can be moved only by her vision of a higher degree of creature comfort than she presently enjoys; her career is an uninterrupted pursuit of material rewards. To underline the destructive simplicity of her motivation, Mrs. Wharton introduces a psychological trait that we have noted previously in Lily Bart and Bessy Westmore. Undine is utterly lacking in self-knowledge; the "chameleon-like" nature of the earlier heroines is repeated in her. Her idea of herself is subject to constant revision based on the opinions of the people surrounding her: "Undine was fiercely independent and yet passionately imitative. She wanted to surprise everyone by her dash and originality, but she could not help modelling herself on the last person she met. . . ." The defection of Peter Van Degen shakes her confidence momentarily, but her social position is reëstablished with the appearance of Raymond de Chelles, and before long "the sense of reviving popularity, and the charm of Chelles' devotion, had almost effaced the ugly memories of failure, and refurbished that image of herself in other minds which was her only notion of self-seeing." No other trait is so consistently used to characterize the shallower women in Edith Wharton's fiction. Lita Wyant, in *Twilight Sleep*, is a later edition of Undine: ". . . All she wanted was to keep on finding herself, immeasurably magnified, in every pair of eyes she met!"

Spiritually, Undine's nature is a wasteland. Mrs. Wharton is satisfied as always that a girlhood in Apex, followed by several years of hotel life with its attendant publicity and bad taste, can hardly be expected to produce a fine spiritual maturity. A thousand years of Western culture have left no faintest imprint on Undine, and because she aspires to a world where manners, taste, and ideas are important, she will be flayed alive for her pretensions. She sums up in herself the ideals of that maverick society of international adventurers and fortune hunters which Ralph Marvell warns her against at St. Moritz—that "sham" society which finds its perfect setting in the imitation grandeur of the Hotel Nouveau Luxe in Paris:

The dining-room of the Nouveau Luxe represented, on such a spring evening, what unbounded material power had devised for the delusion of its leisure: a phantom "society" with all the rules, smirks, gestures of its model, but evoked out of promiscuity and incoherence while the other had been the product of continuity and choice.

It is here that Charles Bowen encounters Undine after she has deserted Ralph Marvell and is setting her traps for Peter Van Degen. Chelles has defined the Nouveau Luxe for him as "a kind of superior Bohemia, where one may be respectable without being bored," and Bowen agrees: "You've put it in a nutshell: the ideal of the American woman is to be respectable without being bored." The remark comes as near as any to providing a kind of thesis for the social commentary of the novel, for it is echoed a second time in an auctorial aside about Undine: "She wanted, passionately and persistently, two things which she believed should subsist together in any well-ordered life: amusement and respectability. . . ."

But Undine's notion of amusement and Edith Wharton's notion of respectability can never be joined, and so Undine blunders ahead, taking one false turn after another, before she realizes that it is her destiny to "find out just too late about the 'something [better] beyond.'" She marries Ralph Marvell to acquire respectability and discovers after three years that she has "given herself to the exclusive and dowdy when the future belonged to the showy and promiscuous." Following her disastrous affair with Van Degen, she retrieves the situation by a second marriage, only to find herself again hemmed in and bored by the feudal discipline of the Chelles family. Finally, after reaching her natural level in the marriage to Elmer Moffat, she learns that a divorced woman can never be an ambassador's wife. She is bound to fall short of her goals because her ideals are incompatible. The ironic spectacle of her blundering must have been a consolation to her creator, who up to a certain point could not legitimately prevent her triumph.

Undine may to a certain extent be understood, and perhaps even sympathized with, as a symbolic victim of the forces which at the turn of the century were shaping the new America. She can hardly be other than what she is, the spirit of materialism incarnate. Edith Wharton knows this. Nevertheless, she finds it impossible, because of her insistence on individual responsibility, to make society ultimately to blame for Undine. More than that, she so clearly despises her protagonist—less for what she is than for what she represents—that she abuses the opportunity to subordinate personalities to the general indictment of a social group and a social ideal, an opportunity that in *The House of Mirth* she had exploited so dispassionately. As the story unfolds, Undine Spragg becomes more visibly an inhuman abstraction. Once again, as in the career of Sophy Viner, one can watch the novelist's prejudices defeat her judgment and trace the slow withdrawal of a sympathy which, even at first, seemed tentative and forced. So clearly is Mrs. Wharton at the mercy of her private feelings that Undine's father and Elmer Moffatt, simply because they are victims of Undine, are treated with proportionately more sympathy than as citizens of Apex they would otherwise have obtained. Their case is instructive. Vulgarity triumphant, represented by Undine, calls forth all the defensive hostility of which Mrs. Wharton is capable; but vulgarity oppressed, in the persons of Abner Spragg and his wife or of Laura Lou Weston in *Hudson River Bracketed,* may even be defended.

That, at least, is the casual impression likely to be entertained by the reader who assumes that Mrs. Wharton is merely a snob. Actually, the discrimination is made upon a deeper, much more valid level. Although vulgarity of manners, like ugliness in the physical scene, is painful to her, pretentiousness—the result, as in Undine, of a failure of self-appraisal—is even more so. It is the absence of pretension in Mrs. Spragg that attracts Ralph Marvell.

The Spraggs had been "plain people" and had not yet learned to be ashamed of it. The fact drew them much closer to the Dagonet ideals than any sham elegance in the past tense. Ralph felt that his mother, who shuddered away from Mrs. Harmon B. Driscoll, would understand and esteem Mrs. Spragg.

Ralph unfortunately generalizes from the character of the parents to that of Undine. It is to safeguard her fictitious innocence that he undertakes the role of Perseus and rescues her, as he imagines, from "the devouring monster Society."

As *The Reef* is the most Jamesian of Edith Wharton's novels, *The Custom of the Country* is the most Balzacian. If the general influence of the French novelist were not everywhere apparent in the early novels, it would still be possible to cite her specific obligations. It is clear, for example, that the method of telling Ethan Frome's story was suggested by "La Grande Bretèche," which Edith Wharton mentioned in the well-known preface to her tale and referred to in *The Writing of Fiction* as "that most perfectly-composed of all short stories." The parallels are more than accidental. Both stories employ the same narrative framework: A stranger (in Balzac's story, a doctor; in Edith Wharton's, an engineer) visits a provincial village and is intrigued by a local ruin (in Balzac, a dilapidated mansion; in Edith Wharton, the gaunt and twisted figure of Ethan Frome). In both stories the situation is gradually revealed as a result of the narrator's inquiries: "Balzac showed what depth, mystery, and verisimilitude may be given to a tale by causing it to be reflected, in fractions, in the minds of a series of accidental participants or mere lookers-on." [1] Edith Wharton's tribute to "La Grande Bretèche" followed *Ethan Frome* by more than a decade, but she had read the story before 1901, for the first tale in *Crucial Instances,* "The Duchess at Prayer," is unmistakably a reworking of Balzac's plot. In her critical writings Balzac is mentioned more frequently than any other novelist. Along with that of James, I believe, his influence is paramount. Between these two poles Edith Wharton found her own equilibrium.

We can assume, I think, that the experience of reading Balzac had a peculiar relevance for her. Although their backgrounds were vastly different, their angle of vision was the same. Edith Wharton was a born aristo-

---

[1] For notes to chap. viii, see p. 257.

crat, while Balzac, as the son of a petty bourgeois family, was an aristocrat in his tastes and aspirations only. A Catholic by birth and a monarchist by choice, he viewed the social world no less conservatively than she did. To Balzac, as to Odo Valsecca in *The Valley of Decision,* the aftermath of the French Revolution was calamitous, since it weakened the influence of those guardians of social stability, the nobility and the clergy, and enlarged that of the *bourgeoisie,* who, like Père Grandet, bought up the property of the clergy and the *émigrés* and, on the strength of their newly acquired wealth, began to seek public office. For Edith Wharton, the comparable event was the Civil War, which cut deeply into the incomes of families like her own while laying the foundations of the Invaders' fortunes. Both writers were born in a period of far-reaching social change in which the boundaries of class began to waver and disappear and the manners and even the ideals of the aristocracy began to be indistinguishable from those of the wealthy bourgeoisie. Balzac emerged as a serious novelist following the July Revolution, which placed control of the government permanently in the hands of the bourgeoisie; Edith Wharton was born in time to witness the slight resistance that her little tribe, weakened by civilized influences and living on its past distinction, offered to the Invaders. As she saw it, one of the weaknesses of the men in her society was "an instinctive shrinking from responsibility," which encouraged them to label politics a dirty game, unfit for gentlemen, and having so rationalized, to withhold their services at a time when, Edith Wharton would have us believe, they were urgently needed to modify the tendencies of the Gilded Age. Ralph Marvell pays rather too high a price for his immunity from the struggle, for the freedom to discriminate finely and to enjoy in a leisurely way what his forebears have accumulated:

The only essential was that he should live "like a gentle-man"—that is, with a tranquil disdain for mere money-getting, a passive openness to the finer sensations, one or two fixed principles as to the quality of wine, and an archaic probity that had not yet learned to distinguish between private and "business" honour.

Similarly in Balzac's France, the tradition of the gentle-man, which left only the army and the diplomatic corps, among the public services, open to the nobility, and which frowned on the better-paying opportunities in business and the professions, made it impossible for the sons of the *ancien régime* to compete materially with the bourgeoisie.

As with their real worlds, so with their fictional. Toward the manifestations of selfishness and greed which accompanied the worship of the five-franc piece and the dollar, they reacted almost identically. The particular truth they chose to represent was the same. In Edith Wharton's world, as in Balzac's, the only crime is disin-terestedness. Loyalty, unselfishness, and simplicity of heart are ruthlessly penalized. The most familiar situa-tion in Balzac is one we have noted in Edith Wharton: the sacrifice of the larger nature to the smaller, of a Père Goriot to his daughters, of Eugénie Grandet and her mother to the miser father, of Cousin Pons and his friend Schmücke to the former's self-appointed heirs, of Baron Hulot to Valérie Marneffe. The ironic fable that Edith Wharton related in *False Dawn* is meant to have the same meaning as *Le Cousin Pons*. After forty years of neglect, the unsurpassed Raycie collection of Italian primitives passes into the hands of a distant relative. An accident reveals its value, and with the proceeds of the sale that follows Netta Cosby and her husband purchase mansions, sables, and Rolls-Royces. So it is with Pons's bric-a-brac collection. The disinterested passion of the collector, the unerring sense of beauty which brought the collection into being, and the hope of preserving it intact are callously sacrificed to the new materialism.

There is an interesting continuity of tradition from the early picaresque novels through the novel of manners as represented by, say, *Père Goriot, Vanity Fair,* and *The Custom of the Country.* The antihero of picaresque fiction was created expressly for the purposes of social satire. A reckless, amoral individual, usually of low birth and reared in a tradition of dishonesty, he moved widely and at will through the social landscape of his time, his eye constantly on the main chance, his hand invariably in the other fellow's pocket. To Eugene Rastignac, Becky Sharp, and Undine Spragg no less than to Gil Blas, society presents itself as a hunting ground where the strong, the amoral, and the calculating, but never the innocent, bring down whatever game is to be had. Traditionally, the *picaro* is most at home in the underworld; his manners are those of the underworld; but in a generally corrupt social world he cannot easily be placed. In a society which zealously preserves the line of demarcation between classes, his opportunities are theoretically —although, for satirical purposes, not actually—somewhat more restricted than in a society whose internal boundaries are becoming fluid and in which an alteration is taking place in the relations of classes. Balzac, Thackeray, and Edith Wharton were alike profoundly aware that the main characteristic of the social structure of their day was its instability, that its hierarchy was being rearranged on a simple pecuniary basis, and that the field was open to the social adventurer. In a stable society, the progress of the *picaro* as he rose or sank in the world could be easily and accurately plotted by relating it to the gradation of manners from class to class. For Edith Wharton, living in an era when manners as she knew them were being "Taylorized" out of existence, the problem presented itself as more difficult. Nevertheless, by thrusting Undine into a world where the old order maintained itself almost inviolate—that of the Dagonets on this side of the Atlantic and of the Chelles in France— she was able, through the conflict of manners, to dramatize her subject successfully.

It seems clear that there is a direct line of descent from the picaresque narrative to the novel of manners, for the characteristic interest of the former, the upward or downward progress of the rogue through the social hierachy, cannot be effectively developed without the constant and precise notation of manners. The picaresque tradition is deeply rooted in American fiction, although not where Edith Wharton would have been apt to find it. From *Modern Chivalry* through *Huckleberry Finn,* wherever it is found it seems to be related directly to the phenomenon of social change and instability. The drifting population and weak law enforcement on the frontier enabled the American *picaro* Simon Suggs to justify his motto, "It's good to be shifty in a new country," and when the frontier vanished and then reappeared, late in the nineteenth century, on the horizon of big business, the *picaro* merely changed the scene of his activity. Less than a decade before *The Custom of the Country*, Robert Herrick set about writing "a new kind of picaresque or rogue story to be told in the first person like the well known rogue stories of Smollett,—only mine was to be of modern life in Chicago, and my hero was to be a successful American 'big business' man who ends his career in the United States Senate. . . ." [2] Herrick's novel, *The Memoirs of an American Citizen* (1905), like most of the serious fiction of the period, helped to show that when the result of social change is disillusionment, literature will dedicate itself to a realistic, critical, frequently satirical appraisal of society. In Spain during the latter half of the sixteenth century this reaction produced the picaresque tale, launched somewhat prematurely by *Lazarillo de Tormes* and established in the period following the Armada's defeat by *Guzmán de Alfarache*. As *The Writing of Fiction* (not to speak of her miscellaneous essays) shows, Edith Wharton was well read in the history of the novel, in the novel literature of the continent, and was self-consciously traditional in her technical approach. To what degree her familiarity with the picaresque tradition may have shaped *The Custom of the Country*, it would be difficult to say; but although she lacked the detachment of the picaresque author, her Undine Spragg is a twentieth-century *picara*, with the mental and moral traits of her prototypes, and her career follows the classic pattern. As far as American fiction is concerned, the originality of *The Custom of the Country* lies, strangely enough, in its traditional fusion of the picaresque with the novel of manners for the purpose of enhancing the social comedy.

The writing of *The Custom of the Country* extended over four years, foreshadowing the decline in Mrs. Wharton's productivity that was to last through the war. The novel may have been projected as early as 1907; at any rate, she was well into it by May of the following year.[3] From then until its publication in October, 1913, she evidently passed through one of the most trying episodes of her life. The act of expatriation was followed by a period of deepening anxiety over the state of her husband's health. Her letters to her editors during this prolonged crisis, supplemented by Henry James's gloomily sympathetic letters to her, barely disguise what must have been a tragic personal dilemma and one which could have been solved, as it was, only by separation and eventual divorce. Less than a year after the publication of *The Custom of the Country*, the war broke suddenly, and Edith Wharton, following a brief and impatient exile in England, returned to Paris to devote all her energies to the relief of the French and Belgian refugees who poured into the capital. Until the day of the Armistice she drove herself tirelessly, organizing her *Accueil Franco-Belge*, soliciting funds, and defending the Allied cause, interpreting the French character, and recording her impressions of the war—many of them obtained at first hand during carefully chaperoned visits to the front—in a series of books and articles aimed at her compatriots, whose lack of moral fervor troubled her as it did her friend James. Under such conditions she could spare little time for reading or writing. "Even had I had the leisure to take up my story-telling," she recalled in *A Backward Glance*, "I should have had no heart for it; yet I was tormented with a fever of creation." The majority of the tales in *Xingu and Other Stories*, published in

October, 1916, were written before the outbreak of the war. The most interesting of the exceptions, a fairly long tale called "Coming Home," adds nothing to her laurels; on the contrary, it proves that a novelist whose detachment was always precariously maintained could, when confronted by the reports of German atrocities, lose her head as easily as the average newspaper reader.

"Coming Home" is the melodramatic story of a young French officer, Jean de Réchamp, who returns to his native village in the Vosges to learn that it has been saved from the depredations of the Boches by the resourcefulness of his fiancée. The surrounding countryside has been systematically laid waste by German troops under the command of the notorious Oberst von Scharlach (played by Erich von Stroheim), who is described by one refugee as a refined sadist and the author of unspeakable crimes against humanity: "His orderly showed me a silver-mounted flute he always travelled with, and a beautiful paintbox mounted in silver too. Before he left he sat down on my doorstep and made a painting of the ruins." Mlle Malo, the fiancée, is the ward of a wealthy old widower in Réchamp, a thoroughly modern and emancipated young woman who before the war had maintained a studio in Paris. Since this is not the kind of background that Mrs. Wharton ordinarily endorses, it is not surprising to learn that Mlle Malo has saved the village by becoming von Scharlach's mistress. When this revelation dawns on the narrator (an American Red Cross worker named H. Macy Greer, who has accompanied Réchamp home), the girl appears to him less attractive. The moral taint has manifested itself in her features overnight: "She looked older for one thing; her face was pinched, and a little sallow, and for the first time I noticed that her cheek-bones were too high." By now it is obvious to Réchamp that he has been betrayed, and Mrs. Wharton, who is never one to let her fallen women off easily, even insinuates that the village gossip which credits Mlle Malo with being the mistress as well as the ward of her aged benefactor may be true. The lovers part without a reconciliation. On the trip back to their base, the narrator and Réchamp pick up a German officer with a serious abdominal wound. Although the fact is never made explicit, we know that by one of the coincidences appropriate to melodrama it is von Scharlach. When the car runs out of gas, the narrator instructs his friend how to use a hypodermic to keep the wounded man alive and then proceeds on foot to the nearest village. When he returns, the prisoner, who it is clear had an excellent chance for survival, is dead. Following the casual post-mortem at the base hospital, Jean de Réchamp is free to join his by now badly shaken American friend for coffee.

Alongside her essays in *Fighting France* and *French Ways and Their Meaning,* "Coming Home" appears to a disadvantage both as literature and as propaganda. Although Mrs. Wharton's indignation had subsided somewhat by the time she wrote her long tale *The Marne* (1918), little was gained by the exchange of one kind of sentimentality for another. The story contains some authentic and touching glimpses of the French countryside and the French people at war which reaffirm Edith Wharton's deep affection for her adopted country, but the chief impression it creates is that the author had a number of grievances against her compatriots to work off and that they would not wait. She has observed and classified a wide variety of slackers, but she has equal

scorn for those who saw the war as a holiday, a business
venture, or an opportunity to transmit the blessings of
American culture abroad and to reform French manners.
In contrast to those Americans who are slow to recognize that the defense of France and the preservation of
Western civilization make common cause, we are introduced to Troy Belknap, a young American who has
spent much of his boyhood in France traveling with his
parents and learning to love the country and its people.
When war is declared, he is fifteen. "France, his France,
attacked, invaded, outraged; and he, a poor helpless
American boy, who adored her, and could do nothing
for her—not even cry, as a girl might! It was bitter."
Back in America, Troy's outspoken devotion to the
Allied cause ("*To save France*—that was the clear duty
of the world, as he saw it") puts him at odds with his
family and friends. On his eighteenth birthday, he asks
to be allowed to return to France to join the American
ambulance service. Several months later his country
enters the war. During the second retreat from the
Marne, he picks up an abandoned rifle, joins a company
of American troops headed for the front, is wounded on
a volunteer mission, and later wakes up in a hospital to
learn that the German advance has been halted.

In the judgment of the most ardent francophile, Edith
Wharton's good intentions would hardly be sufficient to
offset the banality of her fable and the slapdash style in
which it is related. In no other work has she limited
her effects to such broad strokes or so abused the medium of the long tale by compelling it to absorb so many
issues. Because the logic of her theme and treatment
prevented her from adding a single individualizing trait
to the characterization of Troy Belknap, he remains a

name, an ideal, a cause, and nothing more—while his desire for self-immolation on the altar of civilization merely furnishes Mrs. Wharton a pretext for belaboring her compatriots.

One would like to think that she was aware of the excesses of "Coming Home" and *The Marne* when she postponed her third and major attempt to convert her experience of the war years into fiction. "A study of the world at the rear during a long war seemed to me worth doing," she has said, "and I pondered over it till it took shape in 'A Son at the Front.' But before I could settle down to this tale, before I could begin to deal objectively with the stored-up emotions of those years, I had to get away from the present altogether; and though I began planning and brooding over 'A Son at the Front' in 1917 it was not finished until four years later." The novel appeared serially beginning in 1922 and was published in book form in September of the next year, but it was some seven or eight years too late. Not only is it apparent that the old resentments are still alive and the moral fervor of the war years still unabated, but in a curious way the tone of the novel perpetuates the urgent appeal of the recruiting poster. Had H. G. Wells published *Mr. Britling Sees It Through* in 1923 instead of 1916, it would have had the same anachronistic flavor, for one of Wells's less subtle purposes in that novel was to read a quiet sermon to his large American audience. Through his American character, Mr. Direck, who is won over to the Allied cause and joins the Canadian army at a time when his own country prefers to stand aloof as guardian of the future, he made the same point that Edith Wharton seems to be trying to make through the Camptons, father and son, in her novel. But in 1922 the occasion is past, and what one accepts in Wells's novel as propaganda among friends, perhaps justifying in practical terms the additional burden on his plot, is likely to be regarded as tired drumbeating in *A Son at the Front*.

Primarily, the novel examines a case of jealously possessive father love. John Campton's frantic campaign to keep his only son George out of the front lines overrides the moral and humanitarian issues raised by the war. In him we have the ultimate distillation of the self-interests, large and small, which hamper the civilian effort and which in Mrs. Wharton's scheme are variously exhibited in the minor characters who, as in *The Marne*, fail to rise to her large demands. Campton refuses to let himself in for anything that will upset the delicate balance of his existence. His private war with the French authorities on the one hand and with his son's stepfather on the other is deliberately set against the background of world conflict in order to bring out the essential selfishness of his motives and to highlight those acts of cruelty toward other people, and especially Anderson Brant, that in comparison with the larger, inevitable cruelties of the war seem merely gratuitous. It is to Edith Wharton's credit that, following George Campton's death and his father's realization that long before this event the war had in subtle ways estranged them, she does not have John Campton become a booming patriot. He remains to the end unreconstructed, incapable of larger views, and devoid of any real convictions or sympathies. His fiercely protective love for his son is his only motive; when that is removed, his last tie to society is broken.

Although both "Coming Home" and *The Marne* are guilty of presenting the war too narrowly in terms of its impact on the ordinary citizens of France, the perspective is reversed in *A Son at the Front,* where the average Frenchman's stake in the game is only indirectly acknowledged through the glimpses of partings at the depot, of the familiar names on the casualty lists, and of the families in mourning. In fact, the impression inevitably forced upon the reader is that the war is being conducted, and its events arranged in the pattern they present, simply to persuade John Campton that he has a moral duty. In his progress toward final disillusionment, the sons of his French acquaintances are sacrificed at appropriate junctures. The first victim is young Fortin-Lescluse, only son of the physician who has arranged a safe berth at staff headquarters for George Campton. Through his death the elder Campton is made aware of his selfishness, but only transiently. When Madame Lebel, his landlady, loses *her* only son, neither the event itself nor the mother's stolid grief has any meaning apart from its relation to Campton's mean and ineffectual struggle toward the light. The next to go is a young American, Benny Upsher, who like Troy Belknap has viewed the war as his war. But the event that perhaps touches Campton most nearly is the premature death of a promising young French painter whose deathbed he has visited and whose proud and impoverished family he has tried to aid by selling a cherished sketch of George. All novelists run the risk of making their version of causality too obviously subservient to the interests of theme and plot, but it is a risk to which Edith Wharton succumbs with unfortunate regularity in her later novels. *A Son at the Front* is distinguished by a manipulation of coincidence which would strike the reader as less awkward and unfeeling had the events of the story been felt and evaluated by Campton alone rather than with Mrs. Wharton's too evident coöperation.

Edith Wharton's failure to transmute into significant fiction the extraordinary material thrust upon her during the war years may be something more than an object lesson to novelists who would strike while the iron is too hot. It was not simply that she was too close to her subject, or that she felt about it as a partisan human being and not as a novelist; part of her failure must be charged to her oversimplification of the issues. It was a tendency quite natural so long as she stood at the whirling center of events, but unfortunately it carried over into the post-war years she had presumably set aside for reflection before writing her novel. Percy Lubbock, in his portrait, has touched more than once on her refusal to engage in abstract speculation: "The lively leap of her mind stopped dead when she was asked to think, I don't say only about the meaning and the ends of life, but about almost any theoretic enquiry. . . ." And although it was her apparent lack of interest in metaphysical questions that he regretted most, the observation is generally valid. To the situations in her fiction she applied the test of certain inherited values, social, moral, and aesthetic; but when those values proved somehow inadequate to the situation, or when the situation called for a more comprehensive intellectuality which would embrace questions, say, of religion or politics or economics, she was not to be intimidated. With her usual confidence, she cut the material to her pattern.

So it was with the war and its issues. "She was impatient," says Lubbock, "I don't say merely of doubtful or devious hesitation before the challenge of events, but even, as it seemed, of the need to understand, to search

the vast issue and its implications, and to assemble mind
and thought to face it. She knew no such necessity."
The kinds of questions that were to trouble more impar-
tial observers never bothered her. From its beginning,
the war presented itself to her in the simple guise of
a crusade to save Western civilization, symbolized by
France. Germany was the Beast, and so far as her readers could gather, it was France, fighting valiantly with
the aid of a few high-minded foreign volunteers, who
resisted her depredations. Certainly it would be impossible to deduce from *The Marne* that England and
the other Allied powers had any share in the conflict
before 1917. Those who, like the majority of her countrymen, failed to evaluate the issues in these simple terms
and then rush to the barricades immediately, felt the
blunt and undiscriminating impact of her scorn.

When momentarily she turned her attention from the
war and sought relief from its pressures in writing
Summer (1917), the result was salutary. "The tale was
written at a high pitch of creative joy, but amid a thousand interruptions, and while the rest of my being was
steeped in the tragic realities of the war; yet I do not
remember ever visualizing with more intensity the inner
scene, or the people creating it." The novel, which she
regarded as one of her best, is a pendant to *Ethan Frome.*
The setting is roughly the same, with the significant difference of the season and all it means in terms of the
inner drama; the chronicle is one of pinched, defeated
lives; and the central characters are pitted against each
other in a deadly and for the most part inarticulate
struggle of wills that concludes in the usual pathetic
compromise with fate—or, if you will, with the moral

law, since that is Edith Wharton's conception of the real antagonist.

But *Summer* explores an even harsher and, for Edith Wharton, less congenial kind of reality than that of *Ethan Frome* or "Bunner Sisters." The closest precedent is "A Journey," that startling realistic anecdote which took its place uncomfortably among the ironic show-pieces of *The Greater Inclination*. There is nothing in *Ethan Frome* to match the dark, unruly passions of Lawyer Royall and his ward, nor any episodes so frankly sordid as the former's invasion of Charity's bedroom, his drunken insults to her at the Fourth of July celebration, or Charity's last visit to the Mountain when she views the corpse of her mother:

"Mary's over there," someone said; and Mr. Miles, taking the bottle in his hand, passed behind the table. Charity followed him, and they stood before a mattress on the floor in a corner of the room. A woman lay on it, but she did not look like a dead woman; she seemed to have fallen across her squalid bed in a drunken sleep, and to have been left lying where she fell, in her ragged disordered clothes. One arm was flung above her head, one leg drawn up under a torn skirt that left the other bare to the knee: a swollen glistening leg with a ragged stocking rolled down about the ankle. The woman lay on her back, her eyes staring up un-blinkingly at the candle that trembled in Mr. Miles's hand.

It is as if the grim realities of the war in France had momentarily cast their shadow over the countryside of *Ethan Frome*. The dead woman lying on the mattress "like a dead dog in a ditch," her face "thin yet swollen, with lips parted in a frozen gasp above the broken

169

teeth," stresses the physical ugliness of death in a manner appropriate to the combat diary. More clearly than
in *Ethan Frome*, Mrs. Wharton is repelled by her material—perhaps as only a lady and a summer visitor to the
Berkshires could be—and the feeling comes through in
the dogged way she fastens upon its horrors. As before,
the distance from Paris to Lenox lends no enchantment
to the scene, and this time there is no encouragement for
the author to identify herself with her central character.

Charity Royall comes to grief through the same mixture of pride, willfulness, and ignorance that has been
apparent in the characters of Bessy Westmore and
Undine Spragg. Her clash with her guardian makes it
clear that temperamentally they are akin. Both have the
fierce pride of sensitive persons who have known humiliation; both are aloof, consciously superior to their surroundings, and somewhat more vehement than most of
Mrs. Wharton's characters in the nature and exercise of
their feelings; but Lawyer Royall has qualities of mind
and spirit that are thwarted in their expression by his
relationship with his ward. Charity is the most passionate of Edith Wharton's heroines. Channeled into narrow, wayward passages, her emotions run unobstructed,
carrying everything before them. The lawless motions of
the blood which impel her to defy the village code are
her inheritance from the Mountain (shades of *Elsie
Venner*) toward which she must eventually turn for an
explanation of her fate. The Mountain represents Edith
Wharton's one real attempt outside her shorter tales to
come to terms with the racial and subconscious impulses
that seem to have no place in her usual catalogue of
motives. The outlaw community of the Mountain, with

its history of violence, squalor, and intermarriage, remains curiously undefined—a symbol rather than a sociological fact. When Charity learns that she is pregnant,
she sets out on foot for her birthplace. "She supposed it
was something in her blood that made the Mountain the
only answer to her questioning, the inevitable escape
from all that hemmed her in and beset her." Her visit
to her mother's deathbed is made after dark, in the atmosphere of a nightmare. The vaguely menacing figures
of her relatives barely detach themselves from the shad-
ows of the hut's interior, but one is aware of the sounds
of quarreling and drunkenness. The events are real, the
atmosphere unreal; we have been led back by another
extraordinary route into the heart of Conrad's primeval
darkness, whose savage inhabitants are the shapes of
half-forgotten fears and instincts.

Judging by such powerfully realized scenes, Edith
Wharton's remark about the intensity with which she
visualized the "inner scene" of her story would seem to
be valid. Again, as in *Ethan Frome,* her imagination is
able to bring about a fusion of all the elements of her
tale on a symbolic level. The cycle of the human drama
is adjusted to the cycle of the seasons: the promise of
spring and the fulfillment of summer are followed by the
bitter harvest of autumn and the approaching chill of
winter. In no other story is Edith Wharton's attachment
to the rich, unconscious life of nature utilized to such
advantage.

The rare imaginative force with which she was able
to project the inner drama is inseparable from the con-
trolling vision of her characters' destiny. As in *The
House of Mirth* and *Ethan Frome,* the influence of nine-

171

teenth-century determinism is more than simply implied.
One may question, as in *Sanctuary*, the notion of an
hereditary moral attainder, but the symbol of the Mountain manages to suggest another, more credible reason
for Charity's "tainted origin" in her biological inheritance. And the means by which Mrs. Wharton has tried
to stress the influence of environment are not exhausted
by her harmonization, in terms of rhythm and tone, of
the drama of nature with Charity's private drama. One
of the unforgettable episodes in *Summer* is that in which
Charity and Lucius Harney watch the fireworks over the
lake. The gradual crescendo of brilliance in the night
sky has its counterpart in Charity's emotional response
to the scene and, more important, to the challenge of
Harney's presence and the intimacy of their situation.
Her excitement rises with each burst of light and color:
"It was as if all the latent beauty of things had been
unveiled to her." The climax of the display and the
climax of feeling which launches the catastrophe are one.
The extravagant set piece is suddenly illuminated:

A long "Oh-h-h" burst from the spectators: the stand
creaked and shook with their blissful trepidations. "Oh-
h-h," Charity gasped: she had forgotten where she was, had
at last forgotten even Harney's nearness. She seemed to
have been caught up into the stars. . . .
   The picture vanished and darkness came down. In the
obscurity she felt her head clasped by two hands: her face
was drawn backward, and Harney's lips were pressed on
hers. With sudden vehemence he wound his arms about
her, holding her head against his breast while she gave him
back his kisses. An unknown Harney had revealed himself,
a Harney who dominated her and yet over whom she felt
herself possessed of a new mysterious power.

The passage hardly does credit to the generally sensitive and unhackneyed style of the novel, but, aside from that, it would be difficult to cite another episode in naturalistic fiction in which the suggestiveness of the immediate physical environment is so vividly demonstrated. Charity's surrender to Harney is the end result of many factors, but it is touched off by forces beyond the conscious volition of the lovers and in this way merged with the larger drama in which the Fourth of July crowd, the summer night, and the fireworks have their part. It is by such artistry in the treatment that the reader is persuaded to minimize the fact that what he is reading is, after all, a conventional nineteenth-century novel of seduction. Except for the individuality of Lawyer Royall's contribution, it would be hard to find a triter situation in Edith Wharton's novels. But the interest of *Summer*, like that of *Ethan Frome*, lies partly in its development of imaginative resources never called into play by the method to which she was committed in the novel of manners.

Chapter IX

THE RICH LOW MURMUR
OF THE PAST

Although Edith Wharton was in her seventies when she wrote *A Backward Glance,* it was not through weariness but design that her chronicle came to an end, except for a perfunctory postscript, with the Armistice of 1918. The world she knew best, the world that had formed and sustained her, did not survive that event. The change that had begun in the 'eighties when the advance guard of Invaders had appeared on the social horizon of her old New York had been accelerated and finally completed by the war. Suddenly she found herself a lingering stranger in a world she never made, in which the rules of conduct laid down by her zealously proper mother "became . . . observances as quaintly arbitrary as the domestic rites of the Pharaohs." Not until then did she remark the picturesqueness of that simpler age, and by the time she came to write her memoirs she was ready to atone for her former irreverence. When she took stock following the Armistice, it seemed that the eclipse of her world had been emphasized by the passing of its leading spirits and her dearest friends—Henry James, Howard Sturgis, Egerton Winthrop—and of the younger relatives and friends, French and American, who had died in battle. Oppressed by a growing sense of alienation from the present, she tried to make her peace with the gracious shades of her ancestors and to reëstablish a community of spirit with the past. With the patience of an archaeologist she set about, soon after the war, to reconstruct the world of her childhood and youth, first in *The Age of Innocence,* then in a series of long tales collected under the title *Old New York,* and finally in *A Backward Glance* and her posthumous unfinished novel *The Buccaneers.*

Much earlier, however, her consciousness of the change had been memorably recorded in what is probably her best short story, "Autres Temps" (1916). This interesting transition piece deals brilliantly and somewhat wistfully with the return to New York of a woman who eighteen years before had divorced her husband, remarried, and for this transgression had been ostracized by polite society. After years of solitary penance abroad, she is willing to brave the united front of respectable New York society in order to be near her daughter, who, divorced and recently remarried, has ironically duplicated her mother's experience. In the interval of Mrs. Lidcote's expatriation the mores of society have changed, its standards become less severe. She learns from her old friend Franklin Ide that as a result of the mounting divorce rate "it would take an arbitration commission a good many sittings to define the boundaries of society nowadays." When she discovers that, contrary to her expectation, her daughter no longer needs her, Mrs. Lidcote is forced to examine her new position:

Where indeed in this crowded, topsy-turvy world, with its headlong changes and helter-skelter readjustments, its new tolerances and indifferences and accommodations, was there room for a character fashioned by slower sterner processes and a life broken under the inexorable pressure? And then, in a flash, she viewed the chaos from a new angle, and order seemed to move upon the void. If the old processes were changed, her case was changed with them, she, too, was a part of the general readjustment, a tiny fragment of the new pattern worked out in bolder, freer harmonies. Since her daughter had no penalty to pay, was not she herself released by the same stroke?

But although society accepts her daughter's emancipation, it will not reverse its verdict in her own case. For nearly twenty years it has been a tradition to cut Mrs. Lidcote. "The older people have forgotten why," she concludes, "and the younger ones have never really known. . . . And traditions that have lost their meaning are the hardest of all to destroy." Stranded anew, she turns to Franklin Ide, who for years has made it plain that he wants to marry her. But when he involuntarily reveals that his prejudices, if not his judgment, are bound up with those of society, she prepares to return alone to Italy.

Most of the radical social and cultural phenomena which for some reason we like to think of as peculiar to the 'twenties (except those which had their origin in the Eighteenth Amendment) are evident before the war. "Autres Temps" not only serves as a kind of prospectus of the themes and interests of Edith Wharton's later fiction, but it underlines even more sharply than *The Custom of the Country* her awareness that the old "good" society she had known was breaking up under the pressure of changed world conditions and the "new tolerances and indifferences and accommodations."

Moreover, consciously or not, the story manages to strike an intensely personal note. Written probably about the time of Edith Wharton's divorce in 1913 and published nearly a decade after her permanent removal from America,[1] it opens up questions beyond its borders which perhaps illuminate her attitude toward the problem of return and readjustment. To what degree she may have felt that her own domestic misadventure, however extenuating the circumstances, had compromised her reputation at home is an interesting question, particularly in view of the fact that in *The Mother's Recompense* (1925) she repeated the essential plot of "Autres Temps." And whether the personal factor is involved or not, the later novels are filled with the bewilderment of the real and spiritual expatriates at the accelerated changes in American life and manners.

In *The Age of Innocence* (1920) Mrs. Wharton's recoil from the postwar world is felt mainly by indirection, in her choice of setting. Although it is clear that like her hero, Newland Archer, who "cherished his old New York even when he smiled at it," she could reconcile two points of view, the indictment outweighs the defense. In her protest against the deliberately nurtured innocence of old New York she continued in *The Age of Innocence*, as she had done before in *The Reef* and *Ethan Frome*, to rehearse her own complaint against the failures of education and opportunity that had hampered her growth as a human being and as an artist. But underlying her protest was the nostalgia evoked by the setting and manners familiar to her childhood, a nostalgia that was to grow with the years until it effaced what bitterness remained.

---

[1] For notes to chap. ix, see p. 257.

"Unconsciously to us all," one of Edith Wharton's old friends has written in Lubbock's memoir, "life began to change from simplicity to vulgarity somewhere in the late eighties." [2] Significantly, the setting of *The Age of Innocence* antedates that minor social revolution. Although the storm warnings were up, for those who cared to heed them, the mercantile aristocracy in the 'seventies was for the most part impregnable in its complacency. Julius Beaufort, the beefy financier of *The Age of Innocence,* is a disturbing portent, but his financial disgrace only strengthens Washington Square in its self-esteem. Ellen Olenska, who represents another kind of threat to the tribal security, is vanquished when society closes about the Newland Archers like a Roman wall. What one notices about this little world is that it is hermetically sealed against contamination. The question that arises with respect to such novels as *The Fruit of the Tree, A Son at the Front,* and *Hudson River Bracketed* —to what extent was Edith Wharton competent to deal with social and political issues beyond her limited perspective?—is as irrelevant in this instance as it would be for Jane Austen. Nothing in her treatment is more truly representative than its exclusions. We may listen in vain for echoes from the outside world. The crude, boisterous spectacle of postwar expansion, featured by the corruptions of the Grant regime, the rapid extension of the frontier, and the problems posed by labor, immigration, and urbanization, fails to penetrate the consciousness of old New York or to modify in any way its timeless ritual. Never before had Edith Wharton succeeded so well in adapting her subject to her limitations while at the same time allowing full scope for her talents.

There is some advantage to be gained from reading

A Backward Glance as a preface to *The Age of Innocence,* if only to be assured where to locate the novel's emphasis and to be able to trace the origin of some of Mrs. Wharton's most successful details. Although there is a wealth of minor parallels—for example, the old Newbold Madeira, famous in its day, has become "the old Lanning Port," and the great-grandfather of the novelist, General Ebenezer Stevens, who directed the surrender of Burgoyne after Saratoga, has become one of Newland Archer's distinguished ancestors—the general parallels are more helpful. The salient peculiarities of the age of innocence are plainly marked in both. The society reproduced in the novel consisted of a small number of families, ranked in a strict angelic hierarchy according to ancestry and financial means—qualifications which held good only so long as one did not enter retail business, exhibit any form of personal or financial dishonesty, or elope with the first maid or chauffeur. In the 'seventies money was still unable to purchase entrance into the charmed circle; in fact, the mere mention of it was distasteful. The young men had no active interest in adding to their capital. They lived off the enterprise of their forebears and the profits realized from the boom in New York real estate values. None of them, as Edith Wharton recalled, was "in business." They were trained to be lawyers or bankers or stockbrokers, but, like Newland Archer and Ralph Marvell, they kept no office hours and their profession was mainly an ornament.

"It is a singular fact," Henry James remarked of Newport, "that a society that does nothing is decidedly more pictorial, more interesting to the eye of contemplation, than a society which is hard at work." [3] Edith Wharton would have agreed. It was precisely this pictorial quality that attracted her and enabled her to demonstrate once again that she had the "visualizing power" beyond any other novelist of her time. In the intervals between shooting, fishing, and boat racing, the male members of this society lent themselves agreeably to the social strategies of their women. It was a society not merely ingrown, but, judging from the novel, strongly matriarchal, in which the real authority was exerted, blatantly or quietly, and on descending levels, by Mrs. van der Luyden, Mrs. Manson Mingott, and the elder Mrs. Archer. One is reminded, in fact, of the similar view we get of aristocratic French society in the novels of both James and Mrs. Wharton. There too we encounter the formidable old dowagers, narrowly devoted to the ideal of *la famille* and, secondly, the clan, and managing, like the Duchess in *The American* or the Marquise de Malrives in *Madame de Treymes,* to symbolize with immense force the authority residing in the concept of a traditional society. One may even be struck by the unconscious identification which Edith Wharton makes between the Marquise de Malrives and her circle, "who mostly bore the stamp of personal insignificance on their mildly sloping or aristocratically beaked faces," and the Archer women, "tall, pale, and slightly round-shouldered, with long noses, sweet smiles and a kind of drooping distinction like that in certain faded Reynolds portraits." [4]

Edith Wharton's final, balanced judgment of old New York, notably less severe than her earlier judgment, appears in *A Backward Glance* and has been noted frequently. Its virtues, as she saw them, were "social amenity and financial incorruptibility"; its defects were principally two, "an instinctive shrinking from respon-

sibility" and "a blind dread of innovation." Although
the positive values represented by this narrow segment
of American society are implied in *The Age of Innocence,*
its failures are more apparent. Its members were the
descendants of Hamilton's Federalists, but they had no
discernible interest in politics. Following the Civil War
some of these leisured gentlemen began to interest themselves in municipal affairs to the extent of serving on the
boards of museums, libraries, and charities, but beyond
this they could not bring themselves to go. Politics was
out of bounds; consequently, Mrs. Wharton explained,
"none of my friends rendered the public service that a
more enlightened social system would have exacted of
them." Perhaps she was thinking of England, where the
best—and sometimes the worst—abilities of the nobility
were enlisted in the professional branches of government. At any rate, she found a very real criticism of
American democracy in its failure to utilize the best material at hand: "In every society there is the room, and
the need, for a cultivated leisure class; but from the first
the spirit of our institutions has caused us to waste this
class instead of using it." This is one of the bitterest
comments in *A Backward Glance,* representing the ultimate phase of Edith Wharton's conservatism. In the interval following *The Age of Innocence* she moved from
an indictment, however partial, of the class itself to an
indictment of the system which first neglected that class
and then swallowed it whole. And, curiously, the same
contradiction is perpetuated in her memoirs.

It is the "dread of innovation," however, expressed in
a thousand forms of resistance, that characterizes old
New York most completely. When she is describing her
parents' taste in literature, Mrs. Wharton can afford,

even in *A Backward Glance,* to be amused. Repeatedly
in her stories—in *The Age of Innocence, The Old Maid,
Hudson River Bracketed*—she lists the authors, gentlemen all, who were sanctioned by the parlor censor:
Irving, Halleck, Drake, and the elder Dana. The more
vigorous talents, like Poe and Whitman, who were invariably the more disreputable in their antecedents and
associations, were either ignored or dismissed as vulgar.
Mrs. Archer and her daughter, whose tastes were identical, "spoke severely of Dickens, who 'had never drawn
a gentleman,' and considered Thackeray less at home in
the great world than Bulwer." The irony is so unmistakable that one can only smile at the critic who took
Mrs. Wharton's reference to Melville in *A Backward
Glance* as evidence of her snobbishness ("As for Herman
Melville, a cousin of the Van Rensselaers, and qualified
by birth to figure in the best society, he was doubtless
excluded from it by his deplorable Bohemianism, for I
never heard his name mentioned, or saw one of his
books"). The resistance to literature was, in effect a resistance to new and unsettling ideas and new forms of
experience. When this attitude was extended to the more
vital concerns of life, Edith Wharton was no longer
amused. There it meant the substitution of an elaborate
system of conventions for the natural response to situations. "In reality," Edith Wharton wrote of Newland
Archer and his contemporaries, "they all lived in a kind
of hieroglyphic world, where the real thing was never
said or done or even thought, but only represented by a
set of arbitrary signs."

In delineating such a world, the novel of manners is
indispensable. The real drama is played out below the
surface—the impeccable, sophisticated surface—and com-

municates itself, if at all, to the observer by means of signs which only the initiate can read. Hence the significance, to old New York, of certain gestures by which the private drama is made public: that frightening portent of social annihilation, the "cut"; the dinner invitation from the van der Luydens, the invitation to occupy a prominent box at the opera, or the presence of Mrs. Manson Mingott's carriage before the door, all signalizing reinstatement; the sudden flight to Europe, which is the solution to every serious emotional crisis. These are the less arbitrary signs. By and large, however, the acquired manners of old New York lend themselves to what Edith Wharton termed "an elaborate system of mystification." A young girl carefully bred in the tradition, like May Welland, knows the social value of the well-timed blush, the feigned reluctance during courtship, and the long engagement. May is so completely the product of the system that Newland Archer, following their marriage, is forced to admit that she will never surprise him "by a new idea, a weakness, a cruelty or an emotion." Thus the problem for the novelist becomes a difficult if engaging one. If passions are to spin the plot with a minimum of labor for himself, they must be visible. If they are not, the novelist may be forced to rely on certain conventions. The detected rendezvous—Selden's glimpse of Lily Bart emerging from the Trenor mansion, or the interview between Ellen Olenska and Newland Archer which is witnessed by the scandal-mongering Larry Lefferts—becomes as necessary to Edith Wharton's art as the overheard conversation and the intercepted letter are to Shakespeare's.

It is difficult to read *The Age of Innocence* without being struck by its resemblance to that earliest of "modern" novels, *The Princess of Clèves*, which has been described by the author of *The Writing of Fiction* as "a story of hopeless love and mute renunciation in which the stately tenor of the lives depicted is hardly ruffled by the exultations and agonies succeeding each other below the surface." Mrs. Wharton might have been describing *The Age of Innocence*. Both novels train their analysis on the effects of unsatisfied passion, and the heroine in each—Madame de Clèves in the first and Ellen Olenska in the second—is a victim of what Nancy Mitford has defined as "the curious shrinking from happiness . . . a state of mind that has been beautifully observed and recorded by Henry James in *The American* as well as, in a more extraverted way, by Balzac in the *Duchesse de Langeais*, and which is to be found among Frenchwomen to this day." [5] More striking than these incidental parallels is the fact that, however corrupt the court of Henry II may appear in contrast to Washington Square, the members of both societies were trained to disguise their feelings, so that in Madame de Lafayette's novel, as in *The Age of Innocence*, the intricate play and counterplay of motives scarcely, as Edith Wharton noted, disturbs the surface.

But *The Princess of Clèves* is distinctly not a novel of manners. To Madame de Lafayette must go the credit for demonstrating more clearly than anyone before her that the novel, as opposed to the drama, is the perfect vehicle for the presentation of an action in which the conflict is profoundly internal, in which, because their situation requires them to assume a mask, almost nothing can be inferred from what the characters do or say— from their gestures, expressions, tones of voice. Madame de Lafayette is preoccupied directly with the psychology of her characters as it reveals itself in consciousness rather than in action. It remained for a Balzac, following in the tradition, but absorbing the contribution of the picaresque novelists, to capitalize on the value of manners as indicating—to use Trilling's phrase again—"the largest intentions of men's souls as well as the smallest." Like Balzac, and unlike Madame de Lafayette, Edith Wharton is a materialist in fiction. Balzac's endless curiosity about the minutiae of business and legal transactions, property rights, and the arts of decoration is almost matched by Edith Wharton's passion for the detail of costume and decor; and her notation of the manners of her class is as scrupulous as Balzac's notation of bourgeois manners in *César Birotteau* or *Eugénie Grandet.* And both, it might be added, apprehend their characters intellectually. It is difficult to conceive of *The Age of Innocence* ever having been written without the fruitful example of the great French novelist.

The Age of Innocence is not Mrs. Wharton's strongest novel, but, along with *Ethan Frome,* it is the one in which she is most thoroughly the artist. It is a triumph of style, of the perfect adaptation of means to a conception fully grasped from the outset. It would be difficult to say that she faltered or overreached at any point. The movement of her plot may be established by the successive and clearly marked positions taken by Newland Archer in his relations with Ellen Olenska and May Welland. May Welland personifies all the evasions and compromises of his clan; she is the "safe" alternative; whereas Ellen has the "mysterious faculty of suggesting tragic and moving possibilities outside the daily run of experience." Charmed by May's innocence, and about to announce his engagement to her, Archer at first finds it

185

easy to join old New York in condemning the Mingotts for sponsoring Countess Olenska: "Few things seemed to Newland Archer more awful than an offence against 'Taste,' that far-off divinity of whom 'Form' was the mere visible representative and vice-regent." He is the willing accomplice of a society "wholly absorbed in barricading itself against the unpleasant," and his appreciation of May Welland is based on this precarious ideal: "Nothing about his betrothed pleased him more than her resolute determination to carry to its utmost limits that ritual of ignoring the 'unpleasant' in which they had both been brought up." In the story that follows Edith Wharton tries to make clear what this innocence costs. The measure of change wrought in Archer's outlook by his experience with Ellen is suggested by a sentence occurring midway in the novel, before the echo of his earlier belief has quite died away: "Ah, no, he did not want May to have that kind of innocence, the innocence that seals the mind against imagination and the heart against experience!"

His fall from grace is carefully motivated. Old New York's treatment of Countess Olenska eventually arouses the innate sense of chivalry that he shares with Ralph Marvell, and once he has read the divorce evidence his indifference is vanquished: "she stood before him as an exposed and pitiful figure, to be saved at all costs from farther wounding herself in her mad plunges against fate." In spite of his strict notions, he is not entirely unprepared for a sentimental adventure. One of the first things we learn about him is that he has had an affair with a married woman "whose charms had held his fancy through two mildly agitated years." Once he has accepted Ellen's case—ironically at the instigation of the clan—he is compelled by logic and sympathy, and finally by the deeper reasons of love, to adopt her point of view. Nothing in Edith Wharton's treatment of the situation is more subtly expressed than the changes which Archer's affair with Ellen work in his perceptions. But his freedom is won too late. Ellen has at the same time learned something from him. She has accepted seriously one of the lessons he had mastered by rote and passed on to her: that freedom cannot be purchased at another's cost. It makes no difference that he is now prepared to discard it. He has given her an idea by which to live and, in doing so, destroyed the one means of enlarging his new-found freedom. When he returns to May Welland, it is to the ultimate realization that, like John Marcher in James's "The Beast in the Jungle," he is the man "to whom nothing was ever to happen."

Edith Wharton never surpassed the irony in which she enveloped this play of cross-purposes. "It is impossible to be ironical," she once noted, "without having a sense of the infinitudes." [6] To the novelist so equipped, the complacent worldliness of old New York offered fair game. Irony was the method best suited to her temperament and her material. It was her way of telling the world that she had not been taken in, whatever her allegiances: and it was the only alternative to tragedy, which, as she suggested in novel after novel, was impossible in her world. It was an atmosphere, however, in which a reader such as Katherine Mansfield, for all her admiration of *The Age of Innocence,* found it increasingly difficult to breathe, for Mrs. Wharton's self-control got on her nerves until she asked, quite irrelevantly in this instance at least, whether it was vulgar "to entreat a little wildness, a dark place or two in the soul." [7]

The touch of "wildness" may be lacking, but there is no failure of sensibility in the novel. The intimate passages between Newland Archer and Ellen Olenska are as deeply moving as those between Ethan Frome and Mattie Silver, whose dilemma is so curiously repeated under far different circumstances. The frustration of the lovers is expressed with great skill by two main devices. Their affair begins and ends in the glare of publicity, from the moment Archer sees his countess at the opera to the moment he discovers that old New York regards them as lovers. The opening chapter of the novel is superbly conceived from both the novelist's and the social historian's viewpoint. The theater in the 'seventies was just in the process of becoming what it is so clearly today, a social arena in which private dramas could be effectively highlighted. The scene at the opera not only introduces the main characters, together with those secondary characters who will serve as commentators—Sillerton Jackson, the undisputed authority on "family," and Lawrence Lefferts, the arbiter of "form"—but it makes Ellen Olenska a public issue; it establishes her in a position from which she cannot retreat and in which she is subject to the maximum scrutiny. The consciousness of this fact, shared by the lovers, makes their every subsequent encounter a pathetically frustrating one.

The second device I would call attention to is Edith Wharton's insistence on the chaste, almost palpable barrier which divides the lovers from the start and which they maintain, even when they are alone, by the thought of their obligations. Time and again—in Ellen's drawing room, in the carriage coming away from the ferry landing, during the clandestine meeting in the art museum and, finally, during the farewell dinner for Ellen—they

reach out to each other across aching distances. At Newport, following a long separation, Archer has a chance
to see Ellen again when his hostess asks him to fetch her
from the pier. He spots her from a distance and stands
watching her awhile. Then he turns and walks back to
the house. It is a rehearsal of the gesture he will make,
some twenty years later, in the epilogue. At such moments one may measure the force of Edith Wharton's
sudden anguished revelation to Charles du Bos, in the
year that witnessed the climax of her domestic troubles:
"Ah, the poverty, the miserable poverty, of any love
that lies outside of marriage, of any love that is not a
living together, a sharing of all!" [8]

In everything but the quality of its craftsmanship, *The
Age of Innocence* is related most clearly to the novels
which followed it rather than to those Edith Wharton
wrote before the war, and chiefly because the later novels will renew the protest against innocence—the modern
innocence of the 'twenties. Accurately or not, Edith
Wharton found the main impulse of the postwar generation in its desire to throw off every kind of restraint
imposed on conduct, morals, religion—and literary expression. With no such faith in this vision of the individual, solitary and erect, bearing no taint of original sin
and no past to encumber him, she found that the case
she had formulated against her parents' generation was
applicable to their grandchildren's. Each sought in its
own way to escape the common lot; each, in its effort to
avoid pain and responsibility, had weakened its moral
fiber. Where convention was concerned, freedom was
no better than slavery; and so Edith Wharton continued
the search for a compromise on which all of her energies
as a novelist were habitually bent.

Not much can be said, one way or another, for those leftovers from the banquet of *The Age of Innocence*, the quartet of long tales grouped under the title *Old New York* (1924). They are slight but competent pieces ranging in tone from irony to melodrama. Like the long tales of Mrs. Wharton's earlier period, they theoretically treat subjects "too spreading for conciseness yet too light in texture to be stretched into a novel." [9] Actually, the subject of *False Dawn* taxes the dimensions of the long tale, whereas that of *The Spark*, so obviously anecdotal in quality, could be encompassed in a short story. On this occasion, it appears, Edith Wharton has applied rather loosely the rule of thumb which delegates the long tale for actions embracing a period of years and depending for their effect on the reader's sense of passing time and on the gradual revelation of the characters' inner life, rather than the "single retrospective flash." None of these later tales, except possibly *The Old Maid*, takes up moral problems as intricate as those of *The Touchstone* and *Sanctuary* and consequently demanding the same careful exposition of circumstances. In contrast to the early tales with their contemporary setting, a larger proportion of the treatment in such stories as *The Old Maid* and *False Dawn* is devoted to the recreation of the physical milieu and the manners of mid-nineteenth-century New York—an interest generally unadaptable to the long tale.

None of the stories of *Old New York* is as good as *Ethan Frome* or "Bunner Sisters"; none is as bad as *Sanctuary*. The best in many ways, and certainly the most interesting at this stage in Edith Wharton's development, is *False Dawn*, a kind of parable suggested, I would guess, by the career of James Jackson Jarves, the pioneer American collector of Italian primitives, whose attempt to alter the taste of his generation proved as heartbreaking as Lewis Raycie's. The latter's purchase of Giottos, Mantegnas, and della Francescas, in disregard of his father's preference for Raphaels, is foreshadowed by his boyhood attachment to the disreputable Edgar Allan Poe; but this time the indulgence of his *avant-garde* tastes results in nothing less drastic than the extinction of the male Raycie line, preparing the way for the neatly ironic ending in which Lewis Raycie's taste finally pays off in sables and motor cars for his remote collateral descendants. It would be easy enough to summarize the story by saying that the vision and stubborn faith of one generation are converted into dollars for a later, more materialistic generation, and undoubtedly this parable had its share in the treatment.

But Edith Wharton is equally aware, as she was in *The Age of Innocence,* of the shortcomings of her parents' generation, its distrust of novelty and the closed circuit of its human sympathies, and it was to this theme that she returned for another tale in the series, *The Spark*. Again she gave her situation the ironic twist that she always found so difficult to resist. Hayley Delane, hospitalized with a severe wound following Bull Run, is fired with an ideal of human sympathy by the gentle ministrations of a man named Whitman; but although his life is changed by the encounter, he is unmoved by his introduction, thirty years later, to Walt's poetry, finding it incredible that his friend could have written such "stuff." That is not the whole of Delane's story, however. Like *The Old Maid* and *New Year's Day, The Spark* examines a case of misconstrued motives, calling to account the narrow judgments of old New York on the rebels in its ranks—a procedure familiar enough in Edith Wharton's fiction. When Delane, following a polo match, strikes his wife's latest lover for maltreating his horse, the motive assigned by the spectators is jealousy of the lover rather than compassion for the animal. Similarly, when Lizzie Hazeldean, in *New Year's Day*, is seen leaving the Fifth Avenue Hotel with Henry Prest, a society wolf with whom she is rumored to be having an affair, old New York cuts her dead and extends its sympathy to her invalid husband. Following Charles Hazeldean's death, Lizzie wounds her lover's vanity unforgivably by telling him that she never loved him and that she became his mistress to pay the bills which would have destroyed the tranquillity of her husband's last days. Although in the years that follow she remains faithful to her husband's memory, society never gets around to giving her credit for her heroism. The same rather superficial investigation of appearance and reality bolsters the familiar and slightly dated melodrama of *The Old Maid*, with its Victorian emphasis on seduction and mother love. In one way or another, each of the stories takes old New York to task for its imperviousness to light and the cruelty or at best insensitivity of its social verdicts. One reads them today with a certain unresponsiveness, not merely because they mark time in Edith Wharton's development, but because even before they appeared she had demonstrated to her public that she was prone to the same conservatism as her parents.

I should not like to leave these bittersweet evocations of the New York past without glancing at a short story —the most terrible, I believe, of any Edith Wharton wrote—which appeared later in the 'twenties. Lloyd Morris has sketched a portrait of Mrs. Astor shortly be-

fore her death in 1908, when her mind had failed:
". . . Still erect, still heavily gowned and jewelled, she
stood quite alone, greeting imaginary guests long dead,
exchanging pleasantries with ghosts of the utmost social
distinction." [10] It seems to me likely that this appalling
image, which Edith Wharton must have been aware of
at first hand, furnished the idea for "After Holbein"
(1928). Of it she made a heartlessly bad and rather
theatrical joke. Anson Warley, a bachelor of sixty-three
and New York's most indefatigable diner-out, has been
suffering from dizzy spells. On a raw winter evening he
pettishly disregards his valet's plea that he remain at
home, starts on foot for his dinner engagement, has a
lapse of memory en route, and turns in by mistake at the
Fifth Avenue mansion of Mrs. Evelina Jaspar, once the
most influential—and most boring—of New York host-
esses, whose dinners Warley had for forty years sed-
ulously avoided. She is now a victim of softening of the
brain. A shrunken specter, dressed outlandishly and
wearing her jewels and a purple wig, she still stands in
the empty hallway, tottering on swollen feet, to receive
the guests who never come and later, at dinner, divides
her conversation between the vacant chairs on either
side. Warley, whose own mind has suddenly begun to
cloud, seeing the house illuminated, thinks he has engaged himself to dine there. He is greeted formally by
Mrs. Jaspar, escorts her in to dinner, and together, at a
table set with kitchen crockery, they enact a travesty of
her former glory. The conversation is thin and ludicrous,
and the pair wax giddy on Apollinaris: "'Old times,'
bantered Mrs. Jaspar; and the two turned to each other
and bowed their heads and touched glasses." After dinner the hostess retires, presumably abandoning her guest

to his cigar. Warley, as he is leaving, suffers a fatal stroke.

The tone of "After Holbein" is the most chilling Edith Wharton ever assumed. Those who would deny that any bond of sympathy exists between Mrs. Wharton and her characters have their best argument here; not by a word does she betray the least compassion for her actors in this grim morality. But the mood that produced the story seems to have been one of exacerbation. The occasional nostalgia of her earlier pieces has disappeared; there is a ghoulish pleasure evident in her lingering over the details of her *Totentanz*.[11] One thinks of Faulkner in the same self-lacerating mood, when he is moved by the decay of a social tradition he values to deck its last moments with the most loathsome emblems of mortality. It is the normal reaction of one who feels himself betrayed by the past and by the tradition in which he was reared, and even Edith Wharton must have had such moments of revulsion. For this reason it would be a mistake, I believe, to assume that in her caricature of Mrs. Jaspar the writer is merely celebrating the decline of Fifth Avenue. Anson Warley, so far as he is representative, belongs to the old "good" New York society described in *A Backward Glance*. The point of the story apparently resides in the fact that the traditional antagonists meet finally and are reconciled at the brink of mutual disintegration.

Chapter X

THE MONTESSORI SCHOOL

"It is known to comparatively few," Edith Wharton remarked in an early short story, "that the production of successful potboilers is an art in itself." [1] From the early 'twenties to the close of her career, her novels were to underline that proposition. On the basis of the scanty evidence available, it is not easy to account for her sudden fall from grace. The purchase, shortly before the end of the war, of Pavillon Colombe near Paris and subsequently of the summer home near Hyères in southern France, both expensive to maintain, must have helped persuade her to widen the market for her writing. Simultaneously, it was apparent that her world, like Willa Cather's at about the same period, had broken in two. (A single detail in *Hudson River Bracketed* would later summarize her complaint against the postwar world and its values: the Duke of Spartivento, heir to a great Spanish title, turns up selling stocks on the French Riviera to American tourists for the New York firm of Rosenzweig and Blemp.) Her initial reaction from the shock, that mood of nostalgia which produced *The Age of Innocence* and the four vignettes of nineteenth-century New York society, gave way gradually to the only possible alterna-

---

[1] For notes to chap. x, see p. 258.

tive: she would examine the "ultra-modern" postwar civilization in the light of what now seemed to be a discredited social, moral, and aesthetic tradition. In spite of expatriation and her growing inaccessibility, she would make what for her was a valiant effort, although doomed from the start, to understand the new generation. Her friendships with young men and women, from whom admittedly she could learn as much as she could teach, and her encouragement of younger writers form one of the clearest motifs in Lubbock's chronicle of her last two decades.

Whatever the explanation, her decline as a serious novelist could hardly have been more drastically forecast than by the publication, less than two years after *The Age of Innocence*, of the weakest of her novels, *The Glimpses of the Moon* (1922). The thousands of housewives who formed the audiences of *The Pictorial Review*, where it first appeared, may have turned to the first installment with reservations. Although Mrs. Wharton's connection with the fashionable world was a valid passport to the realm of women's fiction, her characteristic irony and the austerity of her social and moral judgments were likely to prove handicaps. Before they finished the first chapter, her audience would have been reassured. If *The Age of Innocence* is a triumph of style in the serious meaning of the term, its successor can claim a different kind of triumph in the perfect accommodation of its style to the slick-writing formula. When the novel opens, the young honeymooners, Nick and Susy Lansing, are discovered in the tritely romantic setting of a moonlit balcony overlooking Lake Como. "His hand still lay on hers, and for a long interval, while they stood silent in the enveloping loveliness of the night, she was aware only of the warm current running from palm to palm, as the moonlight below them drew its line of magic from shore to shore." Following a passage of superficially bright dialogue ("I could bear," Lansing remarked, "even a nightingale at this moment . . ."), there is another interval of enchanted silence.

All about them breathed of peace and beauty and stability, and her happiness was so acute that it was almost a relief to remember the stormy background of bills and borrowing against which its frail structure had been reared. "People with a balance can't be as happy as all this," Susy mused, letting the moonlight filter through her lazy lashes.

Not all of the writing is so meretricious, and there is a noticeable recovery in the later novels, but the touch of corruption apparent even so early as *The Custom of the Country* has spread until the style of *The Glimpses of the Moon,* like its characters and situation, reminds us only intermittently of the author of *Ethan Frome* and *The House of Mirth.* The echoes from the last-named novel are just strong enough, in fact, to force an unhappy comparison. Susy Lansing, thrust into the world at seventeen, with only a weakling father to help her adjust her moral sights, is a later and paler version of Lily Bart. She has been trained to live off her wealthy friends, to exploit her personal gifts in return for loans, a wardrobe, and hospitality. Almost as clearly, her English suitor Strefford, who knows of her shifts and evasions but, unlike her less flexible husband, continues to love her, is a later edition of Lawrence Selden. Functioning in contrast to Nick Lansing, he supplies the touchstone, the alternative, for like his predecessor Selden he is "in the show yet outside of it."

The parallel is superficial, but it points toward an important conclusion. Susy Lansing's predicament lacks the tragic potentialities of Lily Bart's, partly because the social world in which she moves has relaxed its standards and its judgments, partly because like all of Edith Wharton's later protagonists she finds it easier to make her adjustments, compromises, and concessions. In the thinner moral atmosphere of the postwar world her actions have only the faintest reverberations—a fact that suggests, even to Susy, the impossibility of tragedy:

> . . . No one had asked her where she had come from, or why she was alone, or what was the key to the tragedy written on her shrinking face. . . .
> That was the way of the world they lived in. Nobody questioned, nobody wondered any more—because nobody had time to remember. The old risk of prying curiosity, of malicious gossip, was virtually over: one was left with one's drama, one's disaster, on one's hands, because there was nobody to stop and notice the little shrouded object one was carrying.

Susy Lansing's personal dilemma, unlike Lily Bart's, has no wider implications; it involves no real disaster even for Strefford, who is the only person besides Nick whose fate in any way impinges on hers. The moral issue is fought out over Nick, and the triumph of his viewpoint—that of a self-righteous and insufferable prig—would be disagreeable if that were where the emphasis finally came to rest. Clearly, as in the earlier novels, the development of character and event is toward a recognition of the necessity of compromise, and compromise has no place in tragedy. But increasingly the problem in the later novels is not whether to make adjustments, but where to make them. Susy Lansing is merely following the lead of earlier Wharton heroines—Justine Brent, Anna Leath, Ellen Olenska, and Lizzie West of "The Letters"—in swallowing her pride and, by making the first advances toward a reconciliation, protecting the male ego. The heroines of the later novels are more realistic and therefore consistently stronger than the men. "You accept things theoretically," Susy tells her husband, "and then when they happen. . . ." Although she never finishes the statement, it is clear what she means. Ralph Gannett, in the early story "Souls Belated," has lodged the identical complaint under similar circumstances against Lydia Tillotson ("You judge things too theoretically. . . . Life is made up of compromises"), and for a quarter of a century this has been the basis of Edith Wharton's criticism of her more naïve or altruistic characters. But now the roles of the sexes are reversed, and it is the woman who henceforth will remind the man that life is real and earnest and not to be governed by abstract theories of conduct.

To what extent Edith Wharton either inherited or helped to devise the formula that later became identified with radio soap opera, I am not prepared even to guess. But the main ingredients of *The Glimpses of the Moon* are tiresomely familiar: the thinly glamorous backdrop, the gay impecunious young couple, the dialogue which at its best leaves no impression and at its worst is reminiscent of those earnestly sophisticated Broadway comedies in which the curtain rose on juveniles and ingénues bouncing through the French doors clad in sport clothes and carrying tennis rackets, and, most important, the *sine qua non* of the soap-opera formula—the thesis that the female of the species is stronger, morally and spiritually, than the male.

With her next novel, *The Mother's Recompense* (1925), Mrs. Wharton was back on firmer ground, managing a setting more familiar and characters whose kinship she could more readily acknowledge. In its initial and closing episodes, the story recalls that of "Autres Temps." Kate Clephane, after having deserted her husband, the scion of a monstrously respectable New York family, to run away with a lover for a two years' voyage on his yacht, has performed her expiation in the manner of Mrs. Lidcote. For nearly twenty years she has led a nomadic existence among the watering spots of Europe, staying in modest hotels and wondering what to do with a life that has become a monotonous round of minor social diversions punctuated by stretches of loneliness. When the daughter she abandoned at the age of three, now having reached her majority, cables her to come and live with her in New York, Kate gladly takes her leave of the second-rate Riviera society in which she has figured for too many years.

Her homecoming, unlike Mrs. Lidcote's, is an unexpected success. Now that her dragon-like mother-in-law is dead, the past is forgiven, even by members of her husband's family—an example of the "new tolerances and indifference and accommodations" remarked in "Autres Temps." Her daughter Anne is charming, sympathetic, and self-reliant, and they establish an immediate intimacy. Kate Clephane's happiness is complete until she discovers that Anne is in love with Chris Fenno, a dilettante who, during a brief interval before the war, had been Kate's lover. Now older, redder, and stouter (the inevitable token, in Edith Wharton's view as in Howells', of moral decay—witness Peter Van Degen, Elmer Moffatt, and Cliffe Wheater in *The Children*), he has preserved the same mixture of selfishness and charm that Kate had known. When the mother strenuously opposes the match without revealing to Anne the basis of her opposition, the consequent misunderstanding destroys their intimacy. Realizing finally that a confession from her can only prevent a marriage on which Anne's happiness depends, Kate makes the requisite compromise, withdraws her opposition, and then following the wedding rejoins the old shrill, bored Riviera crowd. Not, however, before she has had a chance, like Mrs. Lidcote, to turn down an offer of marriage from a tried and faithful middle-aged suitor.

One can admire the thoroughness with which Mrs. Wharton has canvassed the issues involved in Kate's dilemma without being convinced that she has discovered the basic one. It appears, rather, that she has left it to the reader to disentangle it from the secondary issues and the vagaries of the point of view. Throughout the story we are necessarily seated at the window of Kate's consciousness. Our natural willingness to accept her judgments is reinforced by the immediate and constant assurance that she is reliable, that she can perform the function of the "fine central intelligence" in such a way that, unlike in James, no excess of caution is demanded from the reader in order to get the point. It never occurs to Kate, however, that morally her stand is untenable. She has deserted her husband and daughter; Chris Fenno has deserted her. His disappointment and suffering when she interferes with his marriage to Anne are at least a pale reflection of her own under earlier circumstances.

Yet she will grant him no quarter. There is nothing in the novel which prepares us for this irony. Quite legitimately, it might have been the final, logical, supreme touch in the characterization of Kate Clephane; but I am persuaded that it is unintentional and that we have another occasion, as in *The Reef*, where a certain temporizing with the fundamental issue is present. There would be no problem if we could say with confidence that the ultimate failure of Kate Clephane's moral intelligence *is* the whole point of her story, but the rest of the evidence points away from this conclusion.

To the readers of *The Pictorial Review*, who would have approved the sentimental maneuver which brought the lovers together at the end of *The Glimpses of the Moon*, the conclusion of *The Mother's Recompense* must have been strangely unsatisfactory, for it discards—or at least plays fast and loose with—one of the sacred cows of popular fiction, the idea that real happiness in marriage must be based on mutual frankness and confidence. The issue is not to be resolved so simply. One of the valuable traits of Mrs. Wharton's fiction is her willingness to test the clichés of her fellow novelists in the double light of her obdurate rationalism and what we suppose to be her bitter private experience. *The Mother's Recompense* sets about compromising the truism that marital happiness depends on a candid relationship between partners with the same boldness that *Ethan Frome* or "Bunner Sisters" exhibits in questioning the spiritual value of suffering and self-sacrifice. Kate Clephane has too intelligent a sense of her responsibility to be guided by sentimental clichés. The problem posed by Chris Fenno's essential unworthiness and its bearing on Anne's future happiness is slurred over in favor of a more difficult and complicated problem, one which brings the novel into the major thematic context of Edith Wharton's fiction. At the height of her impasse, Kate Clephane turns for help to an Episcopal rector who on their first encounter had impressed her, despite his social front, as essentially a sympathetic human being, "familiar with the humble realities of pain and perplexity, and experienced in dealing with them." Their second interview, which objectifies and in the end composes the struggle that has been going on in Kate's mind, marks the turning point of the action. Dr. Arklow accepts his visitor's explanation that she is seeking advice for a friend, but in reality he is not deceived. At the close of Kate's recital he declares emphatically: "It is her duty to tell her daughter." For the moment the priest has triumphed at the expense of the human being. But as Kate is about to leave he detains her, and the passage that follows is of unusual interest, because it distills the meaning of the experience which Edith Wharton has presented in story after story and which she has by no means exhausted.

"Unless," the Rector continued uncertainly, his eyes upon her, "she is absolutely convinced that less harm will come to all concerned if she has the courage to keep silence— always." There was a pause. "As far as I can see into the blackness of it," he went on, gaining firmness, "the whole problem turns on that. I may be mistaken; perhaps I am. But when a man has looked for thirty or forty years into pretty nearly every phase of human suffering and error, as men of my cloth have to do, he comes to see that there must be adjustments . . . adjustments in the balance of evil. Compromises, politicians would call them. Well, I'm not afraid of the word." He stood leaning against the jamb of the door; her hand was on the doorknob, and she listened with lowered head.

"The thing I'm most afraid of is sterile pain," he said after a moment. "I should never want anyone to be the cause of that."

Kate preserves her secret. The avoidance of "sterile pain" —a phrase which functions as a refrain throughout the subsequent development—is the paramount wisdom that the novel has to communicate. The discovery proceeds from the same realistic regard for human weakness that motivated George Darrow's protest against "the monstrousness of useless sacrifices," as well as the mute but eloquent protest of Ethan Frome.

In certain of the characters of *The Mother's Recompense* it is possible to discern the prototypes, thinly developed, of many characters in Mrs. Wharton's subsequent novels. Already evident is her dislike of the vulgar, lacquered expatriate crowd of Americans who overran the Riviera, so close to her doorstep at Hyères; in *The Children* and *The Gods Arrive* it will be more emphatic. Toward the English colony at Oubli, living in genteel poverty, enclosed in self-righteousness, and obstinately maintaining its isolation and its provincial manners in the freer atmosphere of the continent, her attitude, here as in *The Gods Arrive,* is less severe and more genially satiric. With Lilla Gates, Anne Clephane's divorced cousin, she attempted the earliest of her jazz-age caricatures—a type shortly to be reproduced with somewhat subtler strokes in Lita Wyant in *Twilight Sleep* and with the broadest possible strokes in Joyce Wheater in *The Children.* Lilla is semiliterate, strident, and frivolous, an inveterate party-goer and night club (Mrs. Wharton calls them "cabarets") habitué, who embellishes her features with green rouge, eye powder, and mascara, and has an omnipresent cigarette dangling from her lips. In her reincarnations she is less gaudy but no less superficial. Her blatant modernity serves as a foil for what one character describes as Anne Clephane's "memorial manner." Anne has kept alive the etiquette of an earlier day. Upon the death of old Mrs. Clephane, for example, she goes into conventional mourning while the Clephane box at the Opera remains decorously empty for a month. "It was awfully 'archaic,' as Nellie Tresselton said; but it somehow suited Anne, was as much in her 'style' as the close braids folded about her temples." This trait of her heroine's, which Edith Wharton is careful to emphasize although it has no significant influence on the development of the action, is later bequeathed to Nona Manford in *Twilight Sleep,* where, as we shall see, its function is notably enhanced.

Twilight Sleep (1927), which forged a third link in Edith Wharton's profitable connection with *The Pictorial Review,* picks up the discussion of the role of women, and particularly wives, in American social life where she had dropped it in *The Custom of the Country.* In the meantime, however, the germ of her thesis in this latest novel could be found in one of the books she had found time to write during the war, *French Ways and Their Meaning.* "Compared with the women of France," she had observed, "the average American woman is still in the kindergarten."

The world she lives in is exactly like the most improved and advanced and scientifically equipped Montessori-method baby-school. At first sight it may seem preposterous to compare the American woman's independent and resonant activities—her "boards" and clubs and sororities, her public investigation of everything under the heaven from "the social evil" to baking-powder, and from "physical culture" to the newest esoteric religion—to compare such free and busy and seemingly influential lives with the artless exercises of the infant class. But what is the fundamental principle of the Montessori system? It is the development of the child's individuality, unrestricted by the traditional nursery discipline: a Montessori school is a baby world where, shut up together in the most improved hygienic surroundings, a number of infants noisily develop their individuality.

By all odds the most dominant and memorable character in *Twilight Sleep* is Pauline Manford, the wealthy, flutter-brained, hyperthyroid daughter of a Midwestern automobile tycoon. Middle-aged and married for the second time to a successful New York lawyer, she has a son, Jim Wyant, by her first husband and a daughter, Nona (who is the protagonist of the novel), by her second. She is a type of the invading race for which Edith Wharton has small regard. Like the eighteenth-century lady of fashion in *The Spectator*, she fills her days with pointless but closely scheduled activity, neglects her family to pursue the intellectual fad of the moment, is afraid to relax, afraid to stop and think about the meaning and direction of her life. She is an easy prey for fortunetellers and faith healers, and because she indiscriminately attaches herself to all the fashionable movements, she can deliver a speech one day on birth control and another a few days later on the joys and privileges of motherhood without being aware of any inconsistency in her position. Rather flamboyantly, she illustrates Edith Wharton's contention about American women in

French Ways, that all their "semblance of freedom, activity and authority bears not much more real likeness to real living than the exercises of the Montessori infant." (Real living, she characteristically adds, "is a deep and complex and slowly-developed thing, the outcome of an old and rich social experience.")

Behind Mrs. Manford's futile display of energy there is a motive more compelling than the mere development of her individuality. "Her whole life (if one chose to look at it from a certain angle) had been a long uninterrupted struggle against the encroachment of every form of pain. . . . All her life she had been used to buying off suffering with money, or denying its existence with words, and her moral muscles had become so atrophied that only some great shock would restore their natural strength." When her daughter-in-law is about to give birth to her first child, Mrs. Manford installs her in the most expensive "Twilight Sleep" establishment in the country, surrounds her with flowers, baskets of fruit, light novels, and the latest tabloid editions—"and Lita drifted into motherhood as lightly and unperceivingly as if the wax doll which suddenly appeared in the cradle at her bedside had been brought there in one of the big bunches of hot-house roses that she found every morning on her pillow." There is an important differentiation of motives to be made between the avoidance of "sterile pain" and the avoidance of all pain. As if anxious not to be misunderstood, Edith Wharton in *Twilight Sleep* seems to be consciously delimiting the thesis of her earlier novel.

Pauline Manford's credo is simple—"Of course there ought to be no Pain . . . nothing but Beauty"—but in practice it plays havoc with the lives of her family. Her first husband, Arthur Wyant, unable to keep up the pace, had agreed to a divorce. The infatuation of her second husband, Dexter Manford, for his stepson's wife—an impasse which Mrs. Manford is too preoccupied to head off—threatens the structure of two marriages, her own and her son's. When her daughter Nona falls in love with a married man whose cold and unimaginatively pious wife refuses him a divorce, she cannot help her, having long since forfeited the role of confidante. In the meantime, her son's marriage is undermined from another direction: Lita Wyant, bored with her husband, her baby, and the Wyant respectability, longs for the purlieus of Hollywood and threatens to drag down the family name by seeking a movie career. It is a combination of circumstances sufficiently charged to set off the only explosion of conventional melodrama in Edith Wharton's novels—the episode in which Arthur Wyant, pursuing his antiquated notion of honor, goes gunning for Dexter Manford and by accident wounds Nona. The revelations consequent upon this event are supposed to provide the shock which will restore Mrs. Manford's moral muscles, but at the close of the novel she is as unreconstructed as ever.

Pauline Manford's persistent course of self-delusion, her determination to evade the responsibilities that any close human relationship entails, suggested to Edith Wharton a new approach to the kind of tragedy she had envisioned in *The House of Mirth*. ". . . A frivolous society," we may be again reminded, "can acquire dramatic significance only through what its frivolity destroys. Its tragic implication lies in its power of debasing people and ideals." Nothing is clearer in *Twilight Sleep*

than the novelist's conviction that the ultimate significance of her story must reside in Nona Manford's vic-
timization at the hands of her irresponsible elders.

Examining the characters and their functions in the
later novels as a group, one is struck by the fact that,
with the gradual disappearance of the stalwarts of Edith
Wharton's own class and generation and with the de-
livery of the *coup de grâce* to their ideals, the sense of
responsibility, and, even more curiously, the adherence
to tradition which distinguished the best representatives
of the old New York society are passed on to some of the
unlikeliest members of the younger generation—to Susy
Lansing, to Nona Manford and Vance Weston, whose
parents are Midwesterners of simple origin, to Judith
Wheater (*The Children*), and to Annabel St. George
(*The Buccaneers*)—in short, to the types of young people with whom Edith Wharton surrounded herself during
her last two decades. Meanwhile, we have in Arthur
Wyant, the faded scion of a once prominent family, a
survival of the old ideals in a direct line. Since he is a
contemporary of Ralph Marvell, his fate may be construed as a revelation of what was in store for the latter
had he lived. That he is a failure his former wife, now
Mrs. Manford, ascribes to the Wyants' "old New York
blood—she spoke of them with mingled contempt and
pride, as if they were the last of the Capetians, exhausted
by a thousand years of sovereignty." His cynicism, his
isolation, his feeble and, in the end, disastrous protest
against the prevailing ethos may be taken, along with the
evidence of such stories as "After Holbein," to indicate
that the job of preserving the old values has been entrusted to the "sports" among the most recent generation,

those who have been born too late, who through some accident of conditioning have reacted against the standards and values of their own and their parents' generations. New blood is needed; the old families are no longer fit to carry out the trust.

Nona Manford is nineteen and extremely serious-minded for her years. Like Anne Clephane, she has "the memorial manner." In contrast to her frivolous mother, or to her father, preoccupied with his profession and his middle-aged infatuation for Lita Wyant, or even to the young people of her own crowd, she seems not merely old-fashioned but, to a pathetic degree, wise and disenchanted before her time. Her fate, as Edith Wharton sees it, is to expiate the sins of her elders. There are no terms more appropriate to describe her role, for the kind of justice which is at work in *Twilight Sleep* is as inexorable as that of the Old Testament.

There were moments when Nona felt oppressed by responsibilities and anxieties not of her age, apprehensions that she could not shake off and yet had not enough experience of life to know how to meet. . . . It was as if, in the beaming determination of the middle-aged, one and all of them, to ignore sorrow and evil, "think them away" as superannuated bogies, survivals of some obsolete European superstition unworthy of enlightened Americans . . . as if the demons the elder generation ignored, baulked of their natural prey, had cast their hungry shadow over the young. After all, somebody in every family had to remember now and then that such things as wickedness, suffering and death had not yet been banished from the earth; and with all those bright-complexioned white-haired mothers mailed in massage and optimism, and behaving as if they had never heard of anything but the Good and the Beautiful, perhaps their children had to serve as vicarious sacrifices.

When the bullet from the temporarily deranged Arthur Wyant's revolver, intended for Dexter Manford, accidentally wounds Nona, the sacrifice demanded of the "bewildered little Iphigenia" is complete; the demons are satisfied; and the adults, who have made a hash of their children's lives as well as their own, are left to their makeshift reconciliations. The pain that Pauline Manford has tried to avoid has been exacted with compound interest from her family.

In the closing pages of *The Gods Arrive* (1932), Edith Wharton evidently recognized the desirability of some final interpretation of Vance Weston's career, which she had traced through two volumes with no very consistent design. The last word belongs to Grandma Scrimser on her deathbed, and it provokes in Vance a belated self-recognition: " 'Maybe we haven't made enough of pain —been too afraid of it. Don't be afraid of it,' she whispered." The warning runs like a refrain through the later novels. This puritanical assertion of the inescapable fact of evil and suffering in the world must be construed as an antidote, and a deliberately strong one, to what she regarded as the moral laxity of the postwar era. It does not seem to me to compromise necessarily her attitude toward "the monstrousness of useless sacrifices" or the inflicting of "sterile pain."

There is an absolute continuity of emphasis from *Twilight Sleep* to *The Children.* Once again, the generation which reached middle age following the war is arraigned, the indictment is on the score of irresponsibility, and their guilt is objectified in the blighting of their children's lives. An early suggestion for the story may be found in *The Glimpses of the Moon,* where the five Fulmer children, in the absence of their parents, have improvised a kind of matriarchal society governed by the eldest girl Junie. There is nothing pathetic about the Fulmer children, however; their acquaintance with life is premature but without bitterness. A more general suggestion is embodied in Clarissa Vanderlyn in the same novel, the only child of mismated parents who are content to leave her in charge of a nurse in their Venetian *palazzo* while they pursue their separate extramarital conquests. Together with Paul Marvell of *The Custom of the Country*, whose loneliness and bewilderment provide the final commentary on his mother's career, the eleven-year-old Clarissa anticipates the Wheater children, that riotous and cosmopolitan brood whose collective martyrdom is one of the major issues of *The Children*.

The protagonist of *The Children*, however, is Martin Boyne, a bachelor in his middle forties, an engineer who has spent most of his adult life on engineering projects in remote countries. When the story opens he is in Algiers, en route by leisurely stages to Italy, where he is to meet an old flame, Rose Sellars. Having laid away a competence, he has begun to long for some deeper personal attachment and a more settled way of life, and to this end he has reached a tentative understanding, by correspondence, with Mrs. Sellars, whom he has not seen for five years. In Algiers a troop of six small children, in the charge of a young-looking mother, comes aboard his ship. He learns upon inquiry that the "mother" is Judith Wheater, eldest daughter of Mrs. Cliffe Wheater, whom Martin had courted briefly during his college days but who, when he left for parts unknown, had married a vigorous extrovert.

The extraordinary, miscellaneous tribe of young

Wheaters is the product of their parents' several marital ventures. Because she has had the responsibility of mothering the younger children, Judith Wheater at fifteen looks and acts older than her years. Her childhood, like that of Nona Manford and Clarissa Vanderlyn, has been robbed of illusions by a forced participation in the emotional difficulties of her elders. Her education has been neglected, so that she is semiliterate and, as events prove, morally and emotionally a child. Immediately below her in the nursery hierarchy are the twins, Terry and Blanca, the former a Jamesian child, thin, pale, and perpetually feverish, with an air of fatality enveloping him—"distinguished," as Martin Boyne decides, even at eleven—and the latter an attractive but detached, selfish, and hypocritical little girl. The three older children are the offspring of the Wheaters' original union. Since then, the parents have been divorced, married briefly to other partners, and then remarried. Later additions to the clan are: a girl, Zinnie, the red-haired, ungovernable, and precociously materialistic daughter of Cliffe Wheater and Zinnia Lacrosse, a movie star; "Bun" and "Beechy," the children of a philandering, impecunious Italian nobleman to whom Joyce Wheater had been married; and Chipstone, an eighteen-months-old boy, who is the first fruit of the Wheaters' remarriage. To a purposely exaggerated degree, the children are supposed to symbolize the currently lax notions of marriage and the responsibility imposed by a family. "Marriage in France," we are told in *French Ways and Their Meaning*, "is regarded as founded for the family and not for the husband and wife." Parenthood, and not the individual happiness of the partners, is its goal. But the Wheater children are a colorful and variegated testimonial to the different concept of marriage in postwar America. Their little community is precariously held together by Judith, who is determined, after repeated separations and the rootless, drifting hotel life they are compelled to lead have taken their psychological toll, that they will remain together forever.

Half against his inclination, Martin Boyne becomes a sort of godfather to the troop. When the party proceeds to Venice to meet the elder Wheaters, he is persuaded to urge on the parents the necessity of a tutor for Terry. Following the success of this assignment, and by now thoroughly charmed with the children, he becomes more and more devoted to their interests. While Rose Sellars awaits their rendezvous in the Dolomites, he lingers in Venice. Judith Wheater looks to him as intermediary and general paterfamilias, and, after years of loneliness, he is flattered to have found a role to play. Moreover, he is strangely attracted to the girl, whose combination of maturity and childishness he finds irresistible.

That is the situation. What grows out of it is Martin's inevitable misunderstanding with his fiancée, his growing involvement with the plight of the children, which fosters a series of crises, the breaking off of his engagement, and, finally, his pathetically circumspect proposal to Judith, whose feeling for him he has totally misconstrued. When she fails to understand and innocently laughs at the idea of marriage, he feels "like a man who has blundered along in the dark to the edge of a precipice." Disillusioned, feeling suddenly old, and after having been forced to stand by while Judith transferred her allegiance to a new savior, he sails for New York and another engineering job. Years later, in an epilogue reminiscent of that in *The Age of Innocence*, he returns to Europe,

learns that the children have been separated, catches a
glimpse of Judith through the window of a hotel ball-
room, but sails again without meeting her.

Martin Boyne's middle-aged passion for the girl Judith
(initially disguised, like that of Dexter Manford for his
stepson's wife, as paternal concern) is an unexpected re-
versal of what E. K. Brown has designated as one of the
most familiar situations in Edith Wharton's stories: the
love affair between an older woman who has retained
her youth, her charm, and her mental and emotional
resiliency, and a younger man.[2] The relationship appears
as early as "The Muse's Tragedy" in *The Greater Inclination*, but it is particularly a feature of the later novels.
Although the difference in years may vary, Mrs. Ralph
Talkett (*A Son at the Front*), Kate Clephane, Susy Lansing, and Halo Tarrant (*Hudson River Bracketed* and
The Gods Arrive) are all older than their lovers. On the
other hand, another, tonally related circumstance which
appears to hold great charm for Mrs. Wharton is present
again in *The Children:* the encounter of former lovers
after years of separation and the renewal—sometimes
only temporary—of the old enchantment. Sometimes the
reunion has an ironic significance, as it does in *The Custom of the Country* when Undine belatedly picks up
where she left off with Elmer Moffatt, but more generally it lends itself, as in "Autres Temps" and *The Reef*,
to the elegiac intent of Mrs. Wharton's later fiction.

Once we are aware of them, the echoes multiply.
Martin Boyne is the middle-aged bachelor who pops up
so conveniently in an emergency which is invariably
the same. His function, like that of Darrow, Strefford,
Newland Archer, John Durham in *Madame de Treymes*,
Franklin Ide, and Fred Landers, is to rescue the widow

or the misunderstood wife—to offer her the tenderness and security that she has been unable to find in her first marriage. In the meantime, while awaiting his cue, he has been accumulating the kind of worldly experience that will make him acceptable as a lover. Celibacy, for instance, has been no part of his regimen. What Edith Wharton says of Martin Boyne applies to his predecessors: "In the course of his life so much easy love had come his way, he had grown so weary of nights without a morrow, that he needed to feel there was one woman in the world whom he was half-afraid to make love to." Even "dear old Fred" Landers, the least worldly of Mrs. Wharton's bachelors, has acquired a certain authority since Kate Clephane last saw him: "Kate thought . . . that he mumbled less, spoke more 'straight from the shoulder,' than he used to." He has become "the four-square sort of man who met her on the pier and disentangled her luggage with so little fuss." As Mrs. Wharton grows older, her attractive bachelors mature at almost the same pace. Selden, Darrow, and Ralph Marvell are noticeably younger than Fred Landers and Martin Boyne. But then the women too are older. In such novels as *The Mother's Recompense, Twilight Sleep,* and *The Children,* the emotional problems of middle age, though by no means the center of interest, are markedly more prominent than in the stories Edith Wharton wrote before the war. The recurrence of these motifs and the suggestions that arise when we try to combine them should provide a fascinating problem for Mrs. Wharton's biographer. They may be simply the conventions she has found useful in expressing her permanent themes. On the other hand, they may have a deeper, more personal significance of the kind which she herself discovered in George Eliot's novels.

The conclusion of *The Children* reminds us that we have been rehearsing a familiar theme. The lonely figure of Martin Boyne at the rail of the ship which is carrying him away forever from the scene of his romantic debacle reillumines some earlier pictures: that of Ethan Frome bound to his exhausted acres and his demanding womenfolk, of Ann Eliza Bunner setting out hopelessly to look for a job, of Newland Archer seated on the bench opposite Ellen Olenska's Paris flat while his son pays the call he cannot bring himself to make, of Kate Clephane and Mrs. Lidcote returning to their exile abroad, and of Nona Manford lying in her hospital bed. By resorting to the same poignant effect, each questions the wisdom of altruism and self-sacrifice.

Whatever interest may attach to the novels following *The Age of Innocence* as extensions and developments of Mrs. Wharton's characteristic themes, they are fragmentary performances viewed alongside *The House of Mirth, The Reef,* or *The Custom of the Country.* The earlier novels not only have the advantage in scope and perception, but they encourage the impression of a clear, inwardly consistent, and developing pattern of attitudes. In each there is a recapitulation of previous themes and an introduction of new ones, so that we find an expanding significance in Mrs. Wharton's view of her world from *The Valley of Decision* through *The Custom of the Country.* This cannot be said of the novels written in the decade before 1929. Along with other novelists of her generation—Willa Cather, Ellen Glasgow, and Robert Herrick, for example—she is on the defensive.

After a preliminary retreat from the seeming chaos and vulgarity of the postwar world, a retreat signaled by *The Age of Innocence,* she takes her stand and tries, in the series of novels we have been considering, to cope with the bewildering cultural manifestations of the postwar period. For the most part, it is a case of rehashing the old attitudes and at the same time searching tentatively for a new point of view that will embrace both the old and new attitudes.

She is not prepared to make many concessions. What we notice particularly in the later novels is that the individual quest for freedom, pursued in the earlier novels within the limitations already described, is curtailed. With increasing severity the emphasis is on a strict sense of individual responsibility, regardless of the mitigating factors that may be involved. The clearest suggestion that carries over from *The Age of Innocence* through *Twilight Sleep* to *Hudson River Bracketed* and *The Gods Arrive* is that the pain of life must be accepted. Grandma Scrimser's valedictory to her grandson may be taken as Edith Wharton's first and last word to the generation which, as she saw it, tried to protect itself against the more painful invasions of reality by means of divorces, twilight sleeps, faddist religions, and the aimless pursuit of pleasure.

Chapter XI

THE NEW AGE OF INNOCENCE

Hudson River Bracketed, serialized in *The Delineator* when Edith Wharton was sixty-six, bears many signs of a valedictory performance. It was her longest novel since *The Valley of Decision.* In fact, her scheme was so ambitious that it had to be extended to a second volume, and, regarded as a single unit, *Hudson River Bracketed* and its sequel are her longest work of fiction. Even though it was in every way an anticlimax, *The Gods Arrive* was not an afterthought: it was promised by the tentative resolution of the first novel. Evidently at some time during the 'twenties it had occurred to Edith Wharton to write a major novel which would summarize her hard-won new position and at the same time try to bring the problems dealt with in her novels from the beginning into relationship with the special problems of the artist. The larger outlines of her plan, sufficiently distinct in *Hudson River Bracketed* but progressively blurred in *The Gods Arrive,* were drawn to include almost anything she might have to say about the relative claims on the artist of the real and the ideal, the present and the past. Taken together, the two novels proposed to carry Vance Weston, "born into a world in which everything had been, or was being, renovated," backwards in time and space, to make him reverse the odyssey of his ancestors by carrying him from Euphoria, Illinois, to the banks of the Hudson, and thence to Europe, so that he would be exposed to successively deeper influences from the past. The project was Balzacian in its scope. As if to stress its importance in her own view of her development, Edith Wharton included both novels in a curious list of her favorites headed by *The Custom of the Country, Summer,* and *The Children.*[1]

The early chapters of *Hudson River Bracketed* and some of the later chapters of *The Gods Arrive* mark Edith Wharton's one attempt to come to grips with the America west of the Hudson which, represented by Undine Spragg's home town, had appeared only in the remote background of *The Custom of the Country.* It is not surprising that her treatment of Midwestern small town life appears to have been modified by the influence of Sinclair Lewis and that she should have had to read *Main Street* and *Arrowsmith* before she could visualize Euphoria. She seems to have admired Lewis above any American novelist of the 'twenties, and she knew nothing about the Midwest. Moreover, Lewis had allied himself, however casually and with whatever failures of insight, with the tradition in which she worked—the novel of manners—so that they looked to the same kinds of evidence for their understanding of the human comedy.

The world into which Advance G. Weston (he is named after a real-estate development, as Undine Spragg is named after a hair curler invented by her father) is born is one of narrow religion, bad cooking, bastard architecture, dull amusements, and a pervasive "go-getting" spirit. Its sins, in religion and culture as well as

---

[1] For notes to chap. xi, see p. 258.

THE NEW AGE OF INNOCENCE ·

decor, are largely those of taste, as implied by the Weston
living room in Euphoria "with its large pink-mouthed
gramophone on a table with a crochet-lace cover, its gold-
and-gray wallpaper hung with the 'Mona Lisa' . . . ,
'The Light of the World' . . . , and the palm in a con-
gested pink china pot on a stained oak milking stool."
("I was always vaguely frightened by ugliness," Edith
Wharton wrote in *A Backward Glance*.) The gross libel
on Midwestern place names and manners proceeds from
the same bias. Henry James once complained that American place names "minister little to the poetry of associa-
tion," and his friend evidently thought so too. Vance
Weston's family moves from Pruneville, Nebraska, to
Hallelujah, Missouri, then to Advance and finally Euphoria, Illinois, where the grandparents occupy an eight-
room colonial cottage and the younger Westons a modern
suburban-style home. Vance, during his college days,
has edited a campus magazine called "Getting Ahead,"
invented a new religion, and read Bliss Carman, James
Whitcomb Riley, and the more tepid New England poets.
But his disillusionment with Euphoria begins only after
he has surprised his Grandpa Scrimser, "the best Fourth
of July orator anywhere in Drake County" and as lecherous an old man as any to be found in Balzac, in a
clandestine meeting with Floss Delaney, the Dulcinea
of Vance's youthful romantic dream.

When the illness consequent upon this discovery per-
suades Vance's parents to send him east, to Paul's Landing on the Hudson, to convalesce at the home of some
cousins, the stage is cleared for the first episode in his
love affair with the Past. Under the combined spell of
the Willows, an aristocratic old house, and the more
tangible presence of Halo Spear, who bears a remarkable

resemblance to the dead mistress of the house and carries the cultural tradition symbolized by the Willows into the living present, the incipient writer in Vance Weston begins to emerge. As a symbol, the Willows is invested with a personal significance for Edith Wharton which may be measured by her account of her grandparents' country place at Hell Gate in the first chapter of *A Backward Glance*. As Hudson River mansions go, the Willows is not old. Built in 1830, in the garish and irregular style known as Hudson River Bracketed, and now deserted, it has preserved its charm and its furnishings intact, down to the volume of Coleridge's poems open on the drawing-room table at the page where the last owner was reading when she died. In its silent rooms the nineteenth century has survived into the twentieth.

Nearby is Eaglewood, the home of Halo Spear's maternal ancestors. Built in 1680, it has managed, in spite of the family's dwindling fortune, to preserve its integrity even longer than the Willows. At this early stage in the story, Eaglewood represents a past too remote for Vance Weston to penetrate, but the question which gently intrudes itself—why didn't he choose it as a symbol of the Past in preference to the Willows?—leads us outside the novel for an answer. The past embodied in the Willows was the chrysalis of Edith Wharton's girlhood. The active life of the old house spanned the period during which her parents and their friends and those Nestors of their generation whose friendship meant so much to Edith Wharton—the Egerton Winthrops and Charles Eliot Nortons—were born, grew up, married and had families, and for a brief interval set the tone of the only society that Edith Wharton could ever bring herself to call "good"—the period commemorated in the early chapters of her memoirs, *The Age of Innocence* and the tales of old New York, and finally in *The Buccaneers*. The library at the Willows, described by Halo Spear as "a fairly good specimen of what used to be called a 'gentleman's library' in my grandfather's time," is the library of George Frederic Jones, affectionately remembered in *A Backward Glance;* the books which Vance discovers there, and which open up for him the rich treasure house of the past, are the books with which Edith Jones as a lonely child "in the kingdom of my father's library" fed an imagination preternaturally stimulated by years of travel abroad and cloistered in protest against the physical ugliness of old New York.

"This is the Past," Vance Weston, musing in the library at the Willows, decides, "if only I could get back into it. . . ." The remark follows on the heels of a significant crisis in his personal life. By now he realizes the full extent of his blunder in marrying his cousin, Laura Lou Tracy. Sickly, ignorant, and remorselessly dependent, she cannot begin to comprehend Vance's world, any more than Zeena Frome, whom she suggests, can begin to comprehend Ethan's. Her recent bout with pneumonia, contracted during a hike with Vance on which she has overexerted herself, has finally destroyed any pretext of good feeling between her husband and her mother. Not only has Vance fallen from grace at home, but his career has reached a dead end. His literary chores on "The New Hour," begun under such auspicious circumstances, have long since become intolerable. Under the renewed influence of the Willows, he begins a short novel, to be called *Instead*. Like Mrs. Wharton's first ambitious work of fiction, *The Valley of Decision,* it is to be a historical novel, a nostalgic evocation of the past as suggested by the history of Miss Elinor Lorburn, the last owner of the Willows. Before the book is well under way, Halo Tarrant (nee Spear) reappears. Her marriage, like his, has tied her to a narrow-souled, unsympathetic partner and has proved equally disastrous. Together they proceed with the novel, Halo supplying the details which Vance's background and experience have denied him.

"What interests me," remarks Vance, in explaining the early chapters to his collaborator, "would be to get back into the minds of the people who lived in these places— to try and see what we came out of. Till I do I'll never understand why we are what we are." His novel is to be a courageous gesture of defiance in the face of his contemporaries who, as we may gather from the essays in criticism of Mrs. Wharton's last two decades, have rejected the past and tried to stand alone, in an isolated and meaningless context. Vance is the spokesman for a rootless, traditionless generation of young Americans:

You see, from the first day I set foot in this house I got that sense of continuity that we folks have missed out of our lives—out where I live, anyway—and it gave me the idea of a different rhythm, a different time-beat: a movement without jerks and breaks, flowing down from ever so far off in the hills, bearing ships to the sea. . . .

Significantly, even his style manages to reflect the sense of continuity. As Lewis Tarrant expresses it, he has "had the nerve to go back to a quiet, almost old-fashioned style: no jerks, no paradoxes—not even afraid of lingering over his transitions." In all this, one readily detects the overtone of self-defense on Mrs. Wharton's part. The Vance Weston of *Hudson River Bracketed* is entrusted with some of her most cherished convictions about art, and the very significance of the trust lies in the fact that he comes to it wholly unprepared, that he is, on the contrary, conditioned by his background and experience to refuse it. He is the virgin soil in which Mrs. Wharton's ideas triumphantly survive transplanting. *Instead* is an immediate critical success and, although Vance's publishers cheat him, a mild financial one. Its readers, "unconsciously tired of incoherence and brutality," are charmed by its "difference."

Nevertheless, it is clear to Vance—and even clearer after a talk with his severest critic, the elderly George Frenside—that *Instead* had been a "side-show," an " 'emanation,' not a reality," and that "he had given very little of . . . his 'tissue' to its making." Suddenly—and here we begin to doubt the sureness of Mrs. Wharton's intentions—the Past appears to the novelist as no more than a convenient refuge from the reality which threatens him on every side: has ailing, slatternly wife, his shabby quarters, his debts, and his stifling employment at "The New Hour" office, to say nothing of his hopeless passion for Halo Tarrant. When on an earlier occasion, before leaving Euphoria, Vance had been forced to confront reality in the form of his betrayal by Grandpa Scrimser and Floss Delaney, he had seriously contemplated suicide. "He was like a captive walled into a dark airless cell, and the walls of that cell were Reality, were the life he would in future be doomed to. The impulse to end it all here and now possessed him." Out of the pain and disillusionment of the experience had emerged his first and most compelling story, "One Day." Now, in a similarly hopeless situation and motivated by despair, he determines to abandon New York and the fashionable literary and artistic circle in which he has cut so awkward a figure, rent a shack in the country, and set to work on a "big" novel. Once he has brought himself to accept reality, the combination of poverty, isolation, and the responsibility of caring for a sickly wife stimulate, rather than defeat, the recovery of his creative powers. The new novel is going ahead successfully when Laura Lou's health takes a critical turn for the worse and she succumbs from the long concealed ravages of tuberculosis. The following week, Halo Tarrant, ignorant of her death, seeks out Vance to tell him she is free of Lewis Tarrant and that they can resume the platonic relationship which, since the success of *Instead,* has hardly satisfied Vance. He informs her of his wife's death, and the novel ends on the presumption that they will come to a deeper understanding.

Interesting as *Hudson River Bracketed* is, for reasons which have very little to do with its intrinsic qualities, it is not a good novel. Its style, as we have more or less come to expect by now, is for the most part glossy, mechanical, never wholly bad, but characterized by a fatal ease and occasionally betraying the hectic flush of the slick-magazine style. Structurally, the novel is misleading; one has to grope, as in *The Reef* and *The Mother's Recompense,* for Mrs. Wharton's intention. The control which she was able to exert over the separate and combined elements of *The Age of Innocence* thanks to her perfect command of her central theme and its implications is missing in *Hudson River Bracketed;* there is no single view of the action that will satisfactorily explain all its parts. The initial supposition that Vance is divided and torn, as it were, between Euphoria and the Willows, between Floss Delaney and Halo Tarrant, between the

real and the ideal, is undermined by the late acknowledgment that the writing of *Instead* has been a side ex-
cursion, during which the real problem facing Vance has
been deferred. The reader has every right to feel let
down and bewildered. The recurrent emphasis on the
Willows as an imaginative symbol has led him to assume
for it a value that, for Vance unfortunately, it never quite
possesses; and it is an assumption that all of Mrs. Wharton's postwar novels have conditioned him to make. It
is not enough simply to be told—and by Vance in a
moment of self-recrimination—that "it's always the same
with you. . . . You see only one thing at a time, and get
into a frenzy about that, and nine times out of ten it's
not the real thing you're chasing after but only something
your brain has faked up." It will take *The Gods Arrive*
to convince the reader finally that Vance's love affair
with the Past has been only a flirtation.

A partial, though by no means sufficient, clue to
Vance's dilemma is revealed in one of his quiet talks
with his literary mentor Frenside, who observes that "it's
a bad time for a creator of any sort to be born, in this
after-war welter, with its new recipe for immortality
every morning." Taken in one light, Vance is the victim
of postwar confusion and the currently unstable values
in conduct as well as art, so that his dilemma is representative and, as such, its own excuse for being. He is
doomed as a writer never to find his subject, even in his
first, successful novel, and from beginning to end his
creative equilibrium is easily upset. All the more reason,
therefore, for the reader who has followed Mrs. Wharton's recent development to attach a special importance,
as a crystallizing influence, to Vance's excited discovery
of the Past.

Although the characterization of Vance Weston as an individual seems to await the final definition that a sequel might be expected to provide, it has some clarity as a type characterization, for it rests in part on certain traits popularly associated with the artist. Mrs. Wharton has caught the latter's consuming but necessary egoism and his inability to cope with the phenomenal world, but also his integrity. Vance is direct, frank, and impulsive. Because of social ignorance or his preoccupation with his work, he constantly blunders into uncomfortable situations. He is at home neither in Euphoria nor in the literary and social circles of New York, and because he can come to terms with neither world he will be victimized by both.

The treatment of two minor characters in the novel, Harrison Delaney and George Frenside (both to reappear in *The Gods Arrive,* the former no longer recognizable), suggests that Edith Wharton is still interested, if only incidentally, in the fate of the more die-hard members of her own generation and cultural tradition—those direct heirs of the Age of Innocence who have resisted change on every front. The question implied in their every appearance is, how do they stack up in comparison to their successors? Arthur Wyant, of *Twilight Sleep,* with his anachronistic notions of honor, his fastidiousness, and his pathetic dependence on the gossip columns and the bottle, perpetuates—and to a purposely exaggerated degree, in keeping with the tone of the novel—only the defects of the tradition. But in the portraits of those two distinguished failures in *Hudson River Bracketed* the opposite view is emphasized. The integrity of a George Frenside, "elderly, poor, and unsuccessful, and yet more masterful, more stimulating than anyone else she [Halo Tarrant] had known," is a constant reproach to the literary faddists who gather in Rebecca Stram's studio or in Jet Pulsifer's *salon*. And in such a community as Euphoria it is to Harrison Delaney's credit that at fifty he is regarded as a failure. Although he treasures "a dog-eared copy of Pope" and quotes Horace on public occasions, the real measure of his distinction, for those who recall Edith Wharton's remarks in *A Backward Glance* on the current debasement of the English language, is in his speech. The young Vance, we are told, "found a strange attraction in listening to Harrison Delaney's low, slightly drawling speech, and noticing the words he used—always good English words, rich and expressive, with hardly a concession to the local vernacular, or the passing epidemics of slang," and the echo of Delaney's conversation will be heard later in Vance's literary style. The repetition of emphasis in the two characterizations calls attention to a question which in the novels immediately preceding *Hudson River Bracketed* has been obscured by more insistent issues, but which seems to have been voiced tentatively in the persons of Fred Landers and Arthur Wyant; and that is: Is Edith Wharton putting a value on failure in a world she has come largely to despise?

In *The Gods Arrive,* the characterization of Vance Weston—never, in its predecessor, adequately defined—goes to pieces in Mrs. Wharton's hands. Although his salient traits are carried over from *Hudson River Bracketed* and he is recognizable by certain exterior signs as the same individual, Mrs. Wharton's attitude toward him has evidently undergone an extensive revision. These sudden and unexpected shifts of sympathy, noticeable as early as *The Fruit of the Tree* and *The Reef* in the treatment of Amherst and Sophy Viner, are particularly obvious in her last two novels and help to confirm the impression that her subject refused to declare itself in time to insure a unified treatment. It is interesting again to observe the way she handles the characters with whom initially she has no common grounds for sympathy, characters such as Laura Lou Tracy, Bunty Hayes, and Lewis Tarrant, whom her prejudices are apt to condemn without a fair hearing. It is only after she has maneuvered them into a situation in which they must inevitably enlist a certain sympathy (and not always even then, as Sophy Viner reminds us) that her humanity comes belatedly into play and she takes the trouble to try to understand the creatures she has had the temerity to bring to life. At such times, they will reveal untapped reserves of feeling and a delicacy wholly unsuspected, and their final gestures will be magnanimous enough to erase the former impression of their meanness. The coexistence in such characters of selfish and generous impulses is not surprising; there is nothing in the logic of human motives to deny the possibility. What is disconcerting is Mrs. Wharton's unstable partisan spirit and the consequently abrupt alterations of tone in the treatment of these characters. With Vance Weston the process is reversed. What, for instance, are we to make of the fact that in *The Gods Arrive* the Vance who in the earlier novel had been permitted to voice some of Mrs. Wharton's maturest reflections on art and life is at times clearly a poseur, whose conversation bristles with most of the cant phrases of his profession? Again, how are we supposed to arbitrate between the two opposing views represented in these novels, where at times Mrs. Wharton seems to be saying that the artist cannot be bound by ordinary rules or judged by ordinary standards, and at other times persists in holding him entirely accountable?

It is the second view—that of the artist as a responsible member of society—which, as we have come to expect, is vindicated in the end. In *Hudson River Bracketed* Vance Weston's integrity, the sense of responsibility which chained him to "The New Hour" desk, to Laura Lou, and to his ideal of craftsmanship, is at the very base of his character. His best work, the chapters of his never-to-be-finished novel *Magic*, is performed during Laura Lou's final illness, when his private suffering and disappointment have bound him most closely to the reality imposed by his sense of responsibility to another human being. And Grandma Scrimser's dying words—"Maybe we haven't made enough of pain"—clinch an argument that has been developing, rather too unobtrusively, throughout the novel. If it is impossible in the sequel to define Mrs. Wharton's attitude toward Vance Weston, it is because the characterization has been warped to the totally new demands made upon it by the story. Vance must be brought to his knees, and in preparation for this event he must be made to behave so irresponsibly that Mrs. Wharton cannot hide her aversion. Actually, it is only at the close of *The Gods Arrive,* in the hastily contrived and rather forced episodes preceding the final reconciliation of Vance and Halo, that the emphasis on the theme of individual responsibility gives a semblance of unity, largely retrospective, to Vance's story.

The final stage of Vance Weston's journey into the past is reached in *The Gods Arrive* when he and Halo, no longer welcome at home because of the scandal they have furnished, pause in Spain. The episode begins with the second chapter of the novel, where already Mrs. Wharton's radically altered view of the character is evident. The process of disintegration gets under way immediately. Vance is overwhelmed by the assault which Spain makes upon his senses, by the myriad new impressions which he cannot assimilate or organize into any coherent pattern. His creative faculties are paralyzed. He must have time, he tells Halo, to ponder and absorb. It occurs to him that he would have made a better painter than writer, a better sculptor than painter, but these notions are supplanted by the conviction that he was destined to be a poet—or, if not a poet, a student, a grammarian, "like the fellow in the Browning poem." The tangible result of the lovers' sojourn in Spain is a thin historical novel which marks a decided falling away from the standards set by *Instead*. There is in Vance's failure to cope with his European experience a curious echo of Henry James's advice to the author of *Madame de Treymes*, not to "go in too much for the French or the 'Franco-American' subject," [2] and of his famous earlier (1902) remark about the apprentice, that "she must be tethered in native pastures, even if it reduces her to a back-yard in New York." [3] The restriction might be applied more nearly to Vance, pathetically unequipped as he is to deal with Europe, whereas Edith Wharton was more at home abroad than in her own country and, so long as she was confined to the American scene, found it difficult after the war to enlarge the scope of her subject and her treatment of manners.

During the remainder of the novel Vance pursues one will-o'-the-wisp after another, in his art and in his private life. Earlier, in *Hudson River Bracketed*, he had tried his hand at a "big" novel of New York social and commercial life to be called *Loot*, then abandoned it in favor of *Magic*, which was destined to be abandoned in turn for his potboiling costume novel of Spain. Now, still vainly casting about for his subject and method, and at the moment following the lead of the Joyceans, he begins a novel called *Colossus*, which is fated to please none but the members of the coterie to which he is currently attached. Halo is no longer his muse; the flattery of readers he formerly despised and a certain self-distrust have combined to destroy her influence. She learns only by accident that he is working on the new novel. Increasingly an appendage in Vance's scheme and the victim of repeated humiliations at the hands of self-righteous compatriots, she withdraws voluntarily into the background, content like the heroine of a sentimental novel to suffer nobly and uncomplainingly (in no other novel is Mrs. Wharton so obviously critical of the double standard). Ultimately, Vance deserts her for Floss Delaney, the siren from Euphoria whose infidelity had first led him to bark his shins against reality. Floss has come into money and is dragging her father about Europe while she looks for the main chance.

By now the symbolic contrast in the roles of the three women among whom Vance divides his loyalty—Halo Tarrant, Laura Lou Tracy, and Floss—is almost too neatly evident. They are the necessary many selves of the novelist which are struggling for expression and dominance. Laura Lou, with her obvious prettiness, her fretfulness and inadequacy, and her devouring possessiveness, is the kind of partner Vance might have lived comfortably with had he never outgrown Euphoria and his job on "The Free Speaker." She represents an ideal of womanhood easily satisfied by the standards of Euphoria, and her influence on the budding novelist is therefore regressive. Halo, on the other hand, calls forth the most permanent and reliable, if not the deepest impulses of his creative imagination; and it is to her, ultimately, that he must return. The attraction exerted by Floss Delaney is wholly irrational—"subliminal," to use Mrs. Wharton's expression—and for that reason powerful and dangerous; it must be exorcised before Vance can return to Halo. The final disillusionment which is his portion from Floss is an extension of Mrs. Wharton's attitude toward the material of her art; it reflects her cautious avoidance of the abyss of the subconscious, into which she peered so tentatively in *Summer* and certain of her ghost stories. If Laura Lou projects the most banal and undeveloped aspect of his talent and personality, Halo represents the solid basis on which they must grow or perish. Vance's reconciliation with Halo is a return to safe ground, to the rational ideal which Edith Wharton once expressed in her little book on French manners and which governed her own approach to experience, both real and fictional. Her unwillingness to explore the primitive levels of consciousness is too easily justified by making Floss a disagreeable and wholly immoral character, in the image of Undine Spragg.

By the time *The Gods Arrive* reaches its embarrassingly theatrical close in the tableau dominated by Halo, big with child, gravely lifting up her arms "in the ancient attitude of prayer" and then, like Tellus the Earthmother, folding her truant husband in an embrace, we may not be entirely convinced that Vance's experiments are ended and that he will return to the mood of *Instead* for the remainder of his career. Both E. K. Brown and Elmer Davis have considered the possibility that Mrs.

Wharton had a sequel in mind, but this may be only another way of saying that a bad novel always seems to require a sequel. Edith Wharton's lack of control, and especially her failure to pursue her themes, means simply that the potentialities for change established in the initial situation of both novels are by no means exhausted, so that the action is not complete and whole. L'affaire Vance is not concluded—but can it ever be? Perhaps it is just as well that after wearily improvising her conclusion Mrs. Wharton let the whole matter drop.

In style, there is little to differentiate *The Gods Arrive* from its predecessor except perhaps an increasing lack of precision and a deafness to prose rhythms.

When Frenside had left her Halo tried to collect her thoughts; but his visit had shaken her too deeply. He had roused her out of her self-imposed torpour into a state of hyper-acute sensibility, and detaching her from the plight in which she was entangled had compelled her to view it objectively.

This is tired writing. It is careless and clogged, much too generalized, and ridden with clichés. Granted that it is an extreme illustration of Mrs. Wharton's later defects, it is still surprising that the careful stylist of *Ethan Frome* and *The House of Mirth,* the advocate of purer English speech, would allow such a passage to escape the painstaking process of revision to which she had submitted her earlier manuscripts. "What has become in America," she once asked, "of the copse, the spinney, the hedgerow, the dale, the vale, the weald? We have reduced all timber to 'woods.' " [4] It is her own most damaging commentary on her later style.

For the aid and comfort of those of her contemporaries

who resented the bewildering variety of experiments which characterized the arts in the 'twenties, Edith Wharton launched, in *The Gods Arrive,* an undiscriminating and surprisingly tasteless attack on every current tendency in art. As in three of her four preceding novels, she found that she could distill her aversions in a description of what she took to be a typical Bohemian party.

The party consisted of Lorry's trump cards—the new composer, Andros Nevsky, who, as soon as he could be persuaded to buckle down to writing the music of "Factories," was to reduce Stravinsky and "The Six" to back numbers; the poet, Yves Tourment, who, after an adolescence of over twenty years, still hung on the verge of success; Sady Lenz, the Berlin ballerina, who was to create the chief part in Lorry's spectacle; Hedstrom, the new Norse novelist, and Brank Heff, the coming American sculptor, whom the knowing were selling their Mestrovics to collect. . . .

The Bohemian party denies every premise of the *salon,* and therefore it becomes as useful a focus for her prejudices in the later novels (including *The Mother's Recompense* and *Twilight Sleep*) as the *salon* was for her beliefs in the earlier. Organized in defiance of reverence, continuity, taste, and intellectual honesty, it provides her with a symbol of social and cultural degeneracy. At the sacrifice of her usual sense of decorum, Edith Wharton amuses herself with the Lilliputian concerns of her enemies. In the inhuman fashion of a Smollett, she can even be very funny at the game:

Down the table, Nevsky, in fluent Russian French, was expounding to Jane Meggs his theory of the effect of the new music on glandular secretions in both sexes, and Brank Heff, the American sculptor, stimulated by numerous preliminary cocktails, broke his usual heavy silence to discuss with Fraulein Sady Lenz her merits as a possible subject for his chisel. "What I want is a woman with big biceps and limp breasts. I guess you'd do first rate. . . . How about your calves, though? They as ugly as your arms? I guess you haven't danced enough yet to develop the particular deformity I'm after. . . ."

Percy Lubbock once called attention to the "unduly light" touch of some of Edith Wharton's early short stories and attributed it in part to her use of irony and her consequent horror of overemphasis—of "blackening the telling line or of carrying the expressive gesture too far."[5] No such scruple governs the style of her later novels. The satire is strained and frequently meretricious. Her voice is pitched too high; it betrays what she once would have regarded as an unladylike irritability. And too often, as in *The Gods Arrive,* her protest is aimed at strawmen of her own manufacture.

This being so, what is one to say when confronted, a year after Mrs. Wharton's death, by *The Buccaneers* (1938), a novel which, had she finished it, would probably have taken its place among her half-dozen best and which even as it stands indicates that with a congenial subject she could subdue her irritability and regain control of her style? According to her literary executor, Gaillard Lapsley, who rescued the novel from her manuscripts and had it published with the addition of a penetrating critical analysis of his own, *The Buccaneers* was "the centre of her creative interest and activity" during the last four or five years of her life. Her productivity during these last years was not much greater than during the First World War. After 1929, when her health broke finally, she was alternately driven to her desk by nagging financial worries and kept away from it by illness and advancing age. Her life at this time was threatened by loneliness, especially after the deaths of her servant-companions.

There is nevertheless a kind of serenity in the pages of both *The Buccaneers* and *A Backward Glance* which such facts make it difficult to explain. Whether, as has been frequently suggested, she was reaching out at this time for the consoling certainties of religion or whether she had taken refuge in the stoicism one would have expected of her, is not clear. There are, in *The Buccaneers*, flashes of her old malice, particularly in the portrait of Lady Churt and the descriptions of Saratoga society, but the net effect is a far cry from the strenuous brilliance of her earliest fiction. There is even, here and there, a note of conciliation which helps to counteract the occasional asperities of *A Backward Glance*. Edith Wharton is frankly and in a thoroughly Jamesian sense delighted with her title-hunting American girls. As daughters of the Wall Street parvenus with whom she had never made her peace, they would hardly have appeared in the earlier novels, but if they had, it is unlikely that they would have been endowed with the charms of the St. George and Elmsworth girls. On the other hand, the sole representative in *The Buccaneers* of Edith Wharton's own New York is Mrs. Parmore, and she does not appear to advantage. Viewed through Laura Testvalley's Old World perspective, she is herself a parvenu.

. . . Mrs. Parmore told Miss Testvalley, when the latter called to pay her respects to her former employer, that she for her part hoped her daughters would never consent to an engagement of less than two years. "But I suppose, dear

Miss Testvalley, that among the people you're with now
[the St. Georges] there are no social traditions."

"None except those they are making for themselves," Miss
Testvalley was tempted to rejoin. . . .

Percy Lubbock has written at length of the friendships
with young people which helped to lighten Edith Wharton's declining years. "Indeed there was something new
in her expression . . . as she glanced up to welcome a
new generation, glanced up and caught its eye." That
"something new" made itself felt in *The Buccaneers* in
the partisan feeling with which she embraced the daughters of her old enemies and gave them a Laura Testvalley to befriend their cause.

The period of *The Buccaneers*, like that of *The Age of
Innocence*, is the 'seventies. It is the decade over which
Edith Wharton's memory lingers affectionately in these
later years, but its importance to the novel is that it
witnessed the first organized title-hunting invasion of the
British Isles by the American middle class. "In 1876,"
reports Dixon Wecter, "the eighth Duke of Manchester
married Consuelo Yznaga, a Cuban heiress much in New
York society. . . ." [6] The foray described in *The Buccaneers* is led by Conchita Closson, the Brazilian stepdaughter of a Wall Street entrepreneur, whose marriage
to Lord Richard Marable encourages her friends, the St.
George and Elmsworth girls, to train their sights on the
same objective. Consequently, the action of the novel,
after getting under way at Saratoga—James's "dense,
democratic, vulgar Saratoga" of 1870—and tarrying
briefly in New York, shifts to England for its important
setting. As early as 1906, after reading *Madame de
Treymes*, James had written Edith Wharton from his

adopted country: "The real field of your extension is *here*—it has far more fusability with *our* native and primary material." [7] When, after a quarter of a century, she finally followed his advice, it proved to be sound. She was as much at home in the great English country houses as she had been in the *salons* of the Faubourg St. Germain, and she found that with very little difficulty she could transpose her characteristic later themes.

Nan St. George, who in the novel as it stands is the center of interest (Mr. Lapsley foresees Laura Testvalley as threatening to elbow her aside in the finished version), will remind most readers of Nona Manford in *Twilight Sleep* and, somewhat less directly, of Anne Clephane and Vance Weston. It already has been suggested that there is a strong community of physical types among Mrs. Wharton's characters. In contrast to her dazzling older sisters (or to Bessy Westmore and Undine Spragg), Nan St. George has the plainness of feature and lack of "style" which Mrs. Wharton invariably associates with character. More important, she has the untrained sense of the past which appears here and there, like some miraculous growth, among the younger generation as it is represented in the postwar novels. "To Annabel, the Cornish castle [Tintagel] spoke with that rich low murmur of the past. . . ." In spite of the unhappy experience of her marriage to the Duke of Tintagel, she is brought to acknowledge the uses of tradition: "A year ago Annabel would have laughed at these rules and observances: now, though they chafed her no less, she was beginning to see the use of having one's whims and one's rages submitted to some kind of control." On the other hand, this reverence forms no part of her husband's disposition: "He saw the new Tintagel only as a costly folly of his father's, which family pride obliged him to keep up with fitting state. . . ." The Duke is oppressed by the past and the weight of obligations it has settled on him; but for his wife, fresh young democrat though she is, it provides the means of growth lacking in the society she has known.

It was not the atmosphere of London but of England which had gradually filled her veins and penetrated to her heart. She thought of the thinness of the mental and moral air in her own home; the noisy quarrels about nothing, the paltry preoccupations, her mother's feverish interest in the fashions and follies of a society which had always ignored her. At least life in England had a background, layers and layers of rich deep background, of history, poetry, old traditional observances, beautiful houses, beautiful landscapes, beautiful ancient buildings, palaces, churches, cathedrals.

Here is the central irony we have encountered before. Anne Clephane preserves the "memorial manner" in the face of her elders' "new tolerances and indifferences and accommodations." Nona Manford, the daughter of Middle Western parents, has the old-fashioned sense of rectitude which Edith Wharton has identified with the New York of her parents' generation. And Vance Weston brings from Euphoria a latent reverence for the past which few of his contemporaries can appreciate. Mrs. Wharton had a desperate faith in the generations coming to maturity for which it is difficult to find an adequate basis in reality, especially in the idol-breaking years following the First World War. It was a forced kind of consolation, although possible perhaps to one who lived abroad and saw only that minority of her younger compatriots who were drawn to Europe by its history and monuments and not simply by the devaluation of the franc. To the audience of the 'twenties and 'thirties, however, she seemed merely to be whistling in the dark.

By this time, none of Mrs. Wharton's readers should be surprised to remark that the emotional alignments of the characters in her later novels depend, in a curiously exclusive sense, on what might be called their cultural alignments—their devotion to or rejection of the past. Now, this is a rather unsubstantial basis for the conflict, and the novelist runs the risk of making the moral, as well as emotional, springs of her action too simple—or, to use the term she applied to the same element in Dickens and Thackeray, too "infantile." [8] To Nan St. George, the most attractive fact about Guy Thwarte is his deep affection for Honourslove, the family seat in Gloucestershire: "Tradition, as embodied in the ancient walls and the ancient trees of Honourslove, seemed to him as priceless a quality as it did to Sir Helmsley; and indeed he sometimes said to himself that if ever he succeeded to the baronetcy he would be a safer and more vigilant guardian than his father, who loved the place and yet had so often betrayed it." Guy Thwarte is related, obviously, to that generation of Americans described in the later novels which is struggling to conserve what is left after their parents' wastefulness and irresponsibility have run their course. This conservatism is the immediate and, so far as we know, the whole basis of the sympathy between Guy and Nan. It is tempered, however, by Edith Wharton's awareness (which never deserted her) of what is useless and degrading in the past. The dull, intransigent Duke of Tintagel is bored by what is worth preserving from his heritage but clings to his feudal notions of what he owes his tenants, and his first serious quarrel with Nan stems from her enlightened effort to better the latter's condition. If Edith Wharton had been half as alive to the encouraging signs in the present as she was to the wrongs of the past, the schizophrenic tendencies in her later fiction might have been averted.

Only tentative judgments can be passed on *The Buccaneers* because it is impossible to know how successfully Mrs. Wharton would have met the problems still unsolved in the published version. The novel as we have it is marred by certain failures of continuity and emphasis and by a lack of proportion which the author was undoubtedly aware of, but it can be recommended on the strength of several superbly finished scenes, among which Mr. Lapsley has chosen for analysis three—Laura Testvalley's arrival at Saratoga, Lady Churt's unexpected appearance at Runnymede cottage, and the Christmas ball at Longlands—because they help bring into relief the main design of the novel. There is, in fact, only one reason to regret Mr. Lapsley's decision to publish *The Buccaneers,* and that is its revelation that, in the years following 1920, Edith Wharton's powers had not deteriorated so much as they had been abused. Prior to *The Buccaneers,* the evidence of nearly twenty years had suggested incontrovertibly that she had lost her feeling for the right subject, the right tone, and even more surprising, for the subtleties and resources of the English language. As one of the spiritually dispossessed, she could only follow the bent of her protest; but it now seems particularly unfortunate that she chose the forum of the women's magazines. Their conservatism must have agreed with her, but the formula to which they reduced human life and human behavior encouraged certain weaknesses in her writing that she had once managed to control. It is possible that *The Buccaneers* was written for the same audience (Mrs. Wharton's most marketable asset, her familiarity with the great world, was, after all, still very much in evidence), but if so, it avoided the usual damaging concessions.

Chapter XII

A QUESTION OF LIMITS

Percy Lubbock, in his *Portrait,* has given us a final glimpse of Edith Wharton bringing up the rear of the main procession of American novelists, a procession led off by Hawthorne and featuring James and Howells, but strangely devoid of a rank and file and closed evidently to such writers as Twain and Melville. Included are the novelists whose affiliation with Europe was a condition of their art and who "had no thought of a declaration of independence," to say nothing of a "Boston tea-party" like that staged by the young writers of the 'twenties. Edmund Wilson has already criticized this procession on the grounds of its exclusiveness and has pointed out that Mrs. Wharton was as much a forerunner of twentieth-century realism as she was a follower of James. More-over, he adds, it is quite wrong to suppose that the postwar novelists simply cast overboard the imported wares of Europe.[1]

I would like to raise another and perhaps stronger ob-jection to Mr. Lubbock's view of Edith Wharton's place in the history of American fiction. She is, I have already suggested, a markedly solitary figure: the difference be-tween her and every major American novelist of the

[1] For notes to chap. xii, see p. 258.

nineteenth century except James seems to me more important than the fact of their common debt to Europe. Latent in everything she wrote was an attitude her predecessors would in varying degrees have found repugnant, and which, with due respect for the pitfalls in the term, I can only describe as classical. Although she never stated her conviction in so many words, it is inescapable. To read her is to be made constantly aware of her distrust of human nature and her denial of the perfectibility of man and the doctrine of inevitable progress, an attitude that makes itself felt in her insistence on order, form, standards, disciplines—all the prescribed means of curbing romantic individualism. From *The Valley of Decision,* with its disillusioned view of the possibilities of reform, to *Twilight Sleep* and *The Gods Arrive,* with their emphasis on the discipline of pain, she was at war with romantic optimism. What aid and comfort she derived from the unpopular dogmas of Irving Babbitt, I do not know, but she read with approval those austere little volumes by her friend and editor W. C. Brownell, *Criticism* (1914) and *Standards* (1917), which were infused with a classicism drawn mainly from Arnold.

From one point of view, her whole program, in her life as well as in her art, was the subjection of thought and feeling to some kind of formal control. An understanding of the necessity of form she regarded as the mark of the professional in all the arts, including that of daily living. Whether she is speaking of religion, ethics, conduct, manners, language, the physical scene, or the art of fiction, her criterion is the same. Take, for example, the following statements chosen at random from her nonfiction works:

On *religion:* In a passage describing the Episcopalianism of old New York, she speaks of her "reverence for an ordered ritual in which the officiant's personality is strictly subordinated to the rite he performs" (*A Backward Glance,* p. 10).

On *language:* In her desire to stabilize the language, she was as zealous and mistaken as any eighteenth-century lexicographer. Left to itself, she insisted, language "deteriorates into a muddle of unstable dialects. . . . The lover of English need only note what that rich language has shrunk to on the lips, and in the literature, of the heterogeneous hundred millions of American citizens who, without uniformity of tradition or recognized guidance, are being suffered to work their many wills upon it" (*French Ways and Their Meaning,* p. 50). Her solution should surprise no one: "a reverence for the English language as spoken according to the best usage. Usage, in my childhood, was as authoritative an element in speaking English as tradition was in social conduct" (*A Backward Glance,* p. 48).

On the *physical scene:* En route to the front during the First World War, she was again impressed by "the sober disciplined landscape which the traveller's memory is apt to evoke as distinctively French" (*Fighting France,* p. 3), and her lack of interest in the uncultivated scenery of the Alps has already been noted. (One thinks, in this connection, of Henry James, standing at the brink of Niagara and remarking unromantically that "the perfect taste of it is the great characteristic.")

On *manners:* Observing the manners of the French peasantry and the petty bourgeoisie in the villages, she emphasizes "the admirable *fitting into the pattern,* which seems almost as if it were a moral outcome of the universal French sense of form . . ." (*A Motor-Flight through France*, p. 29).

On *conduct:* The French "have another safeguard against excess in their almost Chinese reverence for the ritual of manners" (*French Ways and Their Meaning*, p. 137).

If we grant that France has been the foremost guardian of the classic spirit in modern times, it seems a matter of course that Edith Wharton's attachment to the language, literature, and manners of that country should have been so instinctive and profound, and that both Henry James and Charles du Bos should have found in *The Reef* the special quality of that arch-classicist Racine.

Objecting to the romantic stress on man's infinite potentialities, T. E. Hulme remarked that the classical attitude is "faithful to the conception of a limit." In Edith Wharton that limit is everywhere carefully designated. In her appraisal of human nature it is equated with the idea of Original Sin; in her appraisal of society, with tradition and convention; in her appraisal of art, with taste—"the atmosphere in which art lives, and outside of which it cannot live." When it was disregarded, as it seemed to her to be in the 'twenties, the full depth of her conservatism was revealed in her attacks on the false freedom and romantic self-assurance of a Vance Weston or a Pauline Manford, the latter representing "all those bright-complexioned white-haired mothers mailed in massage and optimism, and behaving as if they had never heard of anything but the Good and the Beautiful. . . ." If, in the heat of battle, her own taste wavered and she was carried by her scorn beyond the self-prescribed limit, she probably was not conscious of the fact.

But this is only half the story. One misses in Edith Wharton the serenity of the classical mood. Whatever vitality and in part whatever weaknesses her fiction may possess are inseparable from her doubts about her own thesis. She is constantly testing her limits, seeking to extend them here and there, discovering that they have more resiliency than she expected, but always finding an ultimate sanction for them at the point where they were originally fixed. It seems undeniable that the stresses in her private life were reproduced in her fiction. The peculiar form of tension in her stories can be traced to her effort to mediate between desire and circumstance, between individual freedom and responsibility. I would hesitate to label her deepest impulse romantic, but it is true that one may find in her the same interest that has been found in those two French masters of her art, Flaubert and Balzac, in whom the romantic imagination found itself harnessed to a view of life ostensibly realistic. The conflict between Flaubert's nostalgic longing for the ideal and his clinical respect for the actual is not so apparent in his art as the conflict between Balzac's professed morality and his individualism, but the testimony of Flaubert's letters is eloquent, for as he nears the end of *Madame Bovary*, the self-identification with his wretched heroine becomes intolerable: ". . . I was so carried away that I groaned aloud, feeling in the depths of my being all that my little woman was then going through. I was afraid I should have a nervous crisis myself." [2] I doubt whether Edith Wharton ever got this close to her characters, but I am persuaded that she took a deeply personal interest in the fortunes of such characters as Ethan Frome, Justine Brent, Anna Leath, and Newland Archer, the rebels and would-be rebels whose predicaments in some way reflected her own. Particularly striking in this context are her remarks on George Eliot. On one level, she was attracted to that novelist by her intellectual and moral vigor, and, more interestingly for the purpose of the immediate argument, by her conservatism: "A deep reverence for family ties, for the sanctities of tradition, the claims of slowly acquired convictions and slowly formed precedents, is revealed in every page of her books." [3] But, as I have tried to indicate in chapter vi, the real source of George Eliot's fascination lay elsewhere, in the relation of her novels to the central problem posed by her experience:

She may have been satisfied that her own course was defensible; but, to all appearances, it was an open contradiction of her teachings, and the seeming inconsistency must have tortured her as social disapproval would have tortured an inferior nature. . . . It is, perhaps, not a paradox to say that if George Eliot had been what the parish calls "respectable," her books would have been a less continuous hymn to respectability. [4]

This was no casual observation. Thirty-four years later, shortly before her death, Edith Wharton repeated it to a newspaper interviewer: "If [George Eliot] hadn't gone to live with George Henry Lewes, and felt obliged in consequence to defend conventional morality, she might have been one of the greatest of English novelists." [5]

In the end, it was the classical—or, if you will, the Christian—view of human nature that triumphed. Edith Wharton never relinquished her belief that the individual who disregards the experience of the ages as it has expressed itself in the form of traditions, standards, institutions, has no surer guides to follow, and can only err.

That the experience of the race changes and must embody itself in new forms, she was certainly aware; and we may never know what it cost her to defer to forms that had lost their meaning. That cost seems to have diminished, however, as the years went by. At the beginning, conventions were simply a means to an end, which was some kind of compromise with one's environment; later, they tended to become an end in themselves. Faced, after the war, with the old question of survival repeated in more decisive terms, Edith Wharton clung to beliefs passed on to her in a form only slightly modified since the Enlightenment. But, as *The Buccaneers* shows, we can discount somewhat the fervor of her later conservatism. Fortunately, she never wholly lost the skepticism with which she had originally taken stock of her inheritance.

Notes

(In an effort to hold the notes to a minimum I have adopted the following device: all direct quotations from Mrs. Wharton which are not specifically identified are from her autobiography A Backward Glance; *similarly, all direct quotations from Percy Lubbock not specifically identified are from his* Portrait of Edith Wharton.)

CHAPTER I

[1] "Innocents Abroad," *Partisan Review,* XVIII (Jan., 1950), 30.
[2] Letter to the author, May 3, 1950.

CHAPTER II

[1] See my article, " 'Pussie' Jones's Verses: A Bibliographical Note on Edith Wharton," *American Literature,* XXIII (Jan., 1952), 494–497.
[2] Lubbock, *Portrait,* p. 19. The writer is Daniel Berkeley Updike, founder of the Merrymount Press, which printed several of Mrs. Wharton's early volumes for Scribner's.
[3] The account which follows is based on Mrs. Wharton's letters to her editors at Scribner's, Burlingame and W. C. Brownell. Burlingame was editor of *Scribner's Magazine,* which published Mrs. Wharton's earliest stories. Brownell supervised the publication of her first book, *The Decoration of Houses,* in 1897.
[4] "Justice to Edith Wharton," in *The Wound and the Bow* (Boston: Houghton Mifflin, 1941), p. 196.
[5] Letter to Edward Burlingame, July 10, 1898. "I may not write any better," she adds, "but at least I hope that I write in a lower key. . . ."
[6] *Sketch for a Self-Portrait* (New York: Pantheon, 1949), p. 125.
[7] "Souvenirs du Bourget d'Outremer," *Revue Hebdomadaire,* XLV (June 21, 1936), 276.
[8] *The Notebooks of Henry James* (New York: Oxford, 1947), p. 24.
[9] *Yale Review,* n.s. XVI (July, 1927), 651.
[10] Letter to Burlingame, November 25, 1893. "I have several more stories which you have not seen, and also the longer one called 'Bunner Sisters' which you may remember my sending you a year or two ago. You then pronounced it too long for one number of the magazine and unsuited to serial publication."
[11] Letter to W. C. Brownell, September 28, 1899.
[12] *Edith Wharton: Étude Critique* (Paris: E. Droz, 1935), p. 1.
[13] *Ibid.,* p. 7. The letter is cited in part by Brown.

[14] "The Novels of Edith Wharton," *Quarterly Review*, CCXXIV (Jan., 1915), 184.

[15] Letter dated June 25, 1904.

[16] "Henry James in His Letters," *Quarterly Review*, CCXXXIV (July, 1920), 197.

[17] "The Art of Fiction," *in* Lyon N. Richardson, ed., *Henry James: Representative Selections* (New York: American Book Co., 1941), p. 96.

[18] Preface to *The Portrait of a Lady, in* Richard P. Blackmur, ed., *The Art of the Novel* (New York: Scribner's, 1934), p. 45.

[19] The quotation is taken from an undated, fragmentary typescript titled "Fiction and Criticism" (p. 6) in the Yale Library collection of Edith Wharton papers.

[20] *Ibid.*, p. 2.

[21] "Marcel Proust," in *The Writing of Fiction* (New York: Scribner's, 1925), pp. 151–178. The essay originally appeared in *The Yale Review*, n.s. XIV (Jan., 1925), 209–222.

[22] Review of Leslie Stephen's *George Eliot*, *Bookman*, XV (May, 1902), 250.

CHAPTER III

[1] The information for this paragraph, as well as the partial list of sources in the following paragraph, has been drawn from Edith Wharton's manuscript notes for *The Valley of Decision*, which are part of the Yale collection.

[2] In a letter to W. C. Brownell, February 14, 1902, Mrs. Wharton summarized her approach: "The Valley . . . is an attempt to picture Italy at the time of the breaking-up of the small principalities at the end of the 18th century, when all the old forms and traditions of court life were still preserved, but the immense intellectual and moral movement of the new regime was at work beneath the surface of things. This work, in Italy, was intellectual rather than political, and found little active expression, owing to the heterogeneous character of the Italian states and the impossibility of any concerted political movement. I have tried to reflect the traditional influences and customs of the day, together with the new ideas, in the mind of a cadet of one of the reigning houses, who is suddenly called to succeed to the dukedom of Pianura, and tries to apply the theories of the French encyclopedists to his small principality. Incidentally, I have given sketches of Venetian life, and glimpses of Sir William Hamilton's circle at Naples, and of the clerical milieu at Rome, where the suppression of the Society of Jesus, and the mysterious death of Ganganelli, had produced a violent reaction toward formalism and superstition. The close of the story pictures the falling to pieces of the whole business at the approach of Napoleon."

[3] George Eliot to Frederic Harrison, *in* J. W. Cross, ed. *George Eliot's Life as Related in her Letters and Journals* (London, 1885), II, 319, quoted in Robert Morss Lovett, *Edith Wharton* (New York: McBride, 1925), p. 53.

[4] Untitled fragment, consisting of three pages in longhand, among Mrs. Wharton's papers in the Yale collection.

[5] *Bookman*, XXII (Sept., 1905), 66.

[6] *Ibid.*, p. 65.

[7] "The Criticism of Fiction," *Times* Literary Supplement, May 14, 1914, p. 230.

CHAPTER IV

[1] *The American Scene,* ed. with introduction by W. H. Auden (New York: Scribner's, 1946), p. 485.
[2] Letter to W. C. Brownell, Aug. 5, 1905 (before publication, Brownell evidently had praised the novel highly): "I was pleased with bits, myself; but as I go over the proofs the whole thing strikes me as so loosely built, with so many dangling threads, and cul-de-sacs, and long dusty stretches, that I had reached the point of wondering how I had ever dared to try my hand at a long thing— So your seeing a certain amount of architecture in it rejoiced me above everything."
[3] *Notes on Novelists, with Some Other Notes* (New York: Scribner's, 1914), p. 155. The society of Balzac's day had, for James, "the inestimable benefit of the accumulated, of strong marks and fine shades, contrasts and complications" (p. 136).
[4] *Forms of Modern Fiction,* ed. by William Van O'Connor (Minneapolis: University of Minnesota Press, 1948), p. 150.
[5] "The Great American Novel," p. 652.
[6] "Art and Fortune," *Partisan Review,* XV (Dec., 1948), 1277.
[7] *The Letters of Henry James,* ed. by Percy Lubbock (New York: Scribner's, 1920), I, 72. The remark is quoted by Mrs. Wharton in her article "Henry James in His Letters," p. 198.
[8] "The Great American Novel," p. 652.
[9] *Ibid.,* p. 651.
[10] *The American Scene,* p. 162.
[11] *Autumn in the Valley* (Boston: Little, Brown, 1936), p. 111.
[12] *French Ways and Their Meaning* (New York: Appleton, 1919), p. 137.
[13] *The American Scene,* p. 197.

CHAPTER V

[1] *The American Scene,* p. 164.
[2] Charles K. Trueblood, "Edith Wharton," *Dial,* LXVIII (Jan., 1920), 80.

CHAPTER VI

[1] Letter to Burlingame, May 15, 1907. Mrs. Wharton had written "ply-room" instead of "fly-room," "superintendent" instead of "manager," and had confused a "loom" with a "card." Her correspondent pointed out further that Dillon's accident (chapter i) could not have happened in a loom, that there were no "loom-rooms" in a mill, only "weave-rooms," and that a "carder" was a man, not a machine.
[2] "Souvenirs du Bourget d'Outremer," p. 284.
[3] The phrase is taken from the unpublished typescript fragment of a novel titled *Disintegration* (p. 23), in the Yale collection.
[4] *The Writing of Fiction,* p. 164.
[5] Review of Leslie Stephen's *George Eliot, Bookman,* XV (May, 1902), 250.
[6] "Characters and Character," *American Review,* VI (Jan., 1936), 271–288.

CHAPTER VII

[1] Only the first, long part of the framework narrative, concluding with "It was that night that I found the clue to Ethan Frome, and began to put together this vision of his story," is preserved among the Yale manuscripts. A few of the improvements:

Manuscript version	Printed version
". . . it was the powerful negligent way in which he carried his inches . . ."	". . . it was the careless powerful look he had . . ."
"The 'smash-up' . . . had so shortened and distorted the whole left side of his body from shoulder to ankle that his powers of locomotion were strained by the brief hobble between his buggy and the post-office window.	"The 'smash-up' . . . had so shortened and warped his right side that it cost him a visible effort to take the few steps from his buggy to the post-office window.
". . . I involuntarily exclaimed . . ."	". . . I exclaimed . . ."
"One would have supposed that such an atmosphere must quicken the emotional as well as the physical circulation . . ."	"One would have supposed that such an atmosphere must quicken the emotions as well as the blood . . ."
"When I had been there a little longer, and had learned that this glittering phase of crystal cold was only the prelude to a long period of biting sunless cold . . ."	"When I had been there a little longer, and had seen this phase of crystal clearness followed by long stretches of sunless cold . . ."
"Then Harmon Gow suggested that Ethan Frome's bay was still valid and that his owner might be willing to come to my rescue."	"Then Harmon Gow suggested that Ethan Frome's bay was still on his legs and that his owner might be glad to drive me over."
"Frome was so devoid of vanity and self-assertion . . ."	"Frome was so simple and straightforward . . ."
"The revelation of tastes and aptitudes so unexpected . . ."	"Such tastes and acquirements . . ."

Another interesting fact is that in the early version the fictional narrator persists in addressing Ethan as "my dear man" and "my dear fellow." This patronizing touch was wisely eliminated from the final version.

[2] "The Novels of Edith Wharton," p. 195.

[3] It has recently been printed. See W. D. MacCallan, "The French Draft

of Ethan Frome," *Yale University Library Gazette*, XXVII (July, 1952), 38–47.
⁴ *The Writing of Fiction*, p. 174.
⁵ *The Letters of Henry James*, II, 283.
⁶ Unpublished fragment, "Fiction and Criticism," p. 5.

CHAPTER VIII

¹ *The Writing of Fiction*, p. 92.
² *Myself*, an unpublished memoir in the collection of Herrick manuscripts at the University of Chicago, p. 79.
³ On June 29, 1907, Mrs. Wharton wrote to Charles Scribner that her "next novel" was under way. On July 17 she described it to Burlingame as "rather a comedy of manners, and of the *gelegenheits Gedicht* order." Five chapters were by this time completed. In a letter dated May 29, 1908, and addressed to Burlingame, occurs the first direct allusion to *The Custom of the Country*, on which Mrs. Wharton has been working during a passage to New York from the continent. It is evidently well along. On June 20, 1908, she writes to Brownell: "Please tell Mr. Burlingame that I have done about 36,000 words of 'The Custom of the Country.' " Between July, 1907, and May, 1908, there is no mention in the correspondence of any other new novel—a fact which seems to eliminate *The Reef* as the "next novel" mentioned in the letter of June 29, 1907.

CHAPTER IX

¹ Letter to Charles Scribner, June 27, 1914. Mrs. Wharton mentions that at the moment she has only four completed stories available for a projected volume. They are "Xingu," "The Long Run," "Autres Temps," and "The Triumph of Night."
² Lubbock, *Portrait*, p. 39. The contributor is Miss Elizabeth Norton, daughter of Charles Eliot Norton.
³ *The American Scene*, p. 485.
⁴ Under whatever national guise they may appear, Edith Wharton's aristocrats are a strongly marked type. There is usually a lack of personal distinction in their appearance if not in their manners, and their dress and circumstances are "dowdy" in a sense calculated to deceive such parvenus as Undine Spragg. Their features are rescued from total mediocrity by the prominences of their noses—the "long noses" of the Archer women being kin to the "aristocratically beaked faces" of the Malrives and their friends. See Mrs. Wharton's half-playful, half-serious digression on noses in *A Motor-Flight through France* (pp. 21–22), where she is describing the tomb of the two Cardinals of Amboise in the Lady Chapel of Rouen: "A magnificent monument—and to my mind the finest thing about it is the Cardinal Uncle's nose. The whole man is fine in his sober dignity, humbly conscious of the altar toward which he faces, arrogantly aware of the purple on his shoulders; and the nose is the epitome of the man. We live in the day of little noses: that once stately feature, intrinsically feudal and aristocratic in character—the *maschio naso* extolled of Dante—has shrunk to democratic insignificance, like many another fine expression of individualism.

257

And so one must look to the old painters and sculptors to see what a nose was meant to be—the prow of the face; the evidence of its owner's standing, of his relation to the world, and his inheritance from the past."

[5] Introduction to her translation of *The Princess of Clèves* (New York: New Directions, 1951), p. xxi.

[6] Unpublished fragment, "Fiction and Criticism," p. 6.

[7] *Novels and Novelists* (New York: Knopf, 1930), p. 320.

[8] Lubbock, *Portrait*, p. 103.

[9] *The Writing of Fiction*, p. 44.

[10] *Postscript to Yesterday* (New York: Random House, 1947), p. 13. The portrait owes much to Dixon Wecter's in *The Saga of American Society*, p. 336.

[11] See the note by William T. Going, "Wharton's 'After Holbein,' " in *The Explicator*, X (Nov., 1951), in which the interesting relationship between Mrs. Wharton's story and Holbein's *Totentanz* is developed.

CHAPTER X

[1] "The Recovery," in *Crucial Instances*, p. 70.

[2] *Edith Wharton: Étude Critique*, p. 5.

CHAPTER XI

[1] Among the clippings in the Yale collection is one from the Paris edition of the New York *Herald Tribune*, Nov. 16, 1936, reporting an interview with the novelist by Loren Carroll, during which Mrs. Wharton announced her favorite five among her novels.

[2] *The Letters of Henry James*, II, 57. James's opinion of *Madame de Treymes*, nevertheless, was that it was "beautifully done . . . and full of felicities and achieved values and pictures."

[3] *Ibid.*, I, 396. James made the remark in a letter to Edith Wharton's sister-in-law, Mrs. Cadwalader Jones, after she had sent him two of Mrs. Wharton's books. The event seems to mark the beginning of the friendship between the two novelists.

[4] *French Ways and Their Meaning*, p. 83.

[5] "The Novels of Edith Wharton," p. 184.

[6] *The Saga of American Society* (New York: Scribner's, 1937), p. 407.

[7] *The Letters of Henry James*, II, 57.

[8] "The Criticism of Fiction," p. 229. It was her complaint against the novels of both Dickens and Thackeray that "the whole immense machinery of the passions is put in motion for causes that a modern school-girl would smile at." In comparison with the novels of Balzac, Stendhal, and Flaubert, one is struck by "the futility of the springs of action and the infantile unreality of the moral conflict. . . . It is as if grown people with faces worn by passion and experience were acting a play written in the nursery." This seems to me a cogent, if somewhat overstated, objection.

CHAPTER XII

[1] *Classics and Commercials* (New York: Farrar, Straus, 1950), pp. 415–416.

[2] *Gustave Flaubert: Letters,* selected, with an introduction by Richard Rumbold, trans. by J. M. Cohen (London: Weidenfeld & Nicolson, 1950), p. 88.

[3] Review of Leslie Stephen's *George Eliot,* p. 250.

[4] *Ibid.,* p. 251.

[5] New York *Herald Tribune* interview, Nov. 16, 1936 (see chap. xi, n. 1).

The Writings of Edith Wharton

Note.—*Although intended primarily for the convenience of the reader, the following is as complete a listing as possible of Mrs. Wharton's writings, except for the many poems scattered through magazines, newspapers, and anthologies, as well as letters to newspapers appealing for funds to carry on her World War charities. There is no satisfactory bibliography of Edith Wharton's writings. My aim here has been to correct errors and omissions in earlier listings and to add material (indicated by asterisks) not previously mentioned in any bibliography.*

I am indebted to Lavinia R. Davis' A Bibliography of the Writings of Edith Wharton, *Portland, Me., 1933, and to the bibliographies in E. K. Brown's* Edith Wharton: Étude Critique, *Paris, 1935, and Fred B. Millet's* Contemporary American Authors, *New York, 1940.*

BOOKS

Verses. Newport: C. E. Hammett, Jr., 1878.
The Decoration of Houses (with Ogden Codman, Jr.). New York: Scribner's, 1897.
The Greater Inclination. New York: Scribner's, 1899.
The Touchstone. New York: Scribner's, 1900. Published in England as *A Gift from the Grave* (London: John Murray, 1900).
Crucial Instances. New York: Scribner's, 1901.
The Valley of Decision. New York: Scribner's, 1902. 2 vols.
Sanctuary. New York: Scribner's, 1903.
The Descent of Man, and Other Stories. New York: Scribner's, 1904. Published in England under the same title (London: Macmillan, 1904) but with the addition of one story, "The Letter."
Italian Villas and Their Gardens. New York: Century, 1904.
Italian Backgrounds. New York: Scribner's, 1905.
The House of Mirth. New York: Scribner's, 1905.
Madame de Treymes. New York: Scribner's, 1907.
The Fruit of the Tree. New York: Scribner's, 1907.
A Motor-Flight through France. New York: Scribner's, 1908.
The Hermit and the Wild Woman and Other Stories. New York: Scribner's, 1908.

260

Artemis to Actaeon and Other Verse. New York: Scribner's, 1909.
Tales of Men and Ghosts. New York: Scribner's, 1910.
Ethan Frome. New York: Scribner's, 1911.
The Reef. New York: Appleton, 1912.
The Custom of the Country. New York: Scribner's, 1913.
Fighting France, from Dunkerque to Belfort. New York: Scribner's, 1915.
Xingu and Other Stories. New York: Scribner's, 1916.
Summer. New York: Appleton, 1917.
The Marne. New York: Appleton, 1918.
French Ways and Their Meaning. New York: Appleton, 1919.
The Age of Innocence. New York: Appleton, 1920.
In Morocco. New York: Scribner's, 1920.
The Glimpses of the Moon. New York: Appleton, 1922.
A Son at the Front. New York: Scribner's, 1923.
Old New York: False Dawn (The 'Forties); *The Old Maid* (The 'Fifties); *The Spark* (The 'Sixties); *New Year's Day* (The 'Seventies). New York: Appleton, 1924. 4 vols.
The Mother's Recompense. New York: Appleton, 1925.
The Writing of Fiction. New York: Scribner's, 1925.
Here and Beyond. New York: Appleton, 1926.
Twelve Poems. London: The Medici Society, 1926.
Twilight Sleep. New York: Appleton, 1927.
The Children. New York: Appleton, 1928.
Hudson River Bracketed. New York: Appleton, 1929.
Certain People. New York: Appleton, 1930.
The Gods Arrive. New York: Appleton, 1932.
Human Nature. New York: Appleton, 1933.
A Backward Glance. New York: Appleton-Century, 1934.
The World Over. New York: Appleton-Century, 1936.
Ghosts. New York: Appleton-Century, 1937.
The Buccaneers. New York: Appleton-Century, 1938.

SHORT STORIES (Uncollected)

"Mrs. Manstey's View," *Scribner's Magazine,* X (July, 1891), 117–122. Appears also in *Stories of New York* (New York: Scribner's, 1893).
"The Fulness of Life," *Scribner's Magazine,* XIV (December, 1893), 699–704.
"That Good May Come," *Scribner's Magazine,* XV (May, 1894), 629–642.
"The Lamp of Psyche," *Scribner's Magazine,* XVIII (October, 1895), 418–428.
"The Valley of Childish Things and Other Emblems," *Century,* LII (July, 1896), 467–469.
° "April Showers," *Youth's Companion,* LXXIV (January 18, 1900), 25–26.
° "Friends," *Youth's Companion,* LXXIV (August 23, 30, 1900), 405–406, 417–418.
"The Line of Least Resistance," *Lippincott's Magazine,* LXVI (October, 1900), 559–570.
"The Letter," *Harper's Magazine,* CVIII (April, 1904), 781–789. Appears in the English edition of *The Descent of Man.*

"The House of the Dead Hand," *Atlantic Monthly*, XCIV (August, 1904), 145–160.
* "The Introducers," *Ainslee's*, XVI (December, 1905; January, 1906), 139–148, 61–67.
"Les Metteurs en Scene," *Revue des Deux Mondes*, XLVII (October, 1908), 692–708. Appears as title story in *Les Metteurs en Scene* (Paris: Plon Nourrit, 1909). Never translated into English.
"Writing a War Story," *Woman's Home Companion*, XLVI (September, 1919), 17–19.
* "In a Day," *Woman's Home Companion*, LX (January, February, 1933), 7–8, 46; 15–16, 104, 106, 118.

ARTICLES (Uncollected)

"The Three Francescas," *North American Review*, CLXXV (July, 1902), 17–30.
"The Vice of Reading," *North American Review*, CLXXVII (October, 1903), 513–521.
"George Cabot Lodge," *Scribner's Magazine*, XLVII (February, 1910), 236–239.
"The Criticism of Fiction," *Times* Literary Supplement (May 14, 1914), 229–230.
* "Jean du Breuil de Saint-Germain," *Revue Hebdomadaire*, XXIV (May 15, 1915), 351–361.
* "Les Français Vus par une Americaine," *Revue Hebdomadaire*, XXVII (January 5, 1918), 5–21.
* "L'Amerique en Guerre," *Revue Hebdomadaire*, XXVII (March 2, 1918), 5–28.
* "How Paris Welcomed the King," *Reveille*, no. 3 (February, 1919), 367–369.
"Henry James in His Letters," *Quarterly Review*, CCXXXIV (July, 1920), 188–202.
"Christmas Tinsel," *Delineator*, CIII (December, 1923), 11.
"The Great American Novel," *Yale Review*, n.s. XVI (July, 1927), 646–656.
"William C. Brownell," *Scribner's Magazine*, LXXXIV (November, 1928), 596–602.
"A Cycle of Reviewing," *Spectator* (London), CXLI (November 23, 1928), supplement, 44.
"Visibility in Fiction," *Yale Review*, n.s. XVIII (March, 1929), 480–488.
"Confessions of a Novelist," *Atlantic Monthly*, CLI (April, 1933), 385–392.
"Tendencies in Modern Fiction," *Saturday Review of Literature*, X (January 27, 1934), 433–444. Also in *Designed for Reading*, ed. H. S. Canby (New York: Macmillan, 1934), 37–42.
"Permanent Values in Fiction," *Saturday Review of Literature*, X (April 7, 1934), 603–604. Also in *Writing for Love or Money*, Norman Cousins, ed. (New York: Longmans, 1949), pp. 52–57.
"A Reconsideration of Proust," *Saturday Review of Literature*, XI (October 27, 1934), 233–234.

* "Souvenirs du Bourget d'Outremer," *Revue Hebdomadaire,* XLV (June 21, 1936), 266–286.
"A Little Girl's New York," *Harper's Magazine,* CLXXVI (March, 1938), 356–364.

INTRODUCTIONS

A Village Romeo and Juliet. By Gottfried Keller. Translated by Anna C. Bahlmann. Introduction by Edith Wharton. New York: Scribner's, 1914.
Futility. By William Gerhardi. Introduction by Edith Wharton. New York: Duffield, 1922.
* *Benediction.* By Comtesse Philomène de Laforest-Divonne [pseud. Claude Silve]. Translated by Robert Norton. Foreword by Edith Wharton. New York: Appleton-Century, 1936.

REVIEWS

* Edwin H. and Evangeline W. Blashfield, *Italian Cities. Bookman,* XIII (August, 1901), 563–564.
Stephen Phillips, *Ulysses. Bookman,* XV (April, 1902), 168–170.
Leslie Stephen, *George Eliot. Bookman,* XV (May, 1902), 247–251.
Howard Sturgis, *Belchamber. Bookman,* XXI (May, 1905), 307–310.
Maurice Hewlett, *The Fool Errant. Bookman,* XXII (September, 1905), 64–67.
Eugene Lee-Hamilton, *The Sonnets of the Wingless Hours. Bookman,* XXVI (November, 1907), 251–253.

MISCELLANEOUS

"More Love Letters of an Englishwoman," *Bookman,* XLI (February, 1901), 562.
* Review of Mrs. Fiske's performance in Lorimer Stoddard's dramatization of Hardy's *Tess of the D'Urbervilles,* New York *Commercial Advertiser,* May 7, 1902, p. 9.
The Joy of Living. By Hermann Sudermann. Translated from the German by Edith Wharton. New York: Scribner's, 1902.
The Book of the Homeless. Edited by Edith Wharton. New York: Scribner's, 1916.
Eternal Passion in English Poetry. Selected by Edith Wharton and Robert Norton, with the collaboration of Gaillard Lapsley. New York: Appleton-Century, 1939.

Bibliography

Note.—*This bibliography includes what I regard as the most useful studies and critical essays on Mrs. Wharton and at the same time represents a variety of judgments on the value of her fiction.*

Auchinloss, Louis. "Edith Wharton and Her New Yorks," *Partisan Review,* XVIII (July–August, 1951), 411–419.

Beach, Joseph Warren. *The Twentieth Century Novel: Studies in Technique.* New York: Appleton-Century, 1932. Pp. 291–303, 311–314.

Björkman, Edwin A. *Voices of Tomorrow.* New York: Mitchell Kennerley, 1913. Pp. 290–304.

Bourget, Paul. Introduction to *Chez les Heureux du Monde* (*The House of Mirth*). Paris: Plon Nourrit, 1908.

Boynton, Percy H. *Some Contemporary Americans.* Chicago: University of Chicago Press, 1924. Pp. 89–107.

Brooks, Van Wyck. *The Confident Years.* New York: Dutton, 1952. Pp. 283–300.

Brown, E. K. *In* Pelham Edgar, *The Art of the Novel from 1700 to the Present Time.* New York: Macmillan, 1933. Pp. 196–205.

———. *Edith Wharton: Étude Critique.* Paris: Librairie E. Droz, 1935.

Canby, H. S. In *Literary History of the United States.* New York: Macmillan, 1948. Vol. II, pp. 1209–1211.

Cooper, Frederic T. *Some American Story Tellers.* New York: Holt, 1911. Pp. 168–195.

Cross, Wilbur L. "Edith Wharton," *Bookman,* LXII (August, 1926), 641–646.

Gerould, Katherine Fullerton. *Edith Wharton: A Critical Study.* New York: Appleton, n.d.

Grant, Robert. *Commemorative Tributes to E. A. Robinson and Others.* New York: Publications of the American Academy of Arts and Letters (no. 95), 1939. Pp. 43–59.

Herrick, Robert. "Mrs. Wharton's World," *New Republic,* II (February 13, 1915), 40–42.

Hoffman, Frederick J. "Points of Moral Reference: A Comparative Study of Edith Wharton and F. Scott Fitzgerald," in *English Institute Essays,* 1949. New York: Columbia University Press, 1950. Pp. 147–176.

———. *The Modern Novel in America: 1900–1950.* Chicago: Regnery, 1951. Pp. 11–20.

James, Henry. *Notes on Novelists, with Some Other Notes.* New York: Scribner's, 1914. Pp. 353–356. Estimate of *The Custom of the Country.*

————. *The Letters of Henry James*, Percy Lubbock, ed. New York: Scribner's, 1920. Vol. II, pp. 281–285. James, in a letter to Mrs. Wharton dated December 4, 1912, analyzes at length her novel, *The Reef*.

Kazin, Alfred. *On Native Grounds*. New York: Reynal & Hitchcock, 1942. Pp. 73–82.

Leavis, Q. D. "Henry James's Heiress: The Importance of Edith Wharton," *Scrutiny*, VII (December, 1938), 261–276.

Lovett, Robert Morss. *Edith Wharton*. New York: McBride, 1925.

Lubbock, Percy. "The Novels of Edith Wharton," *Quarterly Review*, CCXXIV (January, 1915), 182–201.

————. *Portrait of Edith Wharton*. New York: Appleton-Century-Crofts, 1947.

Mansfield, Katherine. *Novels and Novelists*, J. M. Murry, ed. New York: Knopf, 1930. Pp. 316–320. On *The Age of Innocence*.

Michaud, Régis. *Mystiques et Réalistes Anglo-Saxons*. Paris: Colin, 1918. Pp. 215–234.

————. *Panorama de la Littérature Américaine Contemporaine*. Paris: Kra, 1926. Pp. 139–147.

————. *Le Roman Américain d'Aujourd'hui*. Paris: Boivin, 1926. Pp. 39–46, 55–79.

Quinn, Arthur H. Introduction to *An Edith Wharton Treasury*. New York: Appleton-Century-Crofts, 1950. Pp. v–xxvii.

Ransom, John Crowe. "Characters and Character," *American Review*, VI (January, 1936), 271–288.

Sedgwick, Henry Dwight. *The New American Type and Other Essays*. Boston: Houghton Mifflin, 1908. Pp. 53–96.

Sencourt, Robert. "The Poetry of Edith Wharton," *Bookman*, LXXIII (July, 1931), 478–486.

Sherman, Stuart Pratt. *The Main Stream*. New York: Scribner's, 1927. Pp. 204–212.

Trilling, Diana. "The House of Mirth Revisited," *Harper's Bazaar*, LXXXI (December, 1947), 126–127, 181–186.

Trueblood, Charles K. "Edith Wharton," *Dial*, LXVIII (January, 1920), 80–91.

Underwood, John Curtis. *Literature and Insurgency: Ten Studies in Racial Evolution*. New York: Mitchell Kennerley, 1914. Pp. 346–390.

Valdiva, Olga A. de. "Edith Wharton," *Andean Quarterly*, V (Summer, 1944), 8–21, 39–58; VI (Winter, 1944), 56–73.

Van Doren, Carl. *Contemporary American Novelists, 1900–1920*. New York: Macmillan, 1922. Pp. 95–104.

————. *The American Novel, 1789–1939*. New York: Macmillan, 1940. Pp. 260–280.

Waldstein, Charles. "Social Ideals," *North American Review*, CLXXXII (June, 1906), 840–852; CLXXXIII (July, 1906), 125–126.

Wilson, Edmund. *The Wound and the Bow*. Boston: Houghton Mifflin, 1941. Pp. 195–213.

————. *Classics and Commercials*. New York: Farrar, Straus, 1950. Pp. 412–418.

Index